History through Trauma

History through Trauma

History and Counter-History in the Hebrew Bible

TIFFANY HOUCK-LOOMIS

PICKWICK *Publications* · Eugene, Oregon

Pickwick Publications
An Imprint of Wipf and Stock Publishers
199 W. 8th Ave., Suite 3
Eugene, OR 97401

www.wipfandstock.com

PAPERBACK ISBN: 978-1-5326-4209-8
HARDCOVER ISBN: 978-1-5326-4210-4
EBOOK ISBN: 978-1-5326-4211-1

Cataloguing-in-Publication data:

Names: Houck-Loomis, Tiffany, author.

Title: History through trauma : history and counter-history in the Hebrew Bible / Tiffany Houck-Loomis.

Description: Eugene, OR: Pickwick Publications, 2018. | Includes bibliographical references.

Identifiers: ISBN 978-1-5326-4209-8 (paperback). | ISBN 978-1-5326-4210-4 (hardcover). | ISBN 978-1-5326-4211-1 (epub).

Subjects: Bible. Deuteronomy—Criticism, interpretation, etc. | Deuteronomistic history (Biblical criticism) | Jews—History—Babylonian captivity, 598-515 B.C. | Bible. Job—Criticism, interpretation, etc. | Bible—Psychology.

Classification: BS645 H59 2018 (print). | BS645 (epub).

Manufactured in the U.S.A.   03/29/18

To my Blackfoot and Jewish ancestors. For their stories that were not inscribed in a book but remain in the body passed down from generation to generation. And for Lotus, whose life was too short and whose body was never held. Your stories found their way into my text.

What we choose to fight is so tiny!
What fights with us is so great.

—Rainer Maria Rilke

Contents

Acknowledgments

My deepest gratitude to Ann Ulanov who, in more ways than words will ever express, tilled the soil that has continued to nurture my growth. She provided just enough water and sunlight (as well as just enough opposition) and then watched with me as that which always belonged within was allowed to grow roots and has slowly begun to break surface.

My thanks to Alan Cooper for his willingness to serve as reader and guide through the diverse world of biblical scholarship. His attentive read and encouragement of my work with Lamentations my first semester at Union has set the course for the bulk of my work leading to this book.

My gratitude to Alexis Waller who regularly afforded stimulating conversation in the range of fields from biblical studies, depth psychology, critical studies and affect theory. She has been a true friend and companion along the way joining in the suffering and the rejoicing.

To my delightful children, Kadin and Viviana, for keeping me grounded in reality, demanding me to set boundaries, and for reminding me to play both in and outside of my work. Thank you for your continued patience and forgiveness.

Finally, to Brian Houck-Loomis, my friend, partner, and lover who has stayed with me through the ups and downs, provided unending support, been a listening ear, and a helpful reader.

Abbreviations

AB	Anchor Bible
DH	Deuteronomistic History
Dtr	Deuteronomistic
JBL	*Journal of Biblical Literature*
JSOT	*Journal for the Study of the Old Testament*
JSOTSup	Journal for the Study of the Old Testament Supplement Series
OTL	Old Testament Library
VTE	Vassal Treaties of Esarhaddon
WBC	Word Biblical Commentary

1

Introduction

"Our general instinct to seek and learn will, in all reason, set us inquiring into the nature of the instrument with which we search."

—PLOTINUS, *ENNEADS* IV, 3, 1

WHAT IS ONE TO make of the little known though widely referred to traumatic experience of the multitude of exiles Israel underwent at the hands of various surrounding superpowers including Assyria, Egypt, and Babylonia throughout the eighth–sixth centuries BCE? How did history, the process of making a narrative and its repetitious recitation, enable Israel to formulate an identity that structured community living during the traumatic aftermath of the devastating Babylonian Exile in the sixth century BCE? How did this same history simultaneously disable Israel the ability to acknowledge and integrate the actual harrowing reality of these events that undeniably left their mark on the way in which Israel understood its relationship to the land, the community of God's people, and Israel's relationship to other nations?

This study investigates these questions by examining the Covenant in Deuteronomy and its counter-narrative in the book of Job. My inquiry focuses on the psychological effects of trauma on the creation and dissolution of religious, political, and national symbols. My approach draws equally on the methods of historical-critical and ideological biblical criticism and from selected psychoanalytic theory about symbols in order to analyze how individuals and communities construct historical narratives as a way of processing life-shattering circumstances. I show that while the Deuteronomic Covenant—a symbol derived from ancient Near Eastern models—enabled

Israel to survive the trauma of exile,[1] it also blamed the victimized culture, perpetuating an ideology of guilt and shame. In contrast, I argue that the book of Job counters the ideology of the Deuteronomistic History, which follows the tenets of the Deuteronomic Covenant. Reading the book of Job as a symbolic history of Israel that parallels the Deuteronomistic History reveals how the ancient Israelites maintained these two diverse and seemingly disparate stories. When held together, these two contrasting stories provide an alternative way of interpreting the traumatic events of exile that pollute the landscape of Israel's history.

The study I present here examines how Israel articulates its own identity, amidst the shifting social and historical contexts of exile, within its officially recognized *historical* texts and what I consider, its *counter-historical* texts. By *historical* texts I am referring to Joshua, Judges, 1 and 2 Samuel, and 1 and 2 Kings. I italicize *historical* from time to time in order to emphasize the ambiguity of the very category. When referencing the Deuteronomistic History, what I term the national or dominant History the word History will be capitalized. Further arguments regarding the concept of history, historical narratives, and counter-texts are explored in depth throughout this work. Israel's relationship with God and how the Deuteronomic Covenant shaped and informed this relationship throughout its shifting social context is central to Israel's identity. Therefore, at the heart of this study, I investigate how God and Israel are identified within the Deuteronomic Covenant as this Covenant was shaped and reshaped throughout the years of oppression and exile. In the context of the prolific rhetoric of Covenantal ideology articulated in the Deuteronomic Covenant read in Deuteronomy and what are accepted by most biblical scholars as the books that include the Deuteronomistic History (Joshua, Judges, 1 and 2 Samuel, 1 and 2 Kings) I proffer that a counter-narrative runs parallel to this structured and dominant narrative. In contrast to a *Covenantal* relationship between Israel and God a counter-narrative surfaces in later postexilic literature. This counter-narrative that surfaces in the book of Job I call, an *Individuated* relationship or *Individuated* religion. These two narratives, the Covenantal and the Individuated, were simultaneously shaped after the events of the Babylonian Exile. The two narratives exist today side-by-side in the Hebrew canon. One does not supersede or erase the other. Instead, they remain together without collapsing into one another. The Covenantal narrative in Deuteronomy and the

---

1. Acknowledging Israel underwent many exiles, when a specific Exile is being referenced such as the Babylonian Exile, the word Exile will be capitalized to designate its specificity. When referring to exile as an experience or the multiple exiles that both the North and the South underwent throughout the eighth–sixth centuries, exile will be referred to in lowercase.

Deuteronomistic History, and the Individuated narrative in the book of Job exist, in a sense, *for* one another. In their mutual existence, a new symbol arises which allows for the former symbol of the Covenant to be renewed and enlivened in the new symbol found in the character of Job, even after the trauma of exile.

By *Covenantal religion* I am referring to the moral and ethical code of conduct explicitly laid out in the Deuteronomic Covenant that ensures land, prosperity, progeny and protection as a reward for obedience, while promising utter destruction and exile from the land as a consequence of Covenantal disobedience. Covenantal religion provided religious and communal structure for Israel during the sixth and fifth centuries, a time when Israel had lost its land and temple and experienced a profound disruption to its religious ideology. A great deal of literature exists within the field of biblical scholarship regarding the Covenant narrative within Deuteronomy and its formulation and reformulation in and throughout exile as a way in which Israel tried to explain this horrific event.

By *Individuated religion* I am referring to the ability of an individual or a community to grapple with the objective Divine Other outside of his or their subjective experience of this Other, and more importantly outside of the community's rules and expectations of this Other. Individuated religion is not an individual religion or an internalized religion *per se*, but rather, a religion that is able to step aside from the cultural ideologies inscribed within its tenets. In doing this, the Individuated (or individuating) religion interrogates and even deconstructs the social and communal symbols of the stated religion. This deconstruction allows the practitioner (within the ancient and modern community) another entry into the religious symbols that, when socially constructed and not individually experienced, merely reflect a particular culture's god images rather than an experience with what is beyond those images.

Carl Jung speaks of individuation as the life-long journey of an individual in relation to his Self and his culture.[2] Jung's concept of the Self differs from other psychoanalytic notions of the self. He describes the Self as a universal principle, shared by all human beings. The Self, in Jungian thought, is like a different center of gravity that pulls each individual toward it in different ways. It is outside of consciousness though it contains conscious and unconscious contents. The word Self is capitalized in Jungian theory to indicate its objective, universal, and timeless existence as an archetype that is imaged differently within each person's individual psyche and psychic

---

2. Jung, "Conscious, Unconscious, and Individuation"; and Jung, "A Study on the Process of Individuation," in *Archetypes and the Collective Unconscious*, ¶¶489–626.

process and within different myths or fairy tales colored by the cultural elements out of which the story emerges. The Self is not simply within one's personal conscious or even unconscious personality but something bigger than one's conscious self; i.e., personal contents. This is the reason for capitalizing the S when referring to Jung's notion of the Self. An individual on the path of individuation moves into greater relatedness with his whole Self and thus greater and deeper relatedness with others. The term Self is a dense and multivalent concept that is understood differently by varying schools of depth psychology. Throughout this work I refer to the Self, through Jung's articulation, as the totality of a human personality that includes the conscious field of the ego as well as the vast field of unconscious contents, both personal and collective.[3] Jung argues that the ego, while containing the field of consciousness, is only a small portion of the totality of the Self, which includes archetypes of the collective unconscious and one's own personal unconscious. In Jung's map of the psyche the unconscious includes personal contents, repressions, and past memories that have slipped from consciousness, as well as collective contents, including archetypal images and historical or biological instincts outside of a personal nature that are shared by all human beings. These concepts will be explained in greater detail following. Marie-Louise von Franz helps articulate Jung's notion of the Self regarding her analysis of fairy tales saying,

> "After working for many years in this field, I have come to the conclusion that all fairy tales endeavor to describe one and the same psychic fact, but a fact so complex and far-reaching and so difficult for us to realize in all its different aspects that hundreds of tales and thousands of repetitions with a musician's variations are needed until this unknown fact is delivered into consciousness; and even then the theme is not exhausted. This unknown fact is what Jung calls the Self, which is the psychic totality of an individual and also, paradoxically, the regulating center of the collective unconscious. Every individual and every nation has its own modes of experiencing this psychic reality."[4]

Even though Donald Winnicott rejects Jung's notion of the Self, calling it a "dead artifact" he too, recognizes the human self as more than the ego, the totality of being, embodied and in relationship.[5] Winnicott argues that the self "arrives at a significant relationship between the child and the sum of the identifications which (after enough incorporation and introjection

---

3. Jung, *Psychology and Religion*, ¶140.

4. von Franz, *Interpretation of Fairy Tales*, 2.

5. Winnicott, *Psychoanalytic Explorations*, 490–92.

of mental representations) becomes organized in the shape of an internal psychic living reality."[6] Drawing on Jungian analysts' Thomas Singer and Samuel Kimbles notion of cultural complexes and Winnicott's notion of the self as the "sum of identifications," I will refer to Israel in light of its developing identity as a communal Self throughout this work.[7] Both of these notions open the personified, dyadic definitions of Self into cultural and collective experiences of groups.

In light of Jung's notion of the Self, individuation remains a difficult and sometimes lonely process wherein one develops a new relationship to old norms, socially constructed ideas, and communal symbols. The process involves facing that which the individual has cut off from her consciousness, whatever she believes does not belong to her or is not acceptable; i.e., aggression, hate, desire, power, beauty, longing, the feminine, the masculine, all that she considers evil.[8] Facing that which has been dissociated or cut off from consciousness, relegated to the depths of the unconscious, and, as a byproduct, to her enemies be them personal or cultural, she begins to integrate these formerly dissociated parts of her own personality, suffering them rather than exporting them.[9] As a process of de-masking one's own façade, individuation prods an individual to examine the ways in which he hides behind society, religion, culture, or family to protect him from doing his own work, knowing his whole self, and finding his own way.

Through the process of individuation, a person begins to come in contact with and in relation to the parts of the Self, personal and universal, that have been exiled and exported onto others. Jung explains that the term individuation "denotes a process by which a person becomes a psychological 'in-dividual,' that is, a separate, indivisible unity or 'whole.'"[10] As she begins to relate to these previously hidden parts, more space, to hold these parts, is made for her and consequently for others. This concept proved vital for Jung, as he understood the function of religion for the individual. Rather than reducing religion to an Oedipal Complex or a childhood wish fulfillment as Freud does, Jung argues that religion allows the potential for individuation in the symbols and rituals it provides.[11] Through individuation

---

6. Ibid., 271.

7. Singer and Kimbles, "Emerging Theory of Cultural Complexes."

8. Throughout this work I switch gender pronouns purposively to remain gender inclusive.

9. Neumann, *Depth Psychology and a New Ethic*, 33–58.

10. Jung, *Archetypes and the Collective Unconscious*, ¶490.

11. Freud, *Future of an Illusion*, 18–42; Freud, *Totem and Taboo*, 24–124; Jung, "Two Kinds of Thinking," in *Symbols of Transformation*, ¶¶4–46, Jung, "The Undiscovered Self," in *Civilization in Transition*, ¶¶148–588; Jung, "Introduction to the Religious

the individual has an encounter with the Self through symbols that spontaneously arise from within and enable union of conscious and unconscious contents out of which a new consciousness emerges.[12]

Individuated religion, as proffered in the book of Job, stands in contrast to Covenantal religion as it challenges the stated ethical code based on the character of Job wrestling with his own experience therein. A new symbol, an image of *tam* (blameless, complete, finished) and *tamim* (integrity) found in the fictional character of Job and God's final response to this *tam* servant, emerges between these two contrasting narratives and challenges the dominant Covenantal paradigm of conditionality. Job, a man of the Covenant who lived in strict obedience to its code, ends up losing all of his possessions, his children and is rejected by his companions. After being forced to reconcile the disillusioning experience of his trauma in resistance to his culturally accepted structure of the Covenant, which provided a systematic explanation of his suffering, Job becomes the one character in the story who is himself appointed as intercessor on behalf of his friends, the very ones who represent Covenant Religion.

The character of Job can be read allegorically as a symbol of the nation of Israel after the events of the Exile. Reading Job allegorically in this way allows for another understanding of the book as a whole. The book of Job can be understood as a symbolic history of Israel, a history that witnesses to the trauma of the Exile and the dissolution of the god of the Covenant. The character of Job emerges, parallel to the dominant historical narrative articulated throughout the historical books, as a symbol of Israel during exile, containing the eradicated affective experience of the trauma and the refusal to accept blame for its consequences. The book of Job presents an image of God as one not bound by the Covenant, who does not act in accordance with Israel's obedience or disobedience, and does not act solely on behalf of Israel. Through Job's aggression he is able to destroy the Covenantal image of God and simultaneously experience God's survival through his destruction. The act of his aggression enables him to relate to and use the Covenant in the construction of a new identity. This alternative voice, the voice of Individuated religion, emerges not as a dominant voice of ancient Israel, but exists as another narrative that brings to consciousness that which was being etched out within the narrowing and rigidifying formulation of the Deuteronomic Covenant during postexilic Israel.[13]

---

and Psychological Problems of Alchemy," in *Psychology and Alchemy*, ¶¶2–43.

12. Jung, "Conscious, Unconscious, and Individuation," in *Archetypes and the Collective Unconscious*, ¶524.

13. Jacobsen, *Treasures of Darkness*, 163–64.

This shift from Covenantal to Individuated religion arises out of the trauma of exile itself. The presence of both narratives forces some within Israel to re-imagine and re-construct their collective identity as well as their image of and relationship with God. Though I will be talking specifically about the book of Job as a counter-narrative there are many other texts I could have chosen to analyze. Those dominantly analyzed within biblical scholarship regarding similar themes are Jeremiah and Deutero-Isaiah, two portions of the Hebrew Bible that challenge the traditional notion of Covenant. In dialogue with two distinct and different theorists, Carl G Jung and Donald W Winnicott, and those following in their wake, I explore the psychoanalytic notion of symbols and use this to explore how symbols, emerging in Israel's history, both inherited and discovered, are used at various points in the development of Israel's collective identity. I articulate how symbols lose their symbolic value, particularly during times when severe trauma causes regression, splitting, and the marginalization of one's own Self or community and one's external Other.

I draw connections between these theories and the relationship between Deuteronomy 28 and the character of Job in the book of Job, by analyzing the texts diachronically[14], in their historical contexts, and synchronically[15], in relation to one another in the canon. I show the varying images of God that get evoked, crushed, concretized, loosened, and deconstructed within and between the parallel narratives of history being constructed therein. Given that one god-image does not replace the other, but rather they stand in tandem, even though in tension, I explore the ways in which communities today might be able to find how their own stories, intertwined with biblical stories, allow them to find new ways of imaging God and imagining their relationship to the Divine at various and conflicting times within their own lives and within the life of their community.

One of the questions of exploration for the following work asks: Is biblical *history* a literary example of how a community psychologically copes with communal and religious trauma? As has been explained, there is a parallel shift in ideology as we move diachronically through the scriptures. One shift is toward a more structured yet more narrow and rigid interpretation of the Deuteronomic Covenant seen in what I call, Covenantal religion;

14. By diachronic I am referring to the theoretical disposition within the historical-critical field of biblical scholarship that analyzes the various individual components of the text, looking for their historical referents, rather than analyzing the text as a whole or synchronically. Mann, *Book of the Torah*, 7–8.

15. By synchronic I am referring to the theoretical disposition within Canonical, Rhetorical or forms of Ideological criticism that analyzes the Bible as a unified whole. Ibid., 6.

if you do as God has commanded you and teach your children to do, then your God will give you progeny and land at the expense of others who are not part of God's elect. Another shift is found in the counter-narrative read in Job. This shift is what I call Individuated religion and it acknowledges the importance of the Covenant yet allows for different and contrary responses to chaos and destruction seen in the human emotions of aggression, devastation, ambivalence, and mourning, and its resistance to equating reward with obedience. The shift is not conclusive nor is it totalizing. Both views, and perhaps more views, remain articulated in the Hebrew Bible providing a host of god-images and relational modalities to pick up and work with as a way of understanding a given text in its ancient context and as a way of making meaning for today.[16]

These questions draw me simultaneously into the fields of historical and ideological criticism on the Bible side and Jungian Analytical Psychology and Winnicottian Object Relations Theory on the psychoanalytic side. The activity of writing stories, instructions, and creating history was a way in which ancient Israel formulated its identity as Israel processed the trauma of the (many) exile(s). On the one hand God is portrayed in the Hebrew Bible as a participant in the Covenant, urging the Israelites toward obedience and giving them choice land, while enabling them to flourish upon it. Or, conversely, God is imaged as the one who strikes them down and thrusts them into exile because of their disobedience. This image of God serves the community in exile, providing the necessary structure to survive the trauma and find a way to make sense of it, even though at the same time it places blame upon victimized Israel. This narrative ensures the God of Israel was not weak and incompetent, failing to protect Israel from the surrounding super-powers but, rather, was in control of the events of oppression and exile throughout. On the other hand, God seems to stand outside of the Covenant, is not bound by it, acts freely and sometimes in surprising ways. This image of God resists Israel's self-blame, ushers in more mystery and forces the individual and the community to wrestle with new ways of relating to Israel's sense of identity, God, and Other, the Other being Israel's surrounding nations after exile.

I am excavating the formula of the Deuteronomic Covenant as it is articulated in the later stages of development during the later exilic period within Deuteronomy 28 and other portions of the Deuteronomistic History, particularly 2 Kings 23. This Covenant in its earliest formation was fashioned after Israel's vassal treaty with Assyria through a method of hybridity as Israel sought to subvert Assyria by making vows fashioned after

16. Ulanov, *Picturing God*, 164–84.

their vassal with Assyria to Adonai instead.[17] What I explore through the psychoanalytic theories posited by Jung and Winnicott regarding the nature of symbols, their construction and function, is the *symbolic* nature of this Covenant. I analyze through the historical-critical method how the Covenant was constructed within the ancient context. I discuss possible implications behind the Covenant's construction given the proposed reasons for its evolution throughout the Hebrew canon. Then, with the psychoanalytic theories I employ, I analyze the implications for the contrary narratives read between the Covenantal and Individuated outgrowths.

Looking Ahead

In chapter 2 I provide a thorough introduction to the employed method wherein I hold the historical-critical approach of biblical scholarship on equal footing with the psychoanalytic theories of Carl G Jung and Donald W Winnicott regarding the depth psychological perspective on symbols and symbol formation in the process of individual and societal growth and development. My method uses psychoanalytic theory as a lens through which to analyze the historical and literary nuances of the Deuteronomic Covenant and the book of Job. I provide an explanation for how the proposed process functions on three levels: first as a way of reading providing a critical theory for analyzing sacred texts; second as a system of scholarly research; and third as a heuristic approach for teaching.

The method is built upon four assumptions. The first assumption I explore is the universal and timeless reality of the psyche. The second supposition recognizes the process of symbolic formation in the movement toward psychic equilibrium and the beginning process of individuation. The third postulation regards the integrity of the separate and unique fields of biblical scholarship and depth psychology which, when held separate, each in their own space, and yet together, using psychoanalytic theory to explore the historical and literary movements within ancient and sacred scriptures, opens up a third space between the two disciplines to critically analyze the biblical text. The fourth and final statement vital to this work acknowledges that the third space, the space between the two disciplines, between the two narratives (Covenant and Individuated) and between the reader or scholar

---

17. Hybridity is a "concept drawn from post-colonial theory that designates the blending of self-determination with elements drawn from the culture of the past oppressor. It is not identical with mere mixing of different cultural elements in identity. Instead, it refers to the complex identity formed in the midst and wake of the experience of domination." Carr, *Introduction to the Old Testament*, 267.

and the texts themselves, becomes possible by engaging with the shadow of ancient Israel's dominant historical narrative, what will be referred to (and explained below) as the fourth, the aspects of Israel's history that have been left out or massaged away within the Deuteronomistic History.

Chapter 3 analyzes the historical and ideological influence upon the creation of the Deuteronomic Covenant within Deuteronomy and the narrative of finding seper-hatorah in 2 Kings 22–23. It interprets the Covenant, both found and created during the eighth–seventh centuries BCE under the influence of Assyrian Vassal Treaties, symbolically as an object that enabled Israel to experience autonomy in the midst of the vassal relationship with Assyria to whom the community was bound. I provide a thorough background of the vast and contentious field of Deuteronomistic History scholarship. I contend a triple redaction theory, meaning three stages of literary development at three different historical periods, is helpful for analyzing the construction of the dominant historical narrative read within Samuel-Kings, and 2 Kings in particular, that is dependent upon the Covenant in Deuteronomy, specifically Deuteronomy 28. I argue the many exiles Israel experienced in the North and the South played a prominent role in the construction of this history and the development of Covenant Religion. Winnicott's theories of the transitional object and location of cultural experience are employed to analyze the Covenant as an object that enabled Israel to grow, develop, and experience autonomy amongst the surrounding superpowers of the eighth–seventh centuries BCE.

Chapter 4 delves into the archeological evidence of exile in the North at the hands of the Assyrians and most traumatically in the South at the hands of the Babylonians. A brief look at exile studies and historical-critical scholarship during this time period and an in-depth discussion on psychic splitting as a result of severe trauma frame a conversation on the collapse of psychic space needed to maintain a symbolic connection with the Covenant and the god-image therein. In this chapter I contemplate how the trauma of the Exile left Israel void of objects once available for working with toward a sense of cohesive identity amidst the politically tumultuous Near East, and void of the symbols that previously enabled Israel to connect with one another through a growing identity in relation to the outside world and to the God of the Covenant. An argument is made for how the trauma of the Babylonian Exile constellated a cultural complex within ancient Israel that was solidified within the dominant historical narrative now known as the Deuteronomistic History. This complex led the Exiles to locate the evil of the Babylonian Exile within ancient Israel itself, blaming the community for its traumatic events.

Part 2 introduces the concept of Individuated Religion and the notion of symbolic history in contrast to Covenant Religion and the Deuteronomistic History as explained within part one. Chapter 5 explains my contribution of the concept of symbolic history by utilizing theorists Carl Jung, Donald Winnicott, Ann Ulanov, French Lacanian psychoanalysts Françoise Davoine and Jean-Max Guadilliére, and cultural critic Ann Cvetkovitch. What these theorists have in common across diverse fields or schools of study is a radical reorientation to trauma and madness. Their work depathologizes trauma and each, in a different way, finds the synthetic, prospective, and constructive function of madness as a method of research into the unconscious or subterranean aspects of individual and collective culture. I use their theoretical approaches to propose the new category *symbolic history*. I argue the symbolic history of ancient Israel stands beside the Deuteronomistic History as a subtext or counter-text challenging the tenets of the Deuteronomic Covenant that color the dominant historical narrative read in Joshua–Kings. This new category opens up another way to enter the book of Job, a supposedly non-historical wisdom book lacking a specific time stamp or location of origin. Reading the book of Job as a symbolic history, beside the dominant history, creates space to reflect upon the horrific experience of exile and the inexplicable silence of God at the utter devastation of ancient Israel.

In Chapter 6 I delve into the history of biblical interpretation and scholarly analysis of the book of Job. Placing the book within the historical scope of biblical interpretation and modern day scholarly analysis provides a context for further inquiry as it shows the cyclical arch of interpretive possibilities approached from divergent angles.

Chapter 7 tackles the literary parallels between Deuteronomy 28 and the book of Job that render a deconstructive reading of the book of Job. I provide a detailed table graph that highlights the similarities of these two works and then analyze how the book of Job transgresses the Deuteronomic Covenant, and thus Covenant Religion, linguistically and symbolically. I draw special attention to the Hebrew used to describe Adonai's servant Job, and argue that the words *tam* and *tamim* function symbolically to draw the reader's (ancient and present) attention to the chosen, blameless, and righteous servants of Adonai, a community who experienced utter completion, as in decimation, at the hands of their enemies. I discuss Job's actions, seemingly contradictory, between the prosaic *inclusio*, or envelope, and the poetic center. Finally, I analyze the divine speeches at the end of the book for clues to what is the new image of God emerging. This new image is revealed to a postexilic Israel. In Job, God's *tam* (blameless and finished) and *yashar* (righteous) servant *re*members—he brings the affective experience of exile back into—the collective body of Israel.

Chapter 8 explores the psychoanalytic significance of the word and symbol *tam* used to describe the servant Job and how this narrated character is used to symbolize the community of postexilic Israel. I argue that Individuated Religion arises as the story of Job unfolds and as the conclusion reveals a God bound not by or to the Covenant. I conclude that this image allows the Covenant to become usable once again, meaning used as a means through which to relate with that which is beyond the Covenant, the transcendent being toward whom the Covenant points, the objective other outside of Israel's subjective experience of that other. This chapter postulates, through psychoanalytic sensibilities, the necessary and prospective function of madness, aggression, destruction, and the body, prospective in the sense of providing a way toward healing and wholeness.

Finally, chapter 9 brings the salient points made regarding the symbolic nature of the Deuteronomic Covenant, collapse of the symbolic due to the traumatic experience of exile, and re-enlivening of the symbol through the affective and poetic story of Job into the modern-day reading community. In this final chapter I make a case for how the proposed method of research allows for a new understanding of how history and counter-history or counter-texts function together within the Hebrew canon and how this biblical example is applicable and in fact crucial for pastoral theology today. By relating the prominent theme, gleaned from the work of analyzing the Deuteronomic Covenant and Covenant Religion in Deuteronomy and the accepted historical books of the Hebrew Bible and its counter-narrative of Individuated Religion read in the book of Job, to the function of these texts within faith communities today, I make a case for how analyzing the historical and literary nuances within these texts reveal new applicability of the difficult and seemingly contentious stories within the biblical canon, for modern-day reading communities.

2

Methodology

Should I print the earth, the sky, my heart?
The cities burning, my brothers fleeing?
My eyes in tears?
Where should I run and to whom?

—MARC CHAGALL

A Roadmap: An Introduction to the
Psychoanalytic Notion of Symbols

THE GUIDING QUESTION FOR the research of this project surfaced for me while engaged in the study of psychoanalytic theory simultaneous with the scholarly study of the Hebrew Bible. While the field of depth psychology engages with sacred texts including the Hebrew Bible for the purpose of deepening depth psychology's clinical application and working theories, it does not engage the Hebrew Bible with the critical tools of biblical scholarship.[1] These critical tools, which include textual, literary, form, historical, social scientific, archeological, and ideological analysis, have enabled scholars to learn more about the ancient contexts out of which the texts originated, the literary forms of the text itself and the effect of social and cultural history upon any reading of the text in our present context. The growing historical and anthropological perspective as well as the discovery of lost fragments of texts provides a more complex image of the Hebrew canon and the ancient communities by whom it was formulated.

At the same time, newer critical and interdisciplinary methods coming from the fields of literary theory, cultural and postcolonial theory, and

---

1. Edinger, *Bible and Psyche*; Edinger, *Transformation of the God-Image*; and Edinger, *Archetype of the Apocalypse*.

13

psychology, to name just a few, have opened up new avenues into the Hebrew Bible.[2] Reading from different angles, perspectives, voices and through a variety of different lenses has enlarged its picture and accessibility. However, biblical scholars, though growing in their ability to work interdisciplinarily, often lack in-depth training from these other critical fields. The tools from other disciplines the biblical scholar seeks to employ, whether from psychology, cultural studies, literary studies, cultural anthropology, etc. as tools for biblical exegesis and analysis end up yielding a method that inevitably values one discipline over the other.

The method born out of my own research interests and subjectivity acknowledges the inevitability of this imbalance and yet seeks to hold the field of biblical scholarship in equal weight and tension with the field of depth psychology. In this effort, it is necessary that adequate time is spent in the beginning of this work articulating the steps of this method. The method is what emerged from my own research in two distinct fields, it is what guides the present project, and it is what informs a distinct pedagogy. The approach functions on three levels:

1. It is a way of *reading* as it provides a critical theory for analyzing sacred texts.

2. It is a method for scholarly *research*.

3. It is a heuristic method for *teaching*.

Simply put, *the following method uses two psychoanalytic theories as a lens through which to analyze the historical and literary nuances of the Deuteronomic Covenant and the book of Job.* The psychoanalytic theories of Carl Jung and Donald Winnicott, particularly their hypotheses regarding the notion of symbol, symbol formation, and symbolic function provide a new way to understand the *history* behind the development of the Deuteronomic Covenant under the influence of the surrounding ancient Near Eastern cultures and the impact of cumulative exiles, and the alternative (*symbolic*) *historical* narrative, as can be read in the book of Job. As psychoanalytic assumptions provide an additional lens through which to analyze the literary aspects of the history presented within the texts at hand necessary time is spent presenting the historical and literary arguments regarding the Deuteronomic Covenant, Deuteronomistic History, and the many exiles that impacted these constructions from the field of biblical scholarship. Simultaneously, equal time is spent providing the psychoanalytical theoretical

2. McKenzie and Kaltner, eds., *New Meanings for Ancient Texts.*

background and the varied arguments regarding the notion of symbol, symbol formation, and symbolic function.

This method, simply stated above, is built upon these four assumptions:

1. The universal and timeless reality of the psyche.

2. The act of symbolic formation as the way toward psychic equilibrium. This initiates the process of, what Jung calls, individuation, or what Winnicott calls, the inherited process of maturation.[3]

3. The integrity of the separate and unique fields of biblical scholarship and depth psychology, which, when held separate each in their own space, and yet together using the two psychoanalytic theories to explore the historical and literary movements within the biblical texts, opens up a third space between the two disciplines to critically analyze the Scriptures.

4. The third space, the space between the two disciplines, Bible and Psychoanalysis, becomes possible by engaging with the shadow of these ancient texts. The shadow of these ancient texts will be referred to (and explained below) as the fourth, the aspects of Israel's history that have been left out or massaged away within the Deuteronomistic History's dominant motif.[4]

The fourth, a tenet of Jung's analytical paradigm that will be explained more fully in the latter half of this work, refers to all that an individual, society, theological paradigm, religion, etc., deems bad and thus unconsciously dissociates from its consciously lived values.[5] In the third as the space between the two different disciplines, between the two different historical motifs explored in this work, and between the scholar and the text, a new perspective, attitude, or position arises. The new arises in the shadow of the fourth or what was left out of consciousness.[6] By engaging with the shadow one creates and finds the space of imagining. Such imagining opens scholars, readers, and practitioners alike into new space within themselves and simultaneously within the text. This new space becomes the location through which to write, teach, and engage these texts for life today. Thus, these four methodological assumptions: The universal and timeless reality of the psyche; The act of symbolic formation as a move coming from the psyche in

---

3. Winnicott, *Maturational Processes*, 180, 257.

4. Ulanov, *Unshuttered Heart*, 157–78.

5. Jung, *Archetypes and the Collective Unconscious*, ¶¶426–27.

6. Ulanov, *Unshuttered Heart*, 170; Jung, "Psychology and Alchemy," in *Aion*, ¶¶159 and 406.

order to gain psychic equilibrium; The integrity of the separate and unique fields of biblical scholarship and depth psychology; and, The third space that becomes possible by engaging with the fourth, the shadow of these ancient texts—guide this author in the three ways discusses above—the act of reading texts, the work of research, and the formation of a pedagogy.

The Objectivity of the Psyche

First, my method assumes the universal and timeless reality of the psyche. As Ann Ulanov reminds students repeatedly, while we do not have the *same* psychic life, we do have the *same kind* of psychic life. She writes, "the psyche exists prior to and independently of consciousness, which emerges from it. Paradoxically, the psyche is an objective reality which we are accustomed to think of as existing within us or as being a function of our subjective consciousness, but which, in fact, acts in relation to us as an "other.""[7] Psyche exists in all persons regardless of one's background, social, political or historical setting, race, religion or sexuality.[8] While the psyche may speak in relation to one's background it is not utterly determined by these cultural aspects and thus it is a shared level of human experience outside of our differences. The psyche is "not reducible to our subjective experience, nor to social constructions, nor to our historical object relations any more than the body is."[9]

While the universality of the psyche as a shared aspect of human existence and experience is not a generally accepted concept within the field of biblical studies, psychoanalysts propose theories based on this assumption. One of the areas of study this core concept of psychic reality leads Jungian analysts to explore and theorize about regards how the psyche often communicates symbolically, sometimes pre or non verbally, and often autonomously outside of conscious awareness. Carl Jung taught that the psyche, as an objective reality, has a language of its own through which it communicates.[10] Before experiences or ideas have reached consciousness and been represented, and thus made communicable in words and mental concepts like math, one's unconscious is able to communicate through dreams, images, symptoms, and within the field of transference and counter-transference between two individuals mediating to one's consciousness that which cannot be directly or tangibly experienced. The language of the

---

7. Ulanov, *Feminine in Jungian Psychology*, 18.

8. Ulanov, *Spirit in Jung*, 102.

9. Ulanov, *Unshuttered Heart*, 151.

10. Jung, *Symbols of Transformation*, ¶180.

psyche is images that bundle together with impulses and affects. Jung says, "the image is a condensed expression of the psychic situation as a whole."[11] To learn what the psyche has to say we must "learn its language and accept it on its own terms."[12]

In articulating an acknowledgment of the reality of the psyche as one of my methodological assumptions, it can be said that just as the psyche autonomously seeks to communicate through the lives of individuals and communities today so the psyche was active and alive, communicating to and through ancient communities. Evidence of the psyche's work and presence in the life of ancient Israel is seen within the texts that were propagated first through oral tradition and were later written, redacted, and canonized in the Hebrew Bible. This is not to assert anachronistically a modern construction upon an ancient community or text arguing the texts, or movements within the texts, can be reduced to twentieth and twenty-first century psychological categories. Rather, the method proposed begins by reading the text with psychological integrity, combing the history, the text, and the modern community interpreting the text for movements of the psyche.[13] As stated above, the universal and timelessness of the psyche suggests not that we all (i.e., the scribal community of ancient Israel and the present day community of scholars, lay leaders, interested observers, practitioners, etc.) have the *same* psychic life but that we have the *same kind* of psychic life. Meaning, just as someone today will stumble upon personal historical experiences that her psyche had previously managed to repress or dissociate from consciousness, through a dream or association, within the field of transference with another person, or revealing itself through her work, so it was for people in ancient communities. Additionally, just as images arise within one's consciousness, seemingly from out of nowhere, and carry with them meaning that connects one with that which is beyond herself, so it was and is for human beings throughout time. It is an argument of the following work that the way in which the psyche informs a person or community, individually and collectively is a fact that is simply observable.[14]

11. Jung, *Psychological Types*, ¶745.

12. Ulanov, *Spirit in Jung*, 104.

13. See Schneider's *Revelatory Text* for more on the three worlds of the text and Kille's, *Psychological Biblical Criticism* for use of these three worlds within psychological biblical criticism. See also Rollins, *Soul and* Psyche, for more on the ways of reading the text psychologically.

14. Jung, *Analytical Psychology*, 5.

Symbolic Formation and Psychic Equilibrium

Second, the following method is based on the assumption that the psyche communicates through images and forms symbols in the process of seeking balance. The psychoanalytic theories of Jung and Winnicott are applied to discuss the use of symbols and symbol formation as a way in which the psyche enables the human being to live as a subject amongst other objective subjects, that is, others in their own right rather than reflections of one's own self or enmeshed in one's own psyche. Psychic equilibrium refers to the work of the unconscious protruding into consciousness, sometimes hindering one's ability to maintain healthy relationships or leading one to repeat harmful behaviors.

Jung's theory regarding symbols and images that emerge from the unconscious is utilized in this work to analyze the Covenant as a symbol within ancient Israel that functioned as a bridge to what was unknown, namely Adonai and Israel's identity as a people of God, and the effect the concretization of this symbol, due to the trauma of exile, had upon the development of a formalized Covenant Religion.[15] In the second half of this

15. In using Jung here, particularly given the content being analyzed—the symbols and history of ancient Israel—it must be noted that Jung has been accused in the academy of being anti-Semitic. It is important not to ignore or pardon his obvious ignorance and verifiably racist claims that shine through in various letters and works from the 1930's (see *Civilization in Transition*, ¶¶18, 353, 354, 1014). Jung was both fiercely advocating for the responsibility of individual development that required, in a sense, a transgressive move away from society and culture, in order not to be swallowed whole by the collective energy as he saw happening in Germany's National Socialism. At the same time, he too was impacted by the surrounding culture in which he was absorbed. The very thing Jung urged against—mass-minded thinking that eventually led to an elevation of some and the mass extermination of others—he too was influenced by. However, when deciphering this important issue, it is equally important to keep in mind Jung's many professional and personal relationships with Jewish colleagues and the thrust of his theory that urged for independent development and thinking that would ultimately challenge political universalistic thinking. To begin with, Jung's professional development was largely influenced by his relationship with Freud, first as his pupil and later colleague before they split in 1913. Other substantial relationships with Jewish psychiatrists and psychoanalysts maintained by Jung both in advising and collegial relationships included Erich Neumann, Aniela Jaffé, and Gerhard Adler. Also crucial was Jung's decision, as he took the chair of presidency over the General Medical Society for Psychotherapy (1930), to form an International Psychoanalytic Society with a different constitution separate from the exclusive German society influenced by German National Socialism, which excluded Jewish participation in the1930s. This society ensured Jewish participation as its international nature freed it from abiding by the anti-Semitic German policies. Not denying Jung's racist claims, I believe the main reason Jung has been labeled anti-Semitic is a way for the academy, and psychoanalysis in particular, to distance itself from Jung's "dangerous" propositions of the autonomy of the psyche as a reality beyond consciousness that urges for our attention and has a

work Jung's theory of the symbol and the symbolic function help articulate the role the book of Job plays in relation to the Deuteronomistic History, the dominant historical narrative of ancient Israel. His theories are utilized here to help tease out how the psyche can be investigated by observing its own patterns.[16] For example, one may reflect upon her own work and notice how she writes about the same thing over and over again each time in a different way, but at root grappling with the same issue. In this way, the psyche is observed in the repetition, bringing up the point again and again in order to be heard and understood, consciously assimilated. As Jung says,

> The psyche is a self-regulating system that maintains its equilib-rium just as the body does. Every process that goes too far im-mediately and inevitably calls forth compensations, and without these there would be neither a normal metabolism nor a normal psyche. In this sense, we can take the theory of compensation as a basic law of psychic behavior. Too little one side results in too much on the other. Similarly, the relation between conscious and unconscious is compensatory.[17]

Thus, the psyche, both conscious and unconscious, works in a compensa-tory fashion. When one values consciousness above the unconscious the unconscious intrudes as if to balance the overemphasis on consciousness, but one can also be taken over by the unconscious. Without the work of psyche to create images and form symbols one may remain stuck within her inner reality, seeing everything external as a mere reflection of her internal state, a reflection of her subjectivity. If one ignores psyche, one can become bombarded with affect that consciously she cannot make sense of or process without mediation, without the help of an external other or another image that enables the individual to assimilate the new material confronting her. If one receives an image or has a religious experience, but is not able to bring the event into conscious reflection, the experience itself is equated

---

life outside of our control. Anything outside of intellectual control or mastery for the academy is bound to be marginalized. Therefore, while evidence of Jung's racism (just as his sexism) is read within his writings, I do not think this is a reason to discount his work as a whole. We, in the academy, continue to build, challenge, and rework the theories and propositions of most primary texts based on the inevitable limitations they suffered as an influence of society and culture—as our works will also be reworked given our ignorances within this particular culture. For more on this controversial issue see: Wehr, *Jung: A Biography*, 304–35; Maidenbaum and Martin, *Lingering Shadows*; Sherry, *Carl Gustav Jung: Avant-Garde Conservative*; Samuels, "National Psychology, National Socialism, and Analytical Psychology," 3–28.

16. Jung, *Analytical Psychology*, 5.

17. Jung, *Practice of Psychotherapy*, ¶330.

with reality rather than pointing her to greater reality. One way in which psyche is mediated is through the use of images. Images slip into consciousness through the unconscious as symbols that enable a bridge between the unconscious and conscious, what is unknown to what is known, in the life of an individual or community.[18]

Ann and Barry Ulanov explain how the psyche communicates in images and experiences they term primordial experiences that reach up from the depths to awaken, signal, or leave a mark on the life of an individual. They write that in these moments,

> Something from the founder's own experience communicates itself to others through the medium of the imagery, affect, or instinctive impulse of the unconscious . . . The subterranean currents of physical and psychic response of people to such a primordial moment gather together, gestate, and gradually produce a symbol that appears in the accessible dimensions of imagination, feeling, or gesture. This symbol expresses, in turn, our unconscious life, the pressing of reality into our conscious and unconscious perceptions, and our apperceptions of this event—how we tell ourselves and others about it.[19]

Thus, the image that presents itself to one's consciousness has something to say, but it is not the image in and of itself that becomes the symbol. Rather it is the collection of one's responses to the image, a community's imaginings even fantasies regarding the images that come. It is the compilation of and one's affective responses to the images that become, in effect, a symbol nuanced for a particular person or community. This symbol allows one to make meaning of her experiences and connect with others outside of her subjective understanding of them. As Jung says, "A symbol is not a sign for something of which I know . . . A symbol is an expression for a thing of which I only know that it does exist. I don't know it . . . symbols are irreducible to literal explanations."[20] Once the symbol has been explained it loses its symbolic value, in a sense, the symbol dies. Von Franz says, "the only way that gaurentees that the living quality of religious symbols will not be prematurely extinguished, is through the realization that religious symbols do not refer to material and concrete facts but to a collective-psychic unconscious reality."[21]

---

18. Ulanov, *Feminine in Jungian Psychology*, 21.

19. Ulanov, *Religion and the Unconscious*, 5.

20. Jung, *Psychiatric Studies*, ¶414.

21. Von Franz, *Projection and Re-collection*, 84.

Paul Ricoeur, in his essay on *Freud and Philosophy*, speaks of symbols as he works to contribute to the investigation of the key connections between the disciplines of the languages of phenomenology and psychoanalysis.[22] He, building on Freud, yet differing from Freud's reductive understanding,[23] describes the symbol as the region of double meaning in language where, "the dream and its analogues are thus set within a region of language that presents itself as the locus of complex significations where another meaning is both given and hidden in an immediate meaning."[24] For Freud, the symbol conceals its true meaning that always goes back to a repressed wish. For Ricoeur, as for Jung, the symbol carries with it not only a reductive meaning, but also, a prospective or synthetic meaning. In other words, the symbol is the language of the psyche communicating to consciousness a new perspective or meaning that takes the individual's consciousness to a new place, a new understanding. However, Ricoeur draws a distinction between the fields of psychoanalysis and the phenomenology of religion. Where he understands psychoanalysis, particularly Freudian psychoanalysis, to argue that the symbol is a distortion of reality, obscuring the desire or wish latent in the manifest image. He posits that phenomenology regards the double meaning of symbol as expressing a depth, a reality, which both shows and hides itself.[25]

Therefore, Ricoeur does not regard symbols as unrealistic fables but rather as the way in which one places oneself in relation to fundamental reality. Receiving and experiencing what is both shown and hidden is the revelation of the sacred.[26] Ricoeur moves the understanding of symbol outside the confines of describing it via human desire and seeks instead to speak of it ultimately as something beyond one's own self, inhabiting multiple meanings. He explains, "In hermeneutics, symbols have their own semantics, they stimulate an intellectual activity of deciphering, of finding a hidden meaning. Far from falling outside the bounds of language, they raise feeling to meaningful articulation."[27]

I mention Ricoeur because his explanation of the symbol is close to Jung's and compatible with Winnicott's, who will be explained below. Though these theorists did not overlap theoretically, Ricoeur, as more widely accepted and read in the academy, helps relate linguistically and

---

22. Ricoeur, *Freud and Philosophy*, 1–6.

23. Ibid., 18–19.

24. Ibid., 7.

25. Ibid.

26. Ibid., 16–18.

27. Ibid., 19.

philosophically what Jung is explaining psychologically regarding the language of the psyche. Ricoeur argues that the symbol, in essence, holds the manifest and latent meaning. Similar to Jung, Ricoeur understands that the symbol contains the sacred and the profane, the image and its opposite, or the shadow of the image in Jungian terms.[28] As Jung says, "Every Psychological extreme secretly contains its own opposite or stands in some sort of intimate and essential relation to it."[29]

Perhaps at the center of Jung's analytical model regarding symbols is his concept of archetypes, and more specifically the archetype of the Self. Archetypes will be discussed in greater detail in chapter 4. This definition will suffice for now,

> the unconscious, as the totality of all archetypes, is the deposit of all human experience right back to its remotest beginnings. Not, indeed, a dead deposit, a sort of abandoned rubbish heap, but a living system of actions and aptitudes that determine the individual's life in invisible ways—all the more effective because invisible. It is not a gigantic historical prejudice, so to speak, an a priori historical condition; but it is also the source of the instincts, for the archetypes are simply the forms which the instincts assume.[30]

Jung's own understanding of the archetypes developed throughout the course of his life and work, but central to his own understanding of the psyche's structure is the layer of the collective, in which dwells these universal patterns which are presented from the psyche in varying ways based on a particular individual but are nonetheless universally experienced. Jung writes that the Self is an archetype that drives one toward integration and wholeness. The Self is both conscious and unconscious, process and content.[31] "The self is a living symbol because it designates something we know exists; we know there is a totality of consciousness and unconsciousness because we are the living examples of it."[32] Where Ricoeur articulates, based on Freud's language, a symbol is both manifest, as something appears to be, and latent, what lies underneath the appearance, namely, its unconscious wish, he acknowledges that the symbol is both the image and it's opposite. For Jung, the image of the Self contains both what is manifest or conscious or part of the ego complex, and that, which is latent or unknown, and

---

28. Ibid., 28–32.

29. Jung, *Symbols of Transformation*, ¶381.

30. Jung, *Structure and Dynamics of the Psyche*, ¶339.

31. Ulanov, *Unshuttered Heart*, 188.

32. Jung, *Psychiatric Studies*, ¶414.

opposite of the ego's pursuits.[33] As Jung says, "the self is no mere concept or logical postulate; it is a psychic reality, only part of it conscious, while for the rest it embraces the life of the unconscious and is therefore inconceivable except in the form of symbols."[34]

The Self designates a wholeness or totality of being that is larger than the ego, that which makes up consciousness. We are both simultaneously in *it* and *it* in us. The Self's agenda is opposite that of the ego's as it seeks to include the left-out parts, all the aspects and contents of one's psyche. The Self's agenda serves as compensation to the ego's agenda, thus symbolically holding for us our own larger picture, what we are striving toward—namely, integration.[35] As Ann Ulanov says, "to be whole means including all our parts—the loony ones, the mad bits, all that lies undeveloped alongside our most developed skills, talents, and desires."[36] She reminds us that the disorder and chaos in society results from neglecting to address the Self that addresses each of us. Jung expounds upon his notion of the Self articulating how, "the Self is such a disagreeable thing in a way, so realistic, because it is what you really are, not what you want to be or imagine you ought to be; and that reality is so poor, sometimes dangerous, and even disgusting, that you will quite naturally make every effort not to be yourself."[37]

The Self is exposed or shows up in the messy field of transference whether it occurs in the analytic space, in relationships, in one's work environment and even in the process of *writing* and *reading* literature. It shows up in the transference as it replays earlier object-relations and debuts one's particular process of individuation as well.[38] The work of analysis is bringing ego-conscious attention to the work of the Self. So, while, according to Jung, "we would rather accept anything in the world, any devil or any hell, than accept ourselves in our particular concreteness. That is the thing of which we are most afraid . . . [It is] only when we accept the thing which is loathsome to us, have we a real will to change, not before."[39] Jung's notion of the Self will come into play more visibly in the second half of this work when discussing the notion of Individuated Religion and the role the book of Job plays in relation to the dominant history purported within the Hebrew canon.

33. Jung, *Psychology and Religion* ¶¶154, 281.

34. Jung, *Aion*, ¶233.

35. Ulanov, *Unshuttered Heart*, 196.

36. Ulanov, *Spiritual Aspects of Clinical Work*, 326.

37. Jung, *Nietzsche's Zarathustra*, 99.

38. Ulanov, *Spiritual Aspects of Clinical Work*, 323.

39. Jung, *Nietzsche's Zarathustra*, 86–87.

Jung understands symbols as intrinsic to and between people and especially in sacred texts that try to speak of that which transcends human consciousness. However, Jung sees that symbols can lose their potency and fail to connect us to what it is they point us toward.[40] As Jolande Jacobi says, "A symbol is alive as long as it is 'pregnant with meaning' only as long as the opposites form and the raw material of imagery combine in it to make a whole so that its relation to the unconscious remains effective and meaningful."[41] Psychic equilibrium is sacrificed to conscious or unconscious totalitarianism. One's symbols can become rote or dead if one only employs the kind of thinking and reflection that comes from the side of consciousness, what Jung calls directed thinking. "Directed or logical thinking is reality-thinking, a thinking that is adapted to reality, by means of which we imitate the successiveness of objectively real things, so that the images inside our mind follow one another in the same strictly causal sequence as the events taking place outside it. We also call this 'thinking with directed attention.'"[42] If one loses access to imagination, creativity, the uncanny or the messy, symbols that were once alive can become deeds to fulfill or creeds to recite rather than moving one into relationship to that which the symbol is pointing toward. Or, on the other side, one can lose herself in the unconscious swamp, lose access to directed thinking and, in this way, get taken over or drowned in the archetypal energy of the unconscious.

Jung helps us to see how symbols can allow for a channelization of libido, allowing for more space within the individual and between the individual and others. However, he says they can also become rote and dead, suffocating the other or plugging up the flow of the libido, ceasing communication within the individual and between the individual and others if there is not enough space between the symbol and one's own experience.[43] The lack of or collapse of space can lead to a dogmatic use of the symbol, no longer connecting one to one's whole Self or beyond one's Self and toward others. Furthermore, if one mandates there is only one particular way into the experience or one single use of the symbol for others, one thrusts the one meaning of the symbol upon others. Thus, individual experience is disallowed and the symbol dies.

One may also become over-identified with the symbol. Rather than the symbol allowing for movement and growth one can become swallowed whole by the meaning itself, becoming subjectively identified with the

40. Jung, *Symbols of Transformation*, ¶¶28–29.

41. Jacobi, *Complex, Archetype, Symbol*, 97.

42. Jung, *Symbols of Transformation*, ¶11.

43. Ibid., ¶217.

symbol rather than seeing the symbol as the bridging agent.[44] Symbols do not contain one meaning for Jung but rather serve as a container for us to experience what is objectively beyond the symbol. When symbols cease from serving this function they become at best, dead, and at worst, dangerous tools. Jung explains, when the symbol is adopted by society and left in the hands of political or social authority it runs the risk of turning freedom of the individual into slavery. He describes this as a case of the archetypal energy encased in the symbol being wrongly attributed to the subjective level of experience when it should be attributed to the objective level of experience—something outside of an individual or particular group. When we wrongly attribute the emergent symbol merely subjectively without recognizing its objective level this can "bring about dangerous inflations which seem unimportant to the lay (person) only because he has no idea of the inward and outward disasters that may result."[45] One can place too much value upon consciousness, disabling reception from one's unconscious resulting in the death of symbols and atrophy of symbolic life. Jung refers to the space the symbol traverses as a process or function that occurs between conscious and unconscious union.[46] The symbol itself arises and is found in the space between conscious and unconscious. If there is no communication between conscious and unconscious, if one is valued over the other the space between the two collapses and the transcendent is not facilitated or experienced. As Ulanov says, our psyches experience deadness when, "we fall into identification with an archetypal image, with one point of view with one symbolic representation of truth."[47]

Continuing with this second methodological assumption let us turn to Donald Winnicott and his understanding of the formation and function of symbols. Different from Jung, Winnicott describes symbols as objects, external from the individual, yet internal too in that they become imbued with the individual's subjectivity in the space between the subject (individual) and her other (caregiver, lover, friend). As he says,

> In the experience of the more fortunate baby (and small child and adolescent and adult) the question of separation in separating

44. Ibid., ¶¶176–250, Ulanov, *Feminine in Jungian Psychology*, 3–84. Jacobi, *Complex, Archetype, Symbol*, 15.

45. Jung, *Psychology and Alchemy*, ¶29.

46. Jung, "Study in the Process of Individuation," "Two Kinds of Thinking," "Concept of Libido," "Transformation of Libido," "Psychology and Religion," "Psychological Approach to the Dogma of the Trinity," "Introduction to the Religious and Psychological Problems of Alchemy," "Individual Dream Symbolism in Relation to Alchemy," "Basics of Alchemy," "Commentary on 'The Secret of the Golden Flower.'"

47. Ulanov, *Unshuttered Heart*, 207.

does not arise, because in the potential space between the baby and the mother there appears the creative playing that arises naturally out of the relaxed state; it is here that there develops a use of symbols that stand at one and the same time for external world phenomena and for phenomena of the individual person who is being looked at.[48]

Crucial for Winnicott, is the potential space between two subjects, potential because the space is filled with objects for play that enable the individual subject to develop a use of symbols to work out inner and outer reality. I want to make a brief comment about the word play. The word play is jarring in a document such as this that addresses historical realities such as exile that were profoundly devastating. I seek to contribute another way of understanding ancient Israel's process of establishing nationhood and identity in the ANE. When I use the word play throughout this document what I mean essentially is flexibility. Psychoanalytic theory helps us understand how play assumes flexibility, an ability to fantasize and image experiences symbolically. When one is unable to be flexible one is unable to be in relationship with difference—personally or collectively. I resisted eliminating the word entirely from this work because play is what is needed for one to be able to establish a sense of external reality, as will be explained. An important note must be made however that the word play is not void of destruction and the vital work of aggression. There is violence in play and it is precisely the violence that allows one to use the objects one is provided and one finds to help define her sense of self. In this way, there is some violence in using the word play, often thought of as only teddy bears and smiles, when referring to the realities and horrors that will be described throughout. This is precisely why I choose to use *this* word interchangeably with imagining, fantasy, and flexibility.

In chapter 3 it will be argued that the Deuteronomic Covenant can be understood and analyzed as an example of a symbol for ancient Israel created out of Israel's communal experience with something that was both beyond them and in their midst during a formative and precarious time as a community in transition. The Deuteronomic Covenant, originally formulated sometime during the seventh century between the time of Hezekiah and Josiah and "discovered" in the temple in 622 BCE under Josiah's reign (2 Kings 23:1–3), was used to congeal Israel, centralize worship, reconnect Israel to Israel's foundation myths and correct Israel's sinful ways in hopes of staving off inevitable destruction and exile from the surrounding

48. Winnicott, *Playing and Reality*, 146–47.

superpowers of Assyria, Egypt, and Babylonia, warring for Israel's precious land.[49] In the Winnicottian sense of a symbol this Covenant enabled Israel to structure life during a time of political upheaval. It was born out of the cultural milieu of the ancient Near East and out of Israel's own growing religious identity. The Covenant, as a symbol, connected Israel to Adonai and to one another with a particular way of relating within the community and with those outside of the community.[50]

Winnicott understands symbols to be that which emerge from the unity between the mothering one and the baby and stand between the baby and her developing self and her external objective other, her caregiver, and her world. Symbols, first for the young child like a toy or blanket (transitional objects in a transitional space) and later for the adult, like art and religion in culture, create space between self and other that facilitates transition from a merged state of being self and other, to seeing each in their own right, existing independently.[51] With the experience of this other comes also the experience of the external world.

Winnicott explains that symbols and symbolic formation create a path toward differentiation that takes place in the transitional space between subject and object and move the subject from the psychological state of "absolute dependence" "towards independence."[52] He describes the process of differentiation as the young child's transition from a merged state of being with caretaker to a place of being able to experience another as objectively other in his or her own right, independent of and external to the subject's experience of the other, as the transitional space. It is in this transitional space that symbols or transitional objects, can allow or disallow movement into greater openness to one's self and others wherein one has the capacity to experience one's self as increasingly distinct, a subject, and an other as truly other, an objective other rather than as a reflection of one's own subjectivity.

This process of transition from dependence to independence requires the essential linking-up of the aggressive impulse. As the child is slowly introduced with moments of disillusion at the growing realization that she is not omnipotently tied to the mothering-one, nor able to magically control her, she is left with objects with which to play and work out her disappointment and disillusionment. It is through aggression the child is able to experience her own destructive capacity. These toys lying

49. Albertz, *History of Israelite Religion*, 195–231.

50. In order to designate the tetragrammaton, the four-letter unvocalized symbol of the divine name of God, I will use the term Adonai throughout this work. When other names of God are used I will designate those in their Hebrew form.

51. Winnicott, *Playing and Reality*, 1–34.

52. Winnicott, *Maturational Processes*, 29–36.

around in the transitional space between mother and baby stand in for both and in play the child can maim the mother (recognized by the outsider as a teddy bear) as she is able to unleash her fury at her mother for leaving her momentarily or not immediately providing her with what she desires. However, in this transitional space while the child gains access to her aggression she begins to recognize that the object thought to have been destroyed, given what it symbolized (the relationship between she and her mothering one), in fact, survives—the teddy bear is still there! It is the survival of the object through the child's destruction of it that enables the child to experience the world as external to her own being and body. Similarly, it is the mother's or mothering-one's ability to survive the child's destructive impulses that allows the child to experience her mother as objectively other outside of the child's subjective experience of her. The space between child and caregiver and later between two adults, for example between an analyst and analysand, Winnicott says is the space of imagination, creativity, ingenuity, and play. This is the space in which paradoxically the child both finds and creates her self as separate from her caregiver, her environment, and yet in relation to both.[53]

This space created within one's developing self and between one's self and the external world, is the transitional space, or the location of the cultural experience.[54] The space has also been called the third space[55] or the space in *between* subject and object the space of transition between a child's experience of her caregiver as herself toward an experience of her caregiver outside of herself.[56] However, in this transitional space the symbol or transitional object can become rigidified into fetish objects or idols, which can end up collapsing this in-between space and thus interrupt growth and differentiation.[57]

Chapter 4 will discuss the view I advance in this work that the Deuteronomic Covenant became rigidified and concretized due to the trauma of the Exile. The space originally maintained through the work of constructing the Covenant collapsed when the Babylonians captured Judah, demolished the temple, and deported the religious elites. In postexilic Israel, the Covenant that had perhaps at one time encouraged autonomy, growth, and differentiation as a nation in relation to its surrounding superpowers,

53. Winnicott, *Playing and Reality*, 119.

54. Ibid., 128–39.

55. Lacan, *Language of the Self,* 132, 264; Ogden, *Subjects of Analysis,* 61–96; Benjamin, *Bonds of Love,* 16–18; and Benjamin, *Shadow of the Other,* 28.

56. Winnicott, *Playing and Reality*, 115–27.

57. Ibid.,12.

became a weapon, a way of assigning fault and a tool that instructed Israel to imbibe the blame in order to make unbearable suffering of exile bearable. The symbol, the act of "finding" and "making" the Covenant (explained in detail in Part 1 following) that opened up a channel of creative energy for Israel in the context of Israel's own vassal relationship to Assyria to withstand domination and maintain a level of autonomy as a nation, instead began to suffocate and deaden the aliveness once experienced in order to find and create some meaning of the Exile.

Both Jung and Winnicott explain how it is the space between subject and object, inner and outer, conscious and unconscious that is vital for growth. It is in this intermediate space in which binaries recede that something new begins to grow. This leads us into the third assumption of the present operative method. To restate, the method by which the following work proceeds utilizes the psychoanalytic theories of Jung and Winnicott as different lenses through which to analyze the historical and literary nuances of the Deuteronomic Covenant and the book of Job. Thus far it has been articulated that the method employed impacts both how I read sacred texts, undergo scholarly research, and teach the Bible. Two of the four underlying assumptions, the universal and timeless reality of the psyche and the psyche's use of symbol formation as a way to bring psychic balance have, so far, been explained. Now we will move into the third methodological assumption, namely the notion of the space between, or, the third space.

Scholarship in the "Space Between"

The integrity of the separate and unique fields of biblical scholarship and depth psychology which, when held separate and yet conversing together, opens up a third space to critically analyze the biblical text. The third space being referred to can be found on at least three levels. First, there is the space between the biblical text and the scholar. Second is the space between biblical scholarship and psychoanalytic theory, here of Jung and Winnicott on symbols. Third, and specific to the present topic, is the space between the Covenant narrative, or Covenant Religion, found in Deuteronomy and the Deuteronomistic History and its counter-narrative of Individuated religion, read in the book of Job. All three levels will be addressed.

Space between text and scholar

In light of the previous conversation regarding the different and yet congruent psychoanalytic notions of the symbol from the perspective of Jung and

Winnicott and the role of the symbolic in a person's life, it is my view that the Bible, as a sacred text, *can* be analyzed and regarded as a symbol. What makes a text sacred is an entire subject on its own, which is too great a topic to engage with fully at present. However, what is considered sacred in this context is a text that withstands the test of time in its ability to enable individuals and communities to make individual and collective meaning. These texts may include religious texts, books of poetry or literature, and songs—though the examples will vary based on person and culture. The very aliveness of the text as something that connects an individual or community to another and to that which transcends ought to be considered sacred. I believe it could even be contested that, should the text cease to connect one to those outside of one's self or to the transcendent, meaning that which is beyond subjectivity, the text may cease to be held as sacred. However, it must be said that any given text could in fact remain alive; i.e., sacred, for some, while, simultaneously be dead; i.e., cease to be sacred, for others. Of course, this leads to another argument regarding the interconnectedness of sacredness and subjectivity, a topic to be addressed at another time. The sacred text, in and of itself, contains something that is outside of any individual or community's relationship with it.[58] This is an important crux of my following argument. Much like a doctrine, a theological concept, a ritual, an icon, or a liturgy, the Bible was created from a particular group of people, in a particular time with a particular historical reality and yet it continues to be used by people and communities outside of the historical experiences of its creators. The way it is used varies, and yet, it is used by a number of diverse communities all over the world, just as it was used, redacted and shaped by diverse communities within the ancient world—which serves as evidence of the aliveness of the symbol.

Going back to the first methodological assumption described above, while we do not all have the same psyche, we do share the same kind of psyche. This means that while a person's engagement with the Bible today or the way in which one uses the Bible as sacred text to enable connection to reality beyond his own experience, and in order to make meaning in his present circumstances will differ in kind, it will, nevertheless, be similar in form. As explained in the second methodological assumption, one of the ways in which the psyche (individual and collective) seeks equilibrium is through symbol formation. Thus, what is meant by the space between text and scholar is the necessary distinction that must be made between the symbol found to seek psychic equilibrium, and the person or community who found and created that symbol in the first place. The following maintains

---

58. Cooper and Goldstein, "Cult of the Dead," 286.

this space by delving into the socio-historical context out of which the text, understood here as symbol, arose.

In Jungian terms, the text, as a symbol, serves as a bridge that points to that which is beyond one's ego consciousness yet includes it as well as individual and collective unconscious contents.[59] The text becomes an object to which one can relate and eventually use. This object (text) can hold one's unconscious projections and allow the individual to wrestle with them, slowly gaining greater consciousness about his own projections upon the symbol and enabling the individual to begin using the symbol to connect with what is beyond him. The text is outside of us and yet informed by our own subjective experience. We create meaning in and from the text that serves to enlarge and strengthen the ego from the Self's perspective, and what the Self points to and makes more accessible. We learn that we are not as we previously conceived of ourselves from our conscious ego perspective. There is another layer, other parts of us we wish so strongly were not part of us that we have thrown those parts off onto other people or other groups. This is the positive and negative function of projection. We "throw" parts of ourselves off onto others. This throwing off distances us from parts of our self but also, eventually, allows us to see those parts that belong to us which were not tangible or visible when completely unconscious.[60] If we can create meaning in and from the text, as a symbol, it will enable us to come into relationship with that which we believed was not part of us.

A lack of space between text and scholar occurs when one engages the text solely from one's ego consciousness. When consciousness is favored at the expense of the unconscious, the unconscious protrudes even more. Meaning, when one believes himself to be involved in a merely objective scientific endeavor in relation to the text, he is all the more caught up in his own unconscious projections or subjective experience of the text, without the help of consciousness to understand where these projections come from or the power they contain. What is needed in order to create space between the text and the scholar when one is merely conscious driven is time spent in what Jung terms, non-directed thinking. Non-directed thinking is the kind of thinking that occurs when we are asleep, when we are playing, or when we are resting from ego chores. This kind of thinking belongs to the unconscious; it does not require or seek resolution or integration. It is the kind of thinking that does not tire, and is not rational, but, rather, expressively communicates in images or other equivalents such as textures,

---

59. Jung, *Psychological Types*, ¶828.

60. Von Franz, *Projection and Re-collection*, 1–34.

sounds, body gestures, scents, or tastes. This kind of thinking can initiate a conversation between one's own unconscious and conscious life.

Interaction with the sacred text from this other mode of non-directed thinking creates the space between text and scholar. This space will open up new meanings and insights and perhaps restore that which has been silenced within the scholar *and* within the *text itself*. What is discovered in this space is vital for both the text and the scholar of the text. The survival and relevance of the symbol for the individual, community, and future communities, is possible because the symbol does not collapse into and remain in one person's or one community's subjective experience of the symbol but remains outside as a symbol through which meaning is made and self and other are both found and created again and again.

This space is not only pertinent for those who are in relation to this symbol, but it is also significant for the symbol itself and for understanding the history connected to the ancient communities responsible for writing and constructing it. I suggest, by creating space between text and scholar, the scholar may be able to discover clues to parts of Israel's history that have been muted, glossed over, or perhaps even erased. Working to create this psychic space between the text and the scholar may prove significant for the future of historical-critical studies. There is more to be known about the history of Israel than the hypothetical scientific agenda of the historical-critical field will allow us to discover.

In Winnicottian language, to understand the Bible as symbol or what he might call a transitional object, means that the Bible is something other than the one who is reading it and yet psychic material of the reader and her relational matrices with others are imparted into the text and played with, destroyed, and re-created. This process enables the reader to find herself in the experience of Scripture and tradition. It also allows the reader access to who or what it is Scripture and tradition point to as something objectively other rather than merely a sum of what we impart to the text, what Winnicott calls as a subjective object.[61] More time will be spent on these concepts in the following chapters. For now, it suffices to say that the Bible understood as a symbol enables any reader of the text enough space to engage with the multiple meanings gleaned from the text itself and the multiple meanings made on behalf of the reader or reading community today.

A good example of how space between text and scholar is possible and relevant for the text to have its symbolic capacity maintained can be found in Hebrew Bible scholar, Bruce Zuckerman's, work. Bruce Zuckerman calls

---

61. Berne-DeGear, "Revisiting Texts of Tension." Also see Rizzuto, *Birth of the Living God*; Winnicott, *Maturational Processes,* 56—63.

his own method, a metaphor. He acknowledges the insignificant reality of theories as they are so carefully constructed by scholars and boldly put forth but given the lack of concrete evidence with the material one seeks to understand in the Hebrew Bible, these theories can be shattered with the slightest breath of new evidence or critical insight.[62] In other words, there is such limited historical and archeological evidence of the events of Israel's past yet entire theories are proposed in the field of biblical studies. A good example of a theory being proposed based on little to no evidence is the Deuteronomistic History hypothesis proposed by Martin Noth which has become an entire field of study, fraught with division and controversy, within Hebrew Bible studies. This theory and field of research is exactly what will be taken up in the following Chapters.

Zuckermann puts forth a metaphor rather than a hard-earned theory, and argues a metaphor is more malleable. As he says,

> A good metaphor has a certain undefined but concrete quality about it by which it can even transcend the words used to bring it to life. It might even be said that the words used to compose a metaphor really only approximate what it actually means ... and in the final analysis one cannot completely define what makes it seem more tangible than a theory and therefore more real.[63]

He is describing the use and work of a metaphor much like the psychoanalytic understanding of a symbol. The symbol, like the metaphor, has certain concreteness about it, yet is more acquiescent than a theory, and works to direct one into a deeper meaning beyond what is constructed in the symbol itself. Zuckerman articulates that the use of metaphor allows him to start his analysis with something that is more tangible and flexible than a theory.[64] He describes, "It allows me to begin my thinking with a freer play of imagination; and considering the lack of specific evidence, which so severely handicaps scholarly research into the Bible, imagination must always be an essential ingredient in one's analysis, whether this be manifest in metaphor, theory or anything else."[65] The work of the imagination as an essential ingredient to analysis is at the heart of this work, and how one is able to create *space* between the text and her subjective perspective of the text.

---

62. Zuckerman, *Job the Silent*, 3.

63. Ibid., 3-4.

64. Ibid.

65. Ibid.

Space between Biblical Scholarship
and Psychoanalytic Theory

The space between biblical scholarship and psychoanalytic theory is another instance of what is called this third space enabled by placing the two disciplines beside one another without collapsing the space between them by reducing either one of them to the other or privileging one discipline over the other. This notion of the third space, adopted from the field of psychoanalysis, is the space wherein this author's own methodology for research and writing takes place by working between these two fields.

For this project in particular, I engage the text with the historical-critical and literary methods of criticism within the field of biblical scholarship. Simultaneously I take up the psychoanalytic theories of Jung and Winnicott (and in the second half of this work off-shoots of the Lacanian tradition found in Davoine and Guadilliére). This method of setting sources from the two disciplines next to each other has created a third space wherein the psychoanalytic theories urge us to ask different kinds of questions regarding the information gleaned from historical-critical and literary research.

Again, this third space is a space wherein both fields inform my analysis of the texts and concepts at hand. For example, while reading Lacanian psychoanalysts Fraçoise Davoine's and Jean-Max Guadilliére's book entitled *History Beyond Trauma* that provocatively advocates madness as a method for psychological and social/communal discovery and eventual healing, I was struck with the resonances between their psychoanalytic ideas and the literary and, potentially, historical role of the book of Job in relation to the Deuteronomistic History in the Hebrew canon. This idea became a crux of this project and will be discussed at length throughout. This is just one example of how my method, using psychoanalytic theory as a lens through which to analyze the historical and literary nuances of the Deuteronomic Covenant and the book of Job, is possible because of the space created between these two disciplines.

Space between the Covenant and Individuated Narratives

The fourth assumption underlying my method is that this third space between text and scholar, between the two disciplines, and between the two *historical* narratives, Covenant and Individuated Religion, becomes possible by engaging with the shadow of the dominant historical narrative, the aspects of Israel's history that have been left out or massaged away within the Deuteronomistic History's motif. These two threads, Covenant and

Individuated Religion, are both articulated and held in tension within the Hebrew canon. Because they are held together, they help enunciate a new symbol that arises between the two *found precisely in the left-out parts*, the repressed memory and affect of the trauma of the exile(s) negated in the national History based on Deuteronomy and inscribed in Joshua—Kings. The "left-out part" will be explained further down as the "inferior function" in Jungian terms, meaning, the non-dominant function—in a person, community, or body of literature—that has not yet been integrated.

The character of Job and what this character holds in relation to this History is a new image that comes to symbolize a new kind of subjectivity and a new vision of God. Chapter 5 will lay out an argument for the book of Job to be read as a symbolic history, a history that does not speak directly about the atrocious experience of the Exile but rather affectively contains the left-out parts of the Deuteronomistic History. The symbol of the Covenant discussed in Part 1 remains intricately connected to both Covenantal and Individuated narratives. Chapter 7 provides a detailed comparison between Deuteronomy 28 and the book of Job. There, an argument will be made for Job as a symbol of Israel as *tam* (blameless, complete, and finished) and full of *tamim* (integrity). This symbol provides new meaning to Covenantal religion through its individuating aspects. Chapter 8 will analyze this symbol from a psychoanalytic perspective offering new possibilities for interpretation that arise due to the book's engagement with the fourth, the shadow of dominant history's narrative.

Chapter 9 will use this new symbol of Job as representing Israel containing the affective experience of the Babylonian Exile, what I have called the left-out aspects of traumatic suffering in Exile, and thus offers a new way into the covenant by individuating from, or stepping outside of the collective experience. To have now the present two narratives, Covenant and Individuated Religion, maintained in the Hebrew canon provides a model for how an individual or a community today might employ these contrasting and even contradictory god-images.

These differing god-images arise out of one's own place in life, social location, or even one's own time of mourning or trauma. The surprise discovery is not that one narrative usurps or replaces the other, but rather, that the Individuated narrative articulated in the book of Job re-enlivens the symbol originally found in the Covenant narrative. The book of Job becomes a symbol that enables postexilic Israel a way to imagine the God beyond the symbol of the covenant. Rather than imaging God *as* the Covenant, collapsing the space between the two, the postexilic community being imaged in the character of Job is provided a picture of God *beyond* the Covenant that is accessible not through perfect obedience to the covenant but through a complete or whole relationship to Self, other, and God. Ann Ulanov says,

> Our tendency to equate God with our own God-images applies to our group pictures as well. Sometimes we think that when we adopt the God-picture of a group we are moving beyond the narrow strictures of our egos. Unfortunately, this is not necessarily so because there really is such a thing as a collective ego and collective consciousness. The symbol for God in these cases is a particular group's highest value or social cause, which may in fact be a worthy value or cause. But the same dangerous psychological process we have been discussing, of substituting a symbolic equation for a symbol, obtains here. When we want to say that God is justice, or God is peace, or God is ecology . . . we are foisting our group-images onto God.[66]

By holding both perspectives, both narratives, the Hebrew canon contains the dual aspects of the symbol, what in Jung's language is called the ruling principle and the inferior function.[67] It is through inscribing the trauma of the Exile, evil experienced within ancient Israel, in both concretizing (through the Covenant narrative) and symbolic (through the book of Job) forms that the Covenant, while being constrictive and potentially re-traumatizing on the one hand, eventually provides postexilic Israel a way to imagine themselves, and the God of the Covenant, with new and varying relational potential.

Method as Pedagogy:
Biblical Studies and Practical Theology

Working with students as a professor in both the fields of biblical studies and depth psychology, I have found great resonance between the two fields. Students in the Bible classes naturally engage with this sacred text from some other place beyond mere academics whether it be from inside themselves informed by their own life history or from their own cultural and religious tradition; often all of these factors prove relevant for analyzing the text. When the students are allowed space to bring all of their selves into

66. Ulanov, *Picturing God*, 171.

67. Jung, *Red Book*, 253, 287. Also see Ulanov, *Madness and Creativity*, 14–15. Jung's understanding of the ruling principle, essentially that which belongs to ego-consciousness, is discussed first in his, *Archetypes and the Collective Unconscious*, ¶¶489–524. The inferior function is its opposite, the other side of the good in us that lies underdeveloped.

conversation with their own scholarship around a particular text something new inevitably opens up and they learn more about the text, and are intrigued by new discoveries. Thus, they are challenged to question their own hesitancies, biases and fears, and are urged to look deeper. New insights into the text, into their own lives, into their own culture and religious tradition emerge alongside new ideas for biblical research.

The method proposed is equally relevant for the student training in a practical field of ministry as it is for the student training to become a biblical scholar. The space of study ignites, invites, and holds new inquiries about the text, the text's history and meaning within history, and the text's meaning for us today. When disallowed this space and forced to engage purely reductively or historically the students, by and large, go dead doing their work. These students can give the "right" answers, but find no life in the symbols offered in the text. The traditional ways of doing scholarship, while alive and viable, if forced upon a student run the risk of what Jung explains as turning freedom into slavery or what Winnicott suggests as robbing the individual of his own creativity, a truly immoral act.[68]

The Third in the Shadow of the Fourth[69]

In order to get to this space of integration where new discoveries and new solutions can be made and found however, the student and scholar is often first challenged and confronted with that which has been left out within herself. All that fails to get included in consciousness, all that remains hidden in the shadows of the unconscious, is what makes up the fourth. What gets left out of consciousness and remains in the shadow of the unconscious differs from individual to individual and from group to group. This notion of the fourth proposed by Jung is taken up by Ulanov who elucidates that, "Our work personally and collectively . . . is sorting out the fourth that engineers the third wherein healing locates."[70] The space between the two, whether it be between the text and the scholar, biblical studies and psychoanalysis, or Covenant and Individuated Religion emerges as a space wherein healing can happen once the left out parts (of self, community, or history) have been grappled with and integrated.

It is the slow integration of and relationship to the material of the fourth, the parts left out individually, communally and socially, that enable the new

---

68. Jung, *Civilization in Transition*, ¶¶488–588; and Winnicott, *Maturational Processes*, 93–105.

69. Ulanov, *Unshuttered Heart*, 157–78.

70. Ibid., 169.

to be found in the space between the text and the scholar, the two disciplines, or the two narratives of Covenant and Individuated Religion. Within Jung's notion of the third, the dialectical relationship between ego and Self or what Jung calls the transcendent function, there exists a prerequisite. That prerequisite is one's openness and submission to the fourth, that is, to what each of us excludes or wants to omit. Jung suggests we cannot get to the third, the new, without first going through what is in the shadows (for Jung, "the shadow"), all that has not been brought to consciousness. In the fourth lies "the bad, the destructive, whatever is evil, what not only competes with our ideals of the good, but seeks to dismantle the good, exterminate it."[71] The fourth, that which remains in the unconscious, as Jung says is the "fly in the ointment, the skeleton in the cupboard of perfection, the painful lie given to all idealistic pronouncements, the earthiness that clings to our human nature and sadly clouds the crystal clarity we long for . . . but at the same time it is . . . the basis for the preparation of the philosophical gold."[72] By and large biblical scholarship is uncomfortable with methods that honor subjectivity, for they are messy, too open-ended, and lack crystal clarity.

The fourth methodological assumption supporting this project's operative method, which, to summarize again, uses psychoanalytic theory, specifically that of Jung and Winnicott on symbols, as a lens through which to analyze the historical and literary nuances of the Deuteronomic Covenant and the book of Job, takes Jung's notion of the fourth and Ulanov's amplification of it, describing the third in the shadow of the fourth, as an essential starting point. In biblical scholarship, there are methods that hold the fourth for the scholarly world. Biblical criticisms such as ideological, post-colonial, feminist, womanist, socio-cultural, and reader-response criticisms, in a certain way are the fourth—the left-out perspectives and parts of biblical scholarship, the voices from the margins who challenge dominant scholarship's objective pretenses. The method proposed herein brings psychological language to the field of biblical scholarship as a way to engage what has been done and what is still left undone.

It is these critical methods within the biblical field, those that reference that which has been left out, lost, forgotten, repressed, or shamed that the following work seeks to address on three levels:

1. The world behind the text in terms of its historicity.

2. The world of the text itself in terms of literary construction.

---

71. Ibid., 170; and Jung, *Psychology and Alchemy*, ¶¶160, 406.

72. Jung, *Psychology and Alchemy*, ¶207.

3. The world in front of the text in terms of who is reading and how one reads.[73]

As the scholar who engages the ancient text is increasingly aware of his own subjectivity in relation to his research, exegesis, and interpretation of the text, noticing patterns and themes in what he chooses to write about and how he approaches the text, his own method will become more capacious. This increased spaciousness will allow the scholar to hear things from the text he could not hear before. The text is freed from his own projections. Other aspects of its historical or literary construction may begin to surface. With attention to the fourth as described above comes a kind of symbolic death, and it is the "Symbolic death . . . [that] is the gateway to what our symbols symbolize."[74] While I analyze the Deuteronomic Covenant, its symbolic value for the Israelites during the eighth to sixth centuries and its rigidification throughout exile in the sixth and fifth centuries, I also investigate the constructive function of its symbolic death, at the destruction of Job, which serves as a gateway in relation to the dominant history to what it is the symbol of the Covenant symbolizes.

Two Audiences

The following work is written with two fields, two audiences in mind. On the one hand, it is written for the field of biblical scholarship. In it is proffered a hypothesis for how the trauma of the Babylonian Exile, compounded by the many previous exiles amongst Israel and Judah, effected the developing Hebrew identity including, in an integral way, Israel's religious identity amidst the social climate of the ancient Near East. I posit that these effects can be read poignantly in Deuteronomy and the Deuteronomistic History. This idea is not a new one but rather builds on scholars who have come before including, but not limited to, Martin Noth, Rainer Albertz, Thomas Römer, and David Janzen.[75] However, a new contribution this work seeks to make is regarding the counter-narrative read in the book of Job and how this counter-text affects the construction and understanding of the Deuteronomic Covenant.

The field of depth psychology has opened up new avenues of research regarding what is not explicitly spoken, in fact remains unknown to

---

73. Schneider, *Revelatory Text*.

74. Ulanov, *Unshuttered* Heart, 218.

75. Noth, *Deuteronomistic History*; Albertz, *Israel in Exile*; Römer, *So-Called Deuteronomistic History*; Janzen, *Violent Gift*.

consciousness, and yet is articulated clearly even if unconsciously through inscribed theories, histories, ideologies, theologies, and hermeneutical dispositions, within relationships and in works of art. The work of depth psychology helps a patient see what is unconsciously spoken and acted out in relationships and repetitive patterns, what is being projected and introjected within the analytic relationship. That which is projected is the psychic material of the patient (or the analyst!) that is not believed to be part of the individual and thus thrust upon innocent bystanders or important and integral relationships for very nuanced and particular reasons.[76] That which is introjected is what one takes in from the analyst, from society, caregivers, idealized lovers or friends that is then assimilated into one's own psychic makeup and into one's group consciousness unconsciously for good or for ill.[77]

The purpose of "seeing" is so that the individual may experience personal freedom and wholeness. Rather than being bound by repetitive actions and behaviors due to unprocessed unconscious material the individual is able to choose more freely and wholly the kinds of relationships, jobs, work, etc. in which to engage. Freedom and wholeness enable an individual to acknowledge pain, personal or communal trauma, and live in relationship with it rather than unconsciously or desperately trying to rid herself of the memory, resultant repercussions, or the compulsive need to have mastery over the experience.[78] Freedom, wholeness, and consciousness allow one to become aware of the "uninvited guests from the unremembered past," guests that haunt one's unconscious, unbeknownst to her, affecting the way in which she views herself and others and how one is able to live and grow, individually and communally.[79] One may not become free of the complexes that intrude in one's life but will be able to see her complexes as her own unique path toward creative living. This builds on Ann Ulanov's reading of *The Red Book* and her own work as a Jungian analyst over the past 40 years. She says, "The repetition is not just madness that bedevils and rends a gap into which we plunge; it also aims to expand consciousness. This happens not through conceptualization but through affective experience . . . The madness of once again suffering the chaos of unraveling that the complex inflicts gets rescued into emerging meaning."[80]

76. M. Klein, *Envy and Gratitude*, 69, 238, 250, 252–53.

77. Ibid., 2–22.

78. Freud, *Beyond the Pleasure Principle*, 31.

79. Coles, *Uninvited Guest from the Unremembered Past*.

80. Ulanov, *Madness and Creativity*, 4.

Bringing the tools of psychoanalysis and psychoanalytic theory to biblical scholarship will provide the necessary materials for inquiry into the formation of the Deuteronomistic History and its counter-narrative in the book of Job. If the formal history of ancient Israel was written during the Babylonian Exile and canonized during the Hellenistic period, two moments impacted by extreme communal trauma, how were these fundamental and sacred texts informed and reformed by this trauma? How was Israelite identity shaped by these experiences? How was Adonai portrayed as a result of or in light of such atrocities? And what does it mean for the scholar and the practitioner today to gain some awareness of the unconscious affect trauma has on one's own development of self or communal identity, figuring the Divine, and constructing the other?

On the other hand, this work is written for the psychoanalytic community, for those in clinical practice or in the field of pastoral care and counseling. The objective is to use the tools of biblical scholarship to analyze the development of the Deuteronomic Covenant and its theology shaped throughout the Deuteronomistic History. After laying this background the work will continue as it investigates the support and critique of this ideology and the counter position being proffered in the book of Job. What is useful for clinicians in their work with patients is an understanding of a sacred text that moves beyond biblical characters and narratives, and moves deeper into how stories, histories, and ideologies get concretized, sometimes creating more trauma, before consciousness is gained.

The hypothesis examined regarding the formation of a text, or a theology within a text, provides a roadmap for how a community or individual might analyze the construction of his or her or their own life texts. The text then, functions as a symbol, enabling greater connectedness to the Self, others, and the Divine other. Rather than simply providing a story with which to relate or myth by which to be informed, though similar in process, the work here is used to analyze the *way* in which a story is *formed* or *told*. Taking the historical and literary context seriously helps one analyze more objectively how she forms her own stories of being and seeks to communicate them. In essence, this work analyzes how we (qua-human) *play* with history as a way of constructing identity and making meaning out of life's varied experiences. The method, as stated before, engages with that which has been left out or silenced, repressed and regressed, thus urgently seeking out parts of one's self and one's community's story that have been lost and left out in order to bring them into the light of consciousness to work them over, bring them back in conversation with the dominant story making room for more personal freedom.

Thus, the method that again to summarize, uses the psychoanalytic theory of Jung and Winnicott regarding symbols as a lens through which to analyze the historical and literary nuances of the Deuteronomic Covenant and the book of Job, pulls from both fields of biblical scholarship and depth psychology and creates enough space for the scholar to analyze her own subjective experiences that impact her research. Rainer Albertz, a prominent German scholar in the field of Hebrew Bible with a focus on Israelite religion looking particularly at how Israelite religion and ideology was shaped by the Babylonian Exile, made the following comment in a forward to a recently published book of compiled essays entitled, *Interpreting Exile: Displacement and Deportation in Biblical and Modern Contexts*:

> When I wrote *Israel in Exile*, I did not consider that I am a refugee of World War II. I have no memory of my home in Upper Silesia, now Poland, from which my mother carried me westward when I was one and a half years old. Nonetheless, the sense of being a refugee that I felt throughout my life wherever I lived in Germany could have provided a little more sensitivity toward the severe psychological and religious problems that the Babylonian Exiles must have experienced, although they seem to have been economically and legally integrated in a manner similar to what I experienced. I had never thought of this conjunction before, but the present volume revealed to me this possible hermeneutical predisposition.[81]

Here is a prominent biblical scholar indicating how his own subjective experience, if acknowledged, *could* have led or could lead to a different hermeneutical disposition or posture in his scholarship. I would argue that Albertz' experience as a refugee during WWII has indeed had an impact on his scholarship and his hermeneutical disposition, perhaps in ways of which he is not yet conscious. Reading the above statement, he seems to acknowledge that his experience could lead to a different hermeneutical disposition but he fails to see that perhaps his unprocessed experience is *exactly* what gave him the insight into his own book *Israel in Exile* and led him to date most of the texts of the Hebrew canon to the exilic period.[82]

Our life experiences inevitably influence our life's work. To summarize, the four methodological assumptions just expounded upon:

1. The universal and timeless reality of the psyche.

2. The act of symbolic formation as a move coming from the psyche in order to gain psychic equilibrium and begin the process of individuation.

81. Albertz, "Foreword," 2.
82. Albertz, *Israel In Exile*.

3. The integrity of the separate and unique fields of biblical scholarship and depth psychology which, when held separate, each in their own space, and yet together, using psychoanalytic theory to explore the historical and literary movements within scripture, opens up a third space between the two disciplines to critically analyze the biblical text.

4. The third space, the space between the two disciplines, becomes possible by engaging with the fourth, the shadow of Israel's dominant History, the aspects that have been left out or massaged away within the History's dominant motif, ground the operative method.

The following method, employs two psychoanalytic theories on symbols as a lens through which to critically engage the historical and literary nuances of the Deuteronomic Covenant and the book of Job. The four methodological assumptions grounding this method implore the scholar (and the clinician though the training the clinician receives provides this opportunity more readily than the training for the biblical scholar) to use the method on one's own life, a combination of being attentive to one's own history, the movement and nudging of the psyche and the scholar's own affective response to what is being read and engaged, in her analysis of the texts at hand. Thus, by gaining more consciousness of one's own story one will be able to see more clearly the dialectical relationship between the various voices echoed in the text with which one finds oneself working.

Limitations

Given the interdisciplinary focus of this work, that I have spent a great deal of time introducing, I must also admit the limitations of such a focus. By equally engaging biblical scholarship and psychoanalytic theory, and seeking to communicate and remain applicable to both fields, key themes and concepts of this work require in-depth discussion on both sides, which may lose, or perhaps simply bore, one side at a time. On the biblical side, necessary time will be spent articulating some of the main arguments regarding the Deuteronomistic History, exile, and critical scholarship on the books of Deuteronomy and Job. These are all areas of study highly contentious and rich with scholarly material. Some time will be spent first giving a brief review of the literature on each of these topics. Next, I will narrow down the argument as it relates to the text(s) at hand providing a brief review of the history of scholarship regarding each and relating to the main thesis of this project. Then, I will provide my own argument for understanding the function of these texts within the Hebrew canon. This step will predominately use the psychoanalytic theories of Carl Jung and Donald Winnicott as well as Ann Ulanov, and Françoise Davoine and Jean-Max Guadilliére, as lenses through which to analyze the historical and literary nuances of the Deuteronomic Covenant, specifically focused in Deuteronomy 28 and the way it is utilized in 2 Kings 23 and 25, and in the book of Job. Finally, I will provide my interpretation of the texts, given both the biblical and psychoanalytic backgrounds, highlighting the way in which these biblical texts speak to one another regarding the history of ancient Israel.

Performing due diligence in both fields requires me to be attentive to the main arguments at hand, but forces me at times to be selective about the arguments I take up given the limited physical space in which to write and the finite emotional and cognitive space with which to engage fully in both fields, rich with an enormity of literature. Thus, biblical scholars may find themselves wanting more attention to philological or textual nuances of Deuteronomy 28 and the passages with which I work within the book of Job, while psychoanalysts will want more dialogue between the psychoanalytic theories employed or clinical examples.

While there were many biblical examples I could have chosen to analyze as a "prototype" of the Deuteronomistic Covenant or Covenant Religion I limited myself to the blessing and curses section in Deuteronomy 28 as opposed to one of the two introductions within Deuteronomy or the other list of curses preceding Deut 28 or potential later postexilic redactions to Deuteronomy in Chapter 30, any of which could have been chosen. However, my choice to work with Deuteronomy 28 in particular is due to its direct relation to other ancient Near Eastern documents. This will be our starting point for analyzing the symbolic function of the Deuteronomic Covenant and its function for Covenant Religion.

Similarly, regarding the book of Job, one could write an entire book on just the prologue or the epilogue or any one poetic voice within the poetry section.[83] By narrowing one's breadth one is inevitably and commendably able to go much deeper into the nuances of this perplexing and lively text. Given the following argument is looking at the broader picture of the relationship between Job and Deuteronomy and the function of these two books for an understanding of an history of Israel and the application of this for communities who read these texts and are consciously or unconsciously informed by cultural interpretations of them today, my discussion on the book of Job is focused primarily on the literary portrayal of the character of Job and his uncanny relationship with Adonai. I have provided references for anyone interested in doing further research on any of the points discussed.

---

83. Ngwa, *Hermeneutics of the "Happy" Ending in Job 42:7–17.*

Part I

Covenant Religion

*History, Ideology, and the
Symbol of the Covenant*

And the King sent out and gathered unto him all the elders of Judah and Jerusalem. And the King went up to the house of Adonai and all the men of Judah and all those who dwelled in Jerusalem with him and all of the priests and the prophets and all the people from small to great. He proclaimed into their ears all the words of the book of the Covenant, the one found in the house of Adonai. And the King stood amongst the pillars and he made a Covenant before Adonai to walk after Adonai and to keep his commandments and his testimony (reminder), his statues with all his heart and all life force to carry out all the words of this Covenant, the ones written upon this book. And all the people stood with the Covenant.

—2 Kings 23:1–3[1]

Part 1 analyzes the historical and literary nuances of Deuteronomy 28 and the construction of Covenant Religion, formulated in the Deuteronomistic History (henceforth DH). I argue that the narrative in 2 Kings 22–23 about finding the book of the Covenant, an early version of the blessings and curses read in Deuteronomy 28, and the book of the Covenant's revitalization and implementation throughout Israel on the cusp of Judah's down-

---

1. All translations are the author's own, unless otherwise noted.

fall, functioned to formalize Covenant Religion and became a dominant motif characterizing the historical narrative that ensued. This movement, during the eighth–seventh centuries BCE, can be elucidated through the psychoanalytic lens of symbol formation and symbolic equation. Symbol formation occurs in all humans and cultures regardless of age or location, as outlined above in chapter 2. Symbolic equation, a normal stage of human development early on in relation to external objects, can reoccur at later stages when these early symbols formed cease from enabling individuals or a community from engaging with the external world or external objects the symbols were initially created to symbolize. What happens instead is the individual or community forces external reality to match her or their collective internal fantasy. Thus, the symbol ceases from being a symbol used in order to bridge the individual to others and to external reality.

Analyzed through the psychoanalytic theories of Winnicott and Jung, I propose the Covenant is best understood as a symbol created by the community of Israel during the eighth–seventh centuries BCE in developing their Hebrew community independent of the surrounding superpowers and nations to which they served as a vassal.[2] This symbol, originally enabling Israel to formulate an identity and construct a god-image that promised safety, wellbeing, and a prosperous future, that is the tenets of what I term Covenant Religion, eventually ceased from being a symbol and became instead, an object of judgment, blaming Israel for all the events of the steady

2. A note must be made regarding my employment of psychoanalytic theory, which has traditionally been analyzed and constructed within a dyadic or triadic (child/ two–parent) relational context, to an ancient communal and group context particularly regarding the understanding and construction of the community's relationship with the Divine. First of all, I do not wish to slap modern theories upon an ancient context, yet I do not see these two worlds to be entirely incongruous. My attempt is not to personify Israel or God as actual child to actual parent or 'mothering-one' referred to in psychoanalytic theories, yet I discuss how God or the notion of God is adopted symbolically as a love-object, believing the language of psychoanalysis gives universally helpful insights into personal and communal development. Secondly, I do not believe the one–one or two–one relational matrix described during development, from a particularly western individualistic perspective and articulated in psychoanalysis is necessarily incompatible as a *theory* to analyze communal or national development of identity. The primary and tangential theorists I work with have published papers exhibiting how their theories apply to larger society, particularly in terms of the construction of values and ethics within culture. A recent example of this is, Ruth Stein, a psychoanalyst and author of many works including, *For Love of the Father: A Psychoanalytic Study of Religious Terrorism*, who has discussed the notion of triadic evil wherein she describes the triadic structure as the perpetrator, victim, and the ideal. Her perspective broadens the triadic relationship from a personal relation matrix to a larger systemic matrix seeing the third as the religious, social, or cultural idea. Stein's work is helpful methodologically for expanding the traditionally conceived one–one or two–one dynamics of psychoanalysis to communal and national levels.

decline of power and eventual exiles the community suffered. In this reading, the book of the Covenant, and as a result Covenant Religion, functions
within the history of ancient Israel not as a bridge between Israel and the
God of Israel and between Israel and the events of exile, but rather, serves as
a god in and of itself, demanding right action and obedience, placing blame
solely on Israel's (or the Kings') disobedience and inaction as a way to find
some meaning and a way to survive the atrocious events of decimation and
deportation. Understood in this way, Covenant Religion regresses back to
symbolic equation, "because you failed to act obediently, you will be punished by losing your land and having your offspring killed."

In chapter 3 of part 1, I will ground the reader in a new approach to
the DH. This new approach seeks a symbolic understanding of the Deuteronomic Covenant, the Covenant as a symbol that allows for growth and
community development but also gets stuck and equated with that which
it sought to symbolize, namely Israel's relationship with Adonai and the
tenets of this Covenantal relationship. First, the Chapter will introduce the
historical-critical controversies regarding the notion of the Deuteronomic
agenda and postulate a triple-redaction theory. However, the current discussion parts ways with the traditional historical-critical agenda regarding
the DH. Though a triple-redaction theory is argued, as a way to understand
the historical background undergirding the development of key themes
within the history, the main emphasis is ultimately placed on the final form
of the text. While some discussion regarding the field of Deuteronomistic
History studies is necessary, what is of primary importance for the reader to
hold in mind is how this Covenant, formulated specifically in Deuteronomy,
functioned as a symbol for Israel during the eighth–sixth centuries BCE,
enabling Israel to construct a historical narrative, whose dominant trope
is now read within the historical books of the canon, forming the basis of
Covenant Religion. Covenant Religion's trope gives a reason for and assigns
meaning to the atrocious events of the Exile, even if this reason and meaning was destructive in and of itself. Chapter 4 will analyze this destructive
outcome as the symbol, initially providing space to create a unique and particular identity amongst the greater ANE landscape, became equated with
the traumatic events of the exile(s) and operated as an object or narrative of
judgment within exilic and postexilic Israel.

3

People of the Covenant

The Making of a Covenant Religion

This major distortion characterized the transmission of traumas: an insensitivity marks everything reminiscent of the catastrophe, while a pseudo-normality reigns in the family.

—FRANÇOISE DAVOINE AND JEAN-MAX GUADILLIÉRE,
HISTORY BEYOND TRAUMA[1]

Now that[2] you did not serve Adonai your God with joyfulness and with a good heart according to the abundance of everything, therefore you will serve your enemies whom Adonai will send against you, in hunger and in thirst and in nakedness and in want of everything. He will put an iron yoke on your neck until he has exterminated you.

—DEUTERONOMY 28:47–48

1. Davoine and Guadilliére, *History beyond Trauma*, 50.

2. The Hebrew אשר is used here as opposed to כי. While this word is more often translated as *because* I choose to use the word *that* due to the fact that אשר is a relative particle more commonly translated as that, which, or when, as it is used in reference to the object or action preceding it. כי is a conjunctive particle, combining or connecting two thoughts in a sentence. If v. 47 used the כי it would clearly read as it is translated in most biblical translations, indicating that it was *because* of Israel's disobedient actions that they will serve their enemies. The Hebrew carries a slightly more ambiguous tone. While אשר can be translated as the conjunction *because*, it is not translated this way very often. Therefore, אשר more likely ought to be translated as the conjunction *that*.

IN ACCORDANCE WITH MY guiding method that employs the psychoanalytic theories of Jung and Winnicott on symbols as a lens through which to analyze the historical and literary nuances of the Deuteronomic Covenant and the book of Job, we must first begin with the Deuteronomic Covenant. Our first step is to briefly discuss the current scholarly arguments regarding the meaning and usage of the term Deuteronomistic History (DH) in order to lay out the historical landscape now referred to as the Deuteronomic Covenant. The second step, is to articulate key literary themes of this Covenant including the very notion of Covenant, land, obedience and reward versus disobedience and punishment (known now as retribution theology), and perhaps most important, *assignment of responsibility* regarding the events of exile. These themes will be analyzed in relation to parallel themes found in other ANE documents. The third step then carefully analyzes the particularity, prevalence, and purview of these historical-critical and literary themes through the psychoanalytic lens of symbol formation and location of the cultural experience. This method will analyze how the Deuteronomic Covenant became the most prominent construct referred to throughout the historical books (Joshua–Kings) as a way in which Israel constructed meaning out of the experience of oppression, destruction, and then exile. Treating the Covenant through the lens of Winnicott's transitional objects not only provides a new way to understand the importance of the Covenant but makes available another way to interpret how the history is constructed around these Covenantal themes resulting in a Covenant Religion.

Rather than landing on a strict historical or literary argument for or against the existence of a master narrative or master historian or school of historians, the following argument takes a step back to analyze the broad themes that surface within the text as it was formulated within the dominant history.[3] One step in uncovering what the text is communicating is to analyze the symbolic nature of the Covenant as something that was, in the Winnicottian sense, both found and created by Josiah, according to 2 Kgs 22–23, and something that, as it is narrated and reflected upon throughout the history articulated in Joshua–Kings, seemed to allow Judah to stand firm and together as they worked out their sense of being a distinct community amidst the larger ANE. The present chapter will use the psychoanalytic theory presented by Winnicott regarding transitional objects, the transitional space, and location of the cultural experience to discuss the emergence and construction of Covenantal themes within the literary works of the DH. By taking material gleaned from historical-critical research on Deuteronomy 28 and 2 Kings 22–23 and their prominent literary themes,

3. Janzen, *Violent Gift*, 25–44.

the psychoanalytic theories of Donald Winnicott and Carl Jung, along with the four methodological assumptions outlined in chapter 2 regarding the universal nature and movements of the psyche, allows for an analysis, from a psychoanalytic perspective. This analysis shows how the surrounding socio-political background of the ANE during the eighth–sixth centuries BCE impacted the construction and use of this important cultural object in positive and negative ways.

The Deuteronomistic History in Scholarly Review

The DH is a scholarly construction that refers to a history of Israel, ideologically constructed within the historical books of Joshua to Kings. The vocabulary, content, and style that these historical books share have led scholars to hypothesize that these books comprise a specific History influenced by the Covenantal language of Deuteronomy, hence the *Deuteronomistic* History. The historical books are not the only books influenced by this ideological construction of history. Similar vocabulary, content, and style are interpolated throughout the prophets, laments, and wisdom literature within the canon, further suggesting the influence of this historical narrative in the construction of the canon.

The DH describes the time between Moses, or the time just before Moses died on Mount Horeb at the end of the book of Deuteronomy when Israel was on the cusp of the land of Canaan about to exit the wilderness and take up residence, up until the second deportation of the Babylonian Exile and the destruction of the Jerusalem temple in 586 BCE. The DH includes:

1. The stories of the beginning of the Hebrew people in Canaan and the conquest narratives in Joshua.

2. The beginnings of their tribal community, including cyclical rebellion and the savior judges who rescued the Hebrew tribes from their evil ways in the book of Judges.

3. The beginnings of a city-state and burgeoning monarchy in the book of Samuel.

4. The process of division between the Northern and Southern Kingdoms on into the eventual fall of Israel and then Judah in the books of Kings.

This history is a story about exile, deportation, and failed monarchy.[4] It tells a nuanced narrative including preferential opinions of the Southern Davidic line and a foreseen decline of Israel's relationship with Adonai

4. Römer, *So-Called Deuteronomistic History*, 80.

that serves as the rationale for the possibility and then actuality of Israel's eventual demise.[5] This highly politicized construction of a history of Israel, read now throughout the canon, serves both to explain the reasons for such tremendous destruction and loss, as well as to provide hope for a different kind of future.

The DH includes various textual contradictions that scholars have analyzed historically, ideologically, literarily, and sociologically, all of which help us realize there are competing narratives of Israel's history that, though not dominant, remain within the Hebrew canon. The DH, while it is the dominant trope, perhaps even the master narrative, is but one trope, one history within the Hebrew canon.[6] It may be impossible to tease out any other cohesive history within the canon. However, I argue that competing narratives, such as found in the book of Job, still exist standing alongside of and challenging the DH. Scholar David Janzen argues in his book, *The Violent Gift*, for the presence of what he calls a master narrative. He sees this as only one narrative that resides alongside another that one can glean by reading the gaps and intrusions within this narrative, the places where the story falls apart or contradicts itself, fails to hold up or simply silences other parts of the story. As he says, "The master narrative of the Deuteronomistic History . . . places high value on the ability of language to explain past and present."[7] He uses trauma theory in order to read the DH and argues there are traces of trauma that have slipped into or behind the main narrative of the History. He sees these slippages as subversions of the master narrative's attempt to provide an explanation for the exilic community's trauma. He argues that the alternative narrative is the traumatic narrative that subverts the master narrative, less nuanced and idealized, but present nonetheless[8] What I am adding to the field of DH studies is an analysis of the Deuteronomic Covenant and its adaptation throughout the biblical history regarding the universal human experience of the psyche, individual and collective, that speaks in images and symbols as a way to seek equilibrium and to come to an understanding of the difference and fluidity between inner and outer, subjective and objective realities.

The cohesion of a dominant historical narrative told throughout Joshua–Kings and the very explicit reasons this narrative gives for the downfall of Israel, even if there are contradictions within it, led scholars beginning in the early twentieth century to hypothesize about these historical books

5. Ibid., 67–106.
6. Janzen, *Violent Gift* 1–25.
7. Ibid., 34.
8. Ibid., 35.

from various angles.[9] The formal study of the Deuteronomistic History hypothesis, though it originally built upon the scholarship of W. M. de Wette (1780–1849), H. Ewald (1803–1857), Wellhausen (1844–1918) and others, was first formally elaborated and set forth by Martin Noth (1943) who defined the 'Deuteronomistic style' as a style literarily in line with the language and themes in Deuteronomy, and advocated for the evidence of Deuteronomistic redactions or later textual additions added to a former corpus of work inside the historical books and the prophets.[10] Noth was the first to propose the hypothesis that there was perhaps one 'author' or redactor dictating a well-planned historical work.[11] Noth noted that this author, also referred to as the historian or "Deuteronomist,"[12] presented a specific presentation that could be evidenced throughout the books of Joshua–Kings providing a nuanced articulation of Israel's history, a backward and forward reflection upon the causes or reasons for the Babylonian Exile.[13] Noth proposed that this History was written shortly after the release of Jehoiachin from the Babylonian prison in 562 BCE sometime around 560 BCE.[14]

Even into the present, scholars are still finding and/or arguing for Deuteronomistic (Dtr)[15] redactions, Dtr phrases or statements and critiques that can be found throughout the Pentateuch and the prophets. Significant for

9. First proposed by Martin Noth in *Überlieferungsgeschichtliche Studien*. For a survey of adaptations and challenges to this position see: Cross, *Canaanite Myth and Hebrew Epic*, 274–89; Halpern, *First Historians*; Levenson, "Who Inserted the Book of the Torah?"; McKenzie, "Deuteronomistic History," 161; McKenzie and Graham, eds., *History of Israel's Traditions*; O'Brien, *Deuteronomistic History Hypothesis*; Albertz, *Israel in Exile*.

10. Noth, *Deuteronomistic History*. See Coggins, "What Does 'Deuteronomistic' Mean?," 34.

11. Noth, *Deuteronomistic History*, 6.

12. I will use quotes when discussing the "Deuteronomist" to remind the reader that this is merely a scholarly construct. I do not believe there was one person responsible for writing the bulk of Israelite history any more than I believe there is to be found one original Ur-text. Rather, I use the term "Deuteronomist" to recognize the scholarly designation of prominent themes within the Hebrew canon as belonging to an exilic and perhaps more accurately postexilic mindset rather than their pre-monarchic or monarchic literary setting.

13. Noth, *Deuteronomistic History*, 6.

14. Ibid., 12.

15. Originally, Dtr was the abbreviation Noth used for the single author or editor. More recently this designation is used for themes within the Deuteronomistic History. That which is Deuteronomic is found within the book of Deuteronomy and contains parts of the book of the Covenant uncovered and restored by Josiah in 622 (2 Kgs 23:1–3). That which is referred to as Deuteronomistic are texts that relate to Deuteronomy and the Covenant therein but form a particularity of their own nuanced theological, literary, and linguistic lens. Lohfink, "Was There a Deuteronomistic Movement?," 40.

the present work is the understanding that the historical events presented throughout Joshua–Kings present a particular ideology, and as others have noted a certain *theology*.[16] As Noth argued, the "Deuteronomist" "was not merely an editor but the author of a history, which brought together material from highly varied traditions and arranged it according to a carefully conceived plan."[17] His conception of the "Deuteronomist" was that of an editor and an author, editing older materials and authoring his own perspective.[18] The Deuteronomist wanted to explain that the end of Judah, the Exile, was caused by Israel's failure as God's chosen people to uphold the Covenant rather than Adonai's failure to stand-up against the Babylonian gods.[19] Thus the DH's important ideological statement being made concerns Adonai's sovereign control over the traumatic events of the collapse of the Israelite kingdoms, based on Israel's disobedience. The "Deuteronomist" portrayed God sanctioning the capture of Samaria first and Jerusalem second as an act of God against the disobedience of Israel in accordance with the Covenant constructed with Israel through Moses as spelled out in the book of Deuteronomy. Since Noth first proposed his theory, the Deuteronomistic History hypothesis has itself almost reached canonical status according to McKenzie (1992), Y. Kaufmann (1960), and I. Engnell (1969). Though the concept is widely accepted and almost taken for granted within the guild of biblical studies, the diversely varying ways different scholars reconstruct this proposed history are phenomenally disparate.

Deuteronomistic History: Triple-Redaction Theory and the Impact of Exile

Second Kings 23:1–3 recounts the first time in Israel's history that the entire community stood to make a public profession with the book of the Covenant, *seper-hatorah*.[20] By history here I mean the biblical history or history as it is reported within the biblical canon. "2 Kgs 23: 1–3 states that for the first time in the history of the monarchy, the entire community

16. Noth, *Deuteronomistic History*, 4; Clements, *God's Chosen People*; von Rad, *Deuteronomy*.

17. Noth, *Deuteronomistic History*, 10.

18. Ironically, this main point of Noth's, that there was one Deuteronomist who authored the history in light of the Exile, sometime just during and throughout the Exile, is the one aspect that has not been widely accepted according to Coggins, "What Does 'Deuteronomistic' Mean?," 24.

19. Noth, *Deuteronomistic History*, 89–99.

20. Cogan and Tadmor, *II Kings*, 296.

undertook a Covenantal obligation to observe the divine ordinances based upon a Book of Teaching. In this respect, the Josianic covenant can rightly be seen as a new departure in the history of Judah." King Josiah gathered the community of Israel together, after he heard the words of the book of the Torah, *seper-hatorah*, read to him by high priest Hilkiah who "found" the book of the Covenant while cleaning out the temple. What is the significance that the entire community stands with *seper-hatorah*, the words cut in stone that promised utter destruction upon future generations of Israel if the community neglected to obey its words uttered by Adonai unto Moses years past? What is the meaning that this book is purported to have been found during the time Judah experienced a momentary reprieve from servitude to Assyria? And why would Israel choose to adopt a narrative that seemingly ensured their demise during this moment of slight reprieve? I contend that such a narrative is constructed precisely *because* of the moment of foreign political reprieve.

In the late seventh century, as Assyrian power began to wane, the Southern Kingdom of Judah experienced a brief moment of autonomy in which to strengthen and realign their political infrastructure. A key organizing principle during this time was the reconstruction and implementation of the Covenant Code. The narrative about "finding" the Covenant in the temple provided a basis for the reform movement. The reform movement, instigated by Josiah, was modeled after the tenets of the book of the Covenant or what is now referred to as the Deuteronomic Covenant.

The arguments regarding dating, authorship, and location of the book of Deuteronomy (henceforth Deut) and the DH are extensive and inconclusive within the field of biblical scholarship. The following argument assumes a triple-redaction theory, meaning there were, at the very least, three editorial stages to this comprehensive history.[21] The first of these three editorial stages was an initial construction of a Covenant and Covenant story sometime during the eighth–seventh centuries BCE (pre-Babylonian Exile), largely influenced by the Assyrian vassal treaty to which Israel served. This layer was formalized at the time of Josiah and the finding of the book of the Covenant.[22] Characteristics of this initial layer of Deuteronomy and the DH

---

21. Römer, *So-Called Deuteronomistic History.* Cf Cross, "Themes of the Book of Kings"; and Van Seters, *In Search of History.*

22. Cross's double redaction hypothesis proposed an initial Josianic layer within this block of texts with the addition of a secondary layer added by a Deuteronomistic redactor, who finished the history sometime after the events of the exile (exemplified in texts such as 2 Kgs 23:26—25:30, and other selected portions of the DH which include references to the exile). Cross, "Themes of the Book of Kings." Also see Nelson's *Double Redaction of the Deuteronomistic History.*

are known by their closeness to other ANE documents such as the Vassal Treaties of Esarhaddon (VTE). It is possible that the majority of Deuteronomy 28 was formulated as part of this initial layer since its parallels with the VTE are unmistakable. In this initial layer, a key emphasis was the centralization of worship, read within 2 Kgs 22–23, and Josiah's cultic revitalization. Centralization of worship would strengthen Jerusalem as a power center, an important move to ensure the future of the Southern Kingdom after the collapse of the Northern Kingdom in 722 BCE. The construction of a document that mirrored their own vassal treaty with Assyria was a move toward maintaining control, providing a national-religious symbol that sought to guarantee safety and wellbeing during a time of political upheaval.

However, the South was not saved from the conflict between the warring superpowers, even at the attempt of their reorganization. Once Babylonia triumphed over Egypt and Assyria and rose to power Judah was targeted, invaded, and decimated. The exilic redaction to this Covenant narrative during the sixth century BCE was thus influenced by the horrific events of the Babylonian Exile that directly challenged the initial promises of the Covenant. One of the characteristics of the exilic layer of the DH is the reference to exile, as eventual and inevitable—Deut 28:47–48—"Because you did not serve the Lord your God joyfully and with gladness of heart for the abundance of everything, therefore you shall serve your enemies whom the Lord will send against you, in hunger and thirst, in nakedness and lack of everything. He will put an iron yoke on your neck until he has destroyed you . . ."). Another characteristic is the loss of land, and the myth[23] of this land being completely emptied of the Hebrew community (2 Kgs 25:11; and 26).[24]

The latest edition of this history, the postexilic edition, was influenced by the collapse of Babylonia at the hands of the Persian Empire. This postexilic edition, constructed sometime during the late sixth—fourth century BCE, during the time of temple reconstruction and the second temple period, a more comprehensive history was formulated. This more comprehensive history, which includes explicit reasons for Israel's destruction and warnings against such destruction happening again, make up, what I term, a formalized Covenant Religion during the second temple period wherein monotheism and the idea of election were more concretely held.[25]

While I utilize the historical-critical approach in order to understand the construction of Deut and the DH, the ultimate emphasis remains on

23. Carroll, "Myth of the Empty Land," posits the "myth of the empty land" is a second temple construction.

24. See Geoghegan's, *Time, Place, and Purpose.*

25. Berquist, *Judaism in Persia's Shadow.*

the final form of these texts, in the form in which they were canonized and became sacred texts. The discussion following delves into the social and historical realities out of which these key texts arose. However, given the limited historical evidence for how and when these texts were actually formulated, these points are merely conjecture. As you can see above, the time periods I assign to the multiple layers of redaction are very large and inconclusive. Since it is impossible to nail down any exact dating and even more impossible to establish the community of authorship, these dates are given in order to reflect upon the significant moments in Israel's development, collapse, and reconstruction, as a small nation-state. The crux of the argument is not on the texts' historicity or literary nuances but on analyzing—through two particular psychoanalytic lenses—how these various redactions came to be in their final form, through political and social upheaval, and what purpose the ideology constructed amongst them serves within ancient Israel's dominant history.

The Babylonian Exile was paramount in the history of Israel, as told within the historical books. In the exilic and postexilic redactions, the Babylonian Exile is the history's reference point. The Babylonian Exile is the reference point according to the dominant history as it is articulated in the DH, but also in transgressive ways in other works of the canon as will be discussed in the second half of this book. There was Israel before the Exile and Israel after the Exile. The historical books, the books of lament—psalms and lamentations, the prophets, and even portions of the wisdom books, reference this significant event as the dénouement of Israel's history. The history's ideologically informed account of the past is informed in light of and in reference to the Babylonian Exile even though the percentage of victims of the actual exile was a relatively small number of Israelites.[26] The narrative that is shaped within the historical books is what I have termed Covenant Religion. This *historical* narrative is often ascribed to the work or influence of a group of laypeople sometimes known as the "Deuteronomists", but more importantly this narrative is known for its ideological and theological themes that are upheld, nuanced, argued, and used for reprove.[27]

26. While some scholars argue that the Exile itself was not in fact traumatic nor was it, as we now think of it, an historical reality but instead a "geopolitical maelstrom out of which the entire biblical 'mythology' arises" this is not (yet) the dominant view within scholarship"; Smith-Christopher, *Biblical Theology of Exile*, 34. It is true that the percentage of Israelites actually exiled was relatively low, perhaps only 10%, which included the elites, scribes, and priests. As mentioned above, Römer argues that the whole notion of an "exilic" time period is an ideological construction. Yet, when one considers the political and social importance of those who were exiled it is undeniable that all of Israel was, in some way, affected by this historical event.

27. Though the specific personality of the author or authors is not the crux of this

While information has been provided to help historically locate the events that necessarily influenced the construction of this narrative, and the ideological shifts made to the narrative at later points of adaptation, primary attention will be given to a key text, Deut 28, that summarizes the basic tenets, and thus serves as a crux, to the *historical* narrative itself. The argument following is less concerned with direction of dependence than it is with the content of this text and the observation of its prolific presence throughout the canon as a reference point and standard through which other parts of Israel's history is judged.[28]

In sum, historical-critics have argued that the Dtr influence was at its height sometime between the eighth—third centuries, or perhaps during that entire time.[29] While there is undoubtedly evidence of Dtr influence,[30] there is simply nothing historically to validate the evidence of any given person(s) or community who would have comprised the "Deuteronomists."[31] What will be explored later is the symbolic function of this Deuteronomic Covenant. I look at the function of this object (the Covenant) that carried an objective external and concrete reality based on its adaptation from similar ANE documents and also carried subjective inner realities from within the Hebrew community projected or placed onto this document in the making, helping Israel to forge an independent and separate identity from their vassal nations, particularly the Assyrian and later Babylonian superpowers of the ancient Near East during the eighth—sixth centuries. The symbolic function of the Deuteronomic Covenant will be explored both in terms of its initial construction during eighth—seventh centuries and in relation to its later adaptation during exilic and postexilic times, seventh—sixth centuries. The work of Donald W. Winnicott will aid in an analysis of the earliest

---

argument, I will note that Albertz, Weinfeld, Römer and others, assume the DH was written by the scribal community.

28. Direction of dependence refers to deciphering which texts came first between the *historical* texts that utilize Deuteronomic language or Deuteronomy that was formulated based on these *historical* texts. This is one of the principle goals of historical-critical and form-crictical studies within biblical scholarship.

29. Römer, *So-Called Deuteronomistic History*, 26.

30. Though Weinfeld gives a compelling argument for such evidence in his classic book *Deuteronomy and the Deuteronomic School* and in his commentary on Deuteronomy based on his analysis of textual similarities throughout the canon leading him to hypothesize attribution for such work to a group of said scribes, there is simply not enough historical evidence to prove this hypothesis.

31. Lohfink, "Was There a Deuteronomistic Movement?," 47. Weinfeld argues for the existence of a school of Deuteronomists at work during the time between the Northern exile in 722, Josiah's reform in 622, and the Southern exile in 586 BCE.

construction of Deuteronomy and the construction of the narrative about "finding" the *seper-hatorah* in the temple reported in 2 Kgs 22.

Finding *Seper-Hatorah* and Its Foundation of the Reform: The Beginning of Covenant Religion

As a way to begin a discussion on Deuteronomy or the book of the Covenant as a prominent symbol in the life of Israel during eighth—seventh centuries BCE, I will first provide a brief *historical* sketch as it is portrayed in 2 Kgs. Again, while I am working with information provided from historical-critical analysis of this time period, I place historical in italics or quotes because the limited historical records we do have come from marginal references within Egypt and Babylonian Chronicles, neither of which mention Josiah. By *historical* I will be referring to Israel's "history" as it is articulated in the books of Joshua–Kings. Therefore, I am not referring to actual history, but rather reconstructed or metaphorical history. The concept of history is being analyzed throughout this work from the perspective of symbolic formation, how individuals and communities come to understand and then recount their "history" with the use of symbols that enable identity formation—formation of internal and external realities.[32] With this in mind, let us proceed.

Josiah arose to the throne at a timely moment in Israel's history and in the greater context of the ancient Near East. Assyria, the dominant superpower for over a century (eighth—late seventh centuries), began to wane around 630 BCE, around the time 2 Kgs states that Josiah rose to power—promoted to the throne around 639 BCE by the *'am ha'arets*, 'people of the land.' The waning of Neo-Assyria left a momentary power vacuum in the Fertile Crescent in the early seventh century. Having been a vassal of Assyria for over one hundred years, Judah had a brief moment of near autonomy, which coincided with the thirty-one years of Josiah's proposed reign.[33] It was during this time period, that the narrator of 2 Kgs explains how Josiah instituted a political campaign to "cleanse" the religious institution within Israel in light of the discovery of *seper-hatorah*. Part of his campaign attempted to eradicate the sanctuaries and temple

---

32. Having said that, there are a few historically significant pieces to note. The archeological work of Uehlinger has brought attention to the fact that there was a definite shift in political alignment between the eighth and the seventh century as can be seen in Judean glyptic (engravings). While the seals of the seventh century carried astral symbols, the seals dating to the sixth century are void of such symbols (Uehlinger, "Gibt e seine joschijanische Kultreform?," 65–67).

33. Cogan and Tadmor, *II Kings*, 277–302.

sites in the North. Perhaps in an attempt to eliminate, visibly, any presence of the previous oppressor's foreign influence, alongside the attempt to centralize worship in Jerusalem, bolstering the economy of the Judean capital. Given the length of Israel's vassaldom to Assyria and based on the legalities of this vassal relationship, Northern Israelite and Southern Judean worship sites housed alters for Assyrian divinities, as was normal for vassal city-states. In a political move, Josiah reclaims the land and worship sites for the "YHWH cult" removing foreign influence and mandating national worship of Adonai. As Albertz proposes,

> On this hypothesis [referring to the book of the Covenant found being a portion of the book of Deuteronomy constructed at this moment in history] it can be recognized that the so-called Josianic reform was far more than a mere reform of the cult; it was at the same time a broad national, social and religious renewal movement which sought to use the historical opportunity offered by the withdrawal of Assyria to reconstitute the Israelite state fully.[34]

As the story goes in 2 Kings 22, upon *hearing* (*shema*) what was written in *seper-hatorah*, King Josiah tore his garments and commanded Hilkiah the priest, Shaphan, the scribe and his son, Ahikam, and the King's servant, Asiah, to inquire of Adonai on his account. Josiah implored them to find out, whether or not, the words written in the book, which promised disaster upon the inhabitants of the place where they stood as a result of generations before *not hearing* or *doing*[35] according to the words written in *seper-hatorah,* were indeed true. A consult with Hildah, the female prophet, confirmed the words written but promised the safety and wellbeing of Josiah. Seemingly, in an effort to reverse the anticipated consequences, Josiah initiated a reform, which began by gathering all the people unto him in order to join in the making of a covenant according to the book of the Covenant that had been found in the *Be'it Adonai.*[36] The former religious symbols of Assyria, the Baal's and Asherah's that had been mixed and mingled with Israelite YHWH symbols within the sanctuaries were cleaned out and burned outside in the fields of Kidron (2 Kgs 23:4). The

---

34. Rainer, 199. Parenthetical remarks are my own. Many have noted that Judea was not a fledgling monarchy until the downfall of Israel in 722, which forced people and monetary resources into Jerusalem enabling it to gain political strength; Römer, 46.

35. שמעו (they heard/obeyed) and לעשות (doing—though often translated as observing) echoes the exact phrasing of the blessing and cursing formula in Deuteronomy 28:1, 15.

36. House of Adonai.

priests held responsible for such polytheistic or synchronistic allowances were deposed and the high places demolished.

In the construction of "history" as it is written in 2 Kgs, the altars that had been erected by Jeroboam, the renegade who led the Northern split (1 Kgs 11:26–40),[37] and all the religious symbols of the North were destroyed at one fell swoop. Josiah reinstituted the Passover as it was prescribed in the book of the Covenant, which had never before in the time of the monarchy been celebrated as such. The historical account recorded in 2 Kgs 22–23, likely constructed during the time of Josiah, helps paint a picture of some of the external circumstances impacting the life of Israel in the late seventh century, the time at which *seper-hatorah* was initially envisioned. However, more important than the actual accuracy of said events, is learning from 2 Kings 22–23 how the story, portrayed as history, operates within the canon, particularly in relation to the book of Deuteronomy.[38] The story, which recounts the act of finding this covenant, functions, as Jung would say, as something that comes from within—an individual or community— that then serves as a bridge to the outside. As the story is narrated within the dominant history the Covenant, its tenets and obedience to them, are paramount. The Covenant is not simply a manual for community life but is equated with what will ensure life, Judah's salvation in the aftermath of the Northern Kingdom of Israel's exile at the hands of the Assyrians, and the impending threat of a similar fate for the Southern Kingdom.

While I believe there were multiple redactions to this dominant historical narrative, as explained above, the purpose of explaining these layers by analyzing this narrative from a historical-critical perspective is not to try and pinpoint what the exact layers are in order to date the layers and assign to them a specific authoring community. Rather, my purpose is to try and understand how and why such a narrative becomes dominant though it does not tell the whole story of Israel's history. The history formulated within Joshua—Kings, and even more so in Chronicles is decidedly a Southern history; i.e., told from the perspective of the Davidic line. The other reason for postulating about various layers of redaction is to analyze how this dominant history carries with it a rigid conception of who is at fault for the fall of Israel, essentially becoming a self-blaming system as it describes what Israel must do in order to be returned to Adonai or to have Adonai turn back toward Israel.

Thus, the history itself, in the Winnicottian sense is both found (by the priest cleaning out the temple) and created (as it was redacted through

---

37. Albertz, *History of Israelite Religion*, 126–56.

38. Römer, *So-Called Deuteronomic History*, 50–55.

oral and written texts) throughout the eighth—seventh century. The history can be understood ideologically, as a byproduct of the symbolic function of the Covenant, the Covenant as an object that was both found and made by the Hebrew community during the eighth—seventh centuries BCE. The Covenant, functioning as a symbol that led Israel to construct a history and make meaning out of this history, allowed Israel to experience a sense of autonomy and agency in the context of oppression. However, through the traumatic events of the Exile, this symbol ceases from functioning as a symbol and instead becomes a codified belief system that collapsed into the traumatic experience of the Exile while simultaneously silencing the affective reality of this experience.

Richard Horsley challenges traditional genre categories; i.e., historical, apocalyptic, wisdom, lament, held within biblical studies. He argues that the field limits itself to these theological categories neglecting the very real political and economic issues that inevitably affected the writing of ancient Israelite texts of all genres. Though Horsley's book is primarily dealing with second temple period texts his challenge is applicable here as well.

> Almost certainly . . . the production and use of these texts in antiquity did not proceed according to modern theological categories. The contents of texts that have been classified according to different types of theology . . . have concerns much wider and often more "down to earth" than religious ideas. Indeed they are concerned also with political-economic issues, and their religious symbols and ideas are usually related to those political-economic issues.[39]

Horsley's argument emphasizes the crux of this chapter which shows how the religious symbol of the covenant is, in a very real way, related to the political-economic issues most pressing during the eighth—fifth centuries BCE. By analyzing key events of this time period that inevitably influenced the nuances of *seper-hatorah,* the present inquiry examines how this document, and the narrative about its being found, functioned as a religious symbol for the community, which inevitably includes a discussion of its relation to the political and economic historical reality.

Oral tradition was fundamental to Israel's life in community as they constructed an identity that would survive their politically unstable surroundings. Within these oral traditions were nuggets of facts surrounded by fantasy and fiction, shaped and reshaped by subsequent generations. Carr expounds:

39. Horsley, *Scribes, Visionaries,* 5.

Exiles would not have created a deliverer figure like Moses with an Egyptian name and foreign wives. Nevertheless, it appears that the stories as we have them now, including almost all their dialogue and other details, reflect their settings in later periods of Israel's history. As a result, they are more useful as sources for the "truths" learned by Israelites in these later periods than in reconstructing historical "truths" about the times of Abraham and/or Moses . . . They *can* tell us, however, what later Israelites had to say to each other about their identity as a people and God's intentions toward them.[40]

In analyzing Covenant themes as a product of exile it is important to keep in mind the prominent Babylonian Exile in the sixth century as well as the cumulative exiles the Israelites and Judeans faced under the oppression of Assyria in the eight and seventh centuries. Thus, the Deuteronomic Covenant was nuanced from the place of exile, from outside of the land of promise, or inside the land on the cusp of destruction, surrounded by utter desolation, and even from the later period of reconstruction—a time when Israel was moving back into the land and reconstructing community life and temple worship under the foreign influence of Persia.

A brief look at ancient Near Eastern parallels such as the Instruction of Amenomope, the Code of Hammurabi, the Gilgamesh Epic, Hittite loyalty oaths, and Assyrian vassal treaties shows us that the Hebrew texts were not written in a vacuum but rather embedded in a particular culture.[41] The Israelite texts, oral and written, were inevitably influenced by their surrounding cultures both in process and in content. Therefore, rather than gleaning the scriptures for what actually happened in the life of Israel and, most relevant to this study, during the Babylonian Exile, it is more helpful to analyze the Covenantal themes, articulated first in Deuteronomy, regarding reward for obedience and punishment for disobedience, utilized and expounded upon throughout the historical books and within the book of Job, as products of a complex culture that underwent a great disruption in their communal formation. Understanding the historical context out of which these texts arose, though one cannot know exactly when these texts were first written and later redacted, allows us now to think about the Covenant and the *history* born out of it as a product of a particular experience colored by a community's subjective understanding of that experience. Thus, the Covenant symbolized for Israel, Adonai as the God for Israel and Israel's role in relation to this God for future survival as a nation. The image of God and nation

---

40. Carr, *Introduction to the Old Testament*, 202–3.

41. Matthews and Benjamin, *Old Testament Parallels*.

were bound together and the nation was dependent upon the Covenant for health and continued existence.

Sociologist Avery Gordon says, "Complex personhood means that the stories people tell about themselves, about their troubles, about their social worlds, and about their society's problems are entangled and weave between what is immediately available as a story and what their imaginations are reaching toward."[42] In essence, this describes the Deuteronomic Covenant. The Covenant became a web of reality and imagination as Israel worked to construct its national and social identity in the context of the ancient Near East.

Having discussed the relevance of the social and historical setting out of which the Deuteronomic Covenant arose and the historical-critical research as it will pertain to understanding how the Covenant functioned as a symbol during the formation and impending destruction of Israel, now I will turn to the literary themes distinctive of the Deuteronomic Covenant and Covenant Religion.

Deuteronomic Ideology: Key Themes and Textual Evidence

Deuteronomistic theology is perhaps best understood as a retribution theology. What repeats over and over throughout the book of Deuteronomy is the promise of reward for obedience to the Covenant and punishment for disobedience.[43] Aside from this most basic principle other phrases, concepts, ideas and assertions are characteristically Deuteronomistic. For example, within the books of the prophets such repetitive language that references the *Torah* of Adonai (*seper-hatorah*) and his 'statutes' (Amos 2.4), and to 'his servants the prophets' (Amos 3:7) are considered to be typical characteristics of Deuteronomistic vocabulary.[44]

When discussing the literary themes of texts within the DH, I use the designation 'Deuteronomistic' (Dtr) to describe the general shift in focus, tone, and content of exilic and postexilic Israel's spiritual and psychological climate, which inevitably influenced the construction of their historical, prophetic, and even wisdom narratives. What we read through the *History* is a host of themes that appear wed to one another and particularly nuanced as they lead toward the conclusion of exile based on Israel's disobedience and eventual restoration based on a particular set of actions. The result is

42. Gordon, *Ghostly Matters*, 4.

43. Christensen, *Deuteronomy 21:10–34:12*, 673.

44. Coggins, "What Does 'Deuteronomistic' Mean?," 31.

a unified trope, what I call Covenant Religion that was essentially an ideological movement of the constructors of history after the experience of Exile and return.

The Deuteronomic themes, themes that surface within the book of Deuteronomy itself, include:

1. Destruction of the high places—the local sanctuaries throughout the North—in an effort toward cultic centralization wherein all resources would be brought into Jerusalem, in the South.

2. Veneration of Adonai alone, moving closer toward monotheism.

3. The promise of land endangered through disobedience of the Torah.

4. A theological shift from *God* dwelling amongst the people or in the ark to God's *name* dwelling amongst the people and in the house of Adonai.

5. God's abode shifting from earth to the heavens.

6. Sacrificial offerings as personal practices for the purpose of social welfare rather than institutional practices in service to the temple or the priestly class.

7. Jerusalem as the seat of Adonai's name rather than the ark.

8. Non-sacrificial slaughter.

9. Exile and the warning against hubris for the Israelites not to forget where they came from and how they were saved out of slavery by God's mighty hand (Deut 32:10).

10. Sanctity as a consequence of the intentions of the person who consecrates the offering or tithe rather than contingent upon a priest or priestly ceremony.

11. Repentance and return of the Israelites to Adonai and the land promised as the consequence of God's generous love (Deut 30:1–10; 4:29–30).[45]

The reason for including all of these nuances of the Covenant is to show thematic similarities between the Covenant, and thus Covenant Religion, and later, the book of Job and Individuated Religion.

I argue the eleven themes above can be consolidated into these following four major categories that frame Covenant Religion:

---

45. This summary is adapted in conjunction with Weinfeld's summary in *Deuteronomy 1–11*, 37–50.

1. Nationalism versus Sacramentalism

2. Social responsibility

3. Intention versus performance

4. Individual consecration rather than priestly consecration

Later, in relation to the book of Job, these four categories will be referenced in their relationship to the literary allusions used throughout the book. These themes cultivated within the book of Deuteronomy are alluded to explicitly and implicitly, in the book of Job, and while they are paramount for formulating Covenant Religion they are re-imagined and reformulated through the book of Job's ability to address the pain and disillusionment of the Exile.

Josiah, as narrated in 2 Kgs 22–23, was the prototype in the *historical* narrative for this Deuteronomic disposition, as he did what was right in the sight of Adonai, and walked in all the ways of his father David; not turning to the right or to the left (22:2), hearing the words of *seper-hatorah* (22:11), rending his garments (22:11), and instituting a national reform according to the book of the Covenant. However, even with Josiah's Deuteronomic piety, he could not stop the impending collapse and Exile of the Southern Kingdom. Now we shall turn to the literary construction and contents of *seper-hatorah*.

The Deuteronomic Paraenesis[46] within Deuteronomy 28 and Its Relation to the Texts of the Ancient Near East

Deuteronomy, or Mishneh Tôrah, meaning repeated or second law, as it is found within the Hebrew canon is a repetition of a large part of law and history from the Tetrateuch, the first four books of the Torah. This Deuteronomic Covenant is a revised version of the Sinaitic covenant, read in the book of Exodus, revised in part around the time period of Josiah.[47] Chapters 1–30 are written as a long speech of Moses, while chapters 31–34

---

46. An exhortatory composition, advice or counsel.

47. Weinfeld, *Deuteronomy 1–11*, 1. However, this is an area of biblical scholarship where there is little consensus regarding the date and place of the initial Deuteronomic source that only gets more complicated when taking the multiple layers of redaction into account. For the purposes of this work it has been assumed that there was an initial covenant, in contrast to the (Priestly) Sinaitic one reported in Exodus, that was originally constructed, whether orally or inscribed, sometime within mid to late seventh century BCE during the time of waning Assyrian power and before the neo-Babylonian incursion as has been explained above.

report his last actions and his death.[48] Some major themes include cult centralization, emphasizing and institutionalizing worship in Jerusalem and, as an implied consequence, centralization of economics and politics. After the two introductions (Deut 1–4 and 5–11) there is a long collection of laws (Deut 12–26). Deuteronomy 27–28 stand as the conclusion of the collection of laws and purport the blessings and curses according to Israel's obedience of the laws. Moses' conclusion in Deut 29–30 exhorts Israel to choose life by adhering to the instructions preceded. Finally, chapters 31–34 provide a conclusion with Moses' song predicting Israel's eventual rejection of Adonai upon entering the land, the blessing of the twelve tribes and the death and burial of Moses by Adonai.[49]

Joseph Blenkinsopp purports that there is a familiar pattern of the Deuteronomic *paraenesis*, which includes an "appeal to collective experience, immediate or vicarious, followed by the promise of a special relationship contingent on obedience and Covenant-keeping."[50] It is this *paraenesis* that calls for explanation; how it functions within Deuteronomy 28 specifically, within Deuteronomy as a whole, within the Deuteronomistic History (Joshua—Kings) and in the second part of this work, within the book of Job.

The kernel of Deuteronomistic theology is found in Deuteronomy 28:1–19 which articulates Israel's blessing as a result of obedience versus Israel's curse as a result of disobedience.[51] This exhortation, likely constructed within the initial layer of Deuteronomy as it parallels the VTE language of consequences for obedience/disobedience, is what informs Covenant Religion's reasoning for and understanding of the Babylonian Exile. This is the key theme that is crystallized within the national narrative and essentially constructs an image of the wrathful Adonai, angry at Israel's disobedience and thus justified in the action of wiping Israel out through the sixth century Exile. Chapter 28 of Deuteronomy details the Covenantal consequences according to the terms mediated by Moses as written in Chapters 5–26.

Chapter 28 is divided into two main parts, the blessings that will come upon Israel as a consequence of obedience, v. 1–14; and the significantly lengthier second part, which contains the curses that will come upon Israel as a consequence of disobedience, vv. 15–68. Directly parallel to the blessings portion in vs. 1–14, in converse fashion, the curses section in vs. 15–68 describe the consequences of famine, disease, economic downfall, capture by foreign nations, military defeat, oppression, cannibalism, and exile. It has

48. Römer, *So-Called Deuteronomistic History*, 3.

49. Ibid., 4

50. Blenkinsopp, "Narrative in Genesis–Numbers," 87.

51. Christensen, *Deuteronomy 21:10—34:12*, 673.

been postulated that the curses section in vv. 15–68 preceded the blessings section. The argument for this comes from the close parallels the curses section shares with the VTE.

Deuteronomy is unique amongst the other books of the Pentateuch in that its entire contents recount the making and details therein of Israel's Covenantal relationship to Adonai. The books prior to Deuteronomy in the canon place dominant emphasis on God's relationship with the ancestors, Abraham, Jacob and Isaac, God's special calling of Abraham and the promise to make Abraham a great nation as prolific as the sands of the sea and stars of the skies. This calling comes with a certain mandate to consecrate them in order to be God's holy people read in the priestly material of the holiness code throughout Leviticus. Whether one chooses to analyze the construction of the Pentateuch diachronically through historical, source or literary-form analysis indicating earlier strands and later redactions, proto or post Deuteronomic layers within the Tetrateuch or Hexateuch that originated from differing communities at different points in Israel's history,[52] or synchronically through canonical or structural analysis working to understand the literary development of the Israelite identity through the ancestral narratives before Egypt, during Exodus and through the wilderness, it is widely accepted that in Deuteronomy, the tone shifts.[53] Rather than following the former kind of grant-oath formula wherein the sovereign is obligated to his royal servants (Abraham/ancestral narratives) in the Deuteronomic Covenant the vassal, Israel, is obliged to the suzerain, Adonai, in order to receive the blessings promised in the treaty.[54]

One of the reasons for the shift from grant-oath formula to treaty formula and for the existence of such treaty type language, is the result of Assyrian influence upon Israel during the eighth—seventh centuries. The language of the Covenant shares distinctive qualities of the VTE, the documentation of Israel's vassal obligations to Assyria. Deuteronomy 28:20–68 is an expanded definition of what is known within the Iron Age Loyalty Oaths, Hittite and Assyrian, as acts of commission and omission that subject the vassal to the Suzerain by way of the curses laid out.[55]

The basic form of Deuteronomy resembles the structure of these vassal treaties from the ancient Near East, both Hittite loyalty oaths from before 1250 BCE and Assyrian vassal treaties from after 1250 BCE and includes textual similarities with these and even the much later Greek amphictyonic

---

52. Carr, *The Formation of the Hebrew Bible.*

53. Sanders, *Canon and Community.*

54. Weinfeld, *Deuteronomy 1–11*, 58–59.

55. Christensen, *Deuteronomy 21:10—34:12*, 680.

(an association of tribes in ancient Greece who banded together to protect common temple sites) oaths regarding the temple of Apollo of Delphi.[56] These types of oaths were prominent during the Hittite Empire in the fifteenth and fourteenth centuries all the way up through the Roman Empire. These basic elements include a historical introduction providing the background and reasons for the vassal's loyalty (as can be read in the two introductions to Deut in chapters 1–11), the stipulations of the treaty (paralleled in Deut 12–26), a list of divine witnesses, consequences for obedience or disobedience of the treaty (Deut 27:14–28), and a corporate recital of the Covenant and a giving of the tablets (Deut 26:17—27:13).[57]

Deuteronomy shares characteristics of both the earlier form of vassal treaties such as those found in the Hittite documents as well as characteristics from later vassal treaty formulas such as those found in the VTE, 672 BCE, indicating, at the very least, the composition of Deut maintained a blending of the cultural milieu of its time. Features Deut shares with earlier Hittite oaths include the long historical introduction providing reason or cause for such an oath to be initiated and a list of blessings for adherence to the treaty.[58] The VTE did not include such an introduction nor did it include the list of blessings; however, the curses section within Deuteronomy is undeniably similar to those found in the VTE.[59] Within the curses section of Deut 28:23–35 are paralleled in content and order in the VTE that obligate Judea, under the rule of Manasseh, to the Assyrian king Esarhaddon.[60]

Another important similarity Deut shares with the VTE is the tone of self-condemnation in connection with violating the oath.[61] For example, a line that is in the VTE reads, "the people of Arabia asked one another saying: Why is it that such evil has befallen Arabia?" And the people answer, "Because we did not observe the obligation sworn to the god of Ashur." A line from Deut 29: 21–24 parallels this line from the VTE reading, "And the generations to come . . . will ask: Why did Adonai do this to the Land? And they will say: 'because they forsook the Covenant of Adonai.'"[62]

Not only are there similarities in the structure, form and content between these ANE vassal treaties and Deuteronomy. The discovery

56. Weinfeld, *Deuteronomy 1–11*, 6–11.

57. Ibid., 7. Mendenhall, "Covenant Forms," 50–76; Frankena, "Vassal-Treaties of Esarhaddon"; Wiseman, *Vassal-Treaties of Esarhaddon*, 1–28.

58. Weinfeld, *Deuteronomy 1–11*, 8.

59. Wiseman, *Vassal-Treaties of Esarhaddon*, 25–26.

60. Frankena,153; Weinfeld, *Deuteronomy 1–11*, 7.

61. Weinfeld, *Deuteronomy 1–11*, 8

62. Weinfeld, *Deuteronomy 1–11*, 8; Weinfeld, *Deuteronomy and the Deuteronomic School*, 115.

narrative in 2 Kings 22–23 which depicts Josiah's legion uncovering the book of the Covenant in the temple in seventh century BCE parallels the ancient Hittite accounts of the fourteenth and thirteenth centuries BCE when the King Muwatalli submits prayers to the divinity to aid him in rediscovering the written Covenant in order to fulfill it and to confess the sins of the entire country.[63] These similarities connote a ceremonial symbol, of discovery and reform.

Going further, exile itself, along with the desolation of one's land, are specific punishments for vassal treaty disobedience as is evidenced in the VTE lines 538–544, "may your seed and the seed (of your sons) and daughters perish from the land (if you violate the treaty)."[64] Also, Hittite treaties state, "may they break you like reeds, may your name and your seed . . . perish from the land."[65] While the concept of returning to one's land after periods of exile is not peculiar to Hebraic texts specifically, as is attested in Akkadian and Aramaic texts of this period, what is unique is the concept of linking return to land with return to God.[66] An innovation that occurs in Deuteronomy is that return is conditioned by healing which God causes out of God's generous love (Deut 30:1–10; 4:29–30).[67] Weinfeld suggests that the ideas of repentance and return begin in Northern Israel during the time of Hosea on the brink of the Exile in 732, but are later adapted and adopted in Judah during the Judean Exile.[68] Whether or not the idea originated in the North or South is tertiary to the point being made here. Of primary importance is the way in which Israel constructed a particular narrative, similar to the political, religious and historical documents of its time period and yet distinctive of them as well.

Undergoing simultaneously political upheaval and economic consolidation and renewal upon the influx of Northern refugees, the Southern kingdom Judah became the religious, financial, and cultural hub during seventh century BCE. Upon the wake of the Northern kingdom of Israel's destruction (722 BCE), Judah began articulating the events of the Northern exile through the lens of the Southern survival.[69] In an effort to stave off a similar outcome the Book of the Covenant, as described in 2 Kgs 22–23, is

---

63. Weinfeld, *Deuteronomy 1–11*, 19.

64. Ibid., 59 and Weinfeld, *Deuteronomy and the Deuteronomic School*, 133.

65. Wiseman, *Vassal-Treaties of Esarhaddon*, 69–70.

66. Weinfeld, *Dueteronomy 1–11*, 48, Wiseman, *Vassal-Treaties of Esarhaddon*, 26.

67. Weinfeld, *Deuteronomy 1–11*, 48.

68. Ibid., 49. This point is widely contested within the field of Deuteronomstic History studies.

69. Albertz, *History of Israelite Religion*, 198.

elevated from a book of worship which was primarily read in the temple, to a book of state law, "to which all social groups including the king committed themselves in a public legal act, a formal covenant in analogy to the Assyrian vassal treaties (2 Kgs 23:1–3)."[70]

The Deuteronomic *paraenesis* read in Deuteronomy 28 lays the foundation for an *historical* narrative of exile to be born. With the objects lying around from the surrounding ANE culture Israel adopts a narrative that provides a way in which to envision their destruction without losing all hope. It is now time to turn to psychoanalyst D. W. Winnicott regarding the nature of symbols and symbol formation and location of the culture experience to help elucidate the symbolic importance of this political move articulated in the book of Kings regarding the Deuteronomic *paraenesis* of chapter 28.

Winnicottian Explorations into the Nature of a Symbol

In this section I first use Winnicott's theory of the transitional object to analyze the original adaptation of *seper-hatorah* within the life of Israel during the eighth—seventh centuries BCE. Secondly, I introduce Winnicott's notion of the location of cultural experience and the necessity of the intermediate space of play in which meaning is both found and created individually and collectively. Use of these two aspects of Winnicott's theory suggests a new understanding of the construction and use of the Covenant on the cusp of and during the Babylonian Exile.

The Transitional Object

Winnicott contends that in the first few months of life an infant operates under an illusion of omnipotence. In an early state of being merged with the mothering-one, so long as the mothering-one is available and attuned to the infant nurturing this merging, the infant's needs and desires are fluidly met fostering a sense of illusion or what Winnicott calls omnipotence. By omnipotence he means an experience of matching between the infant's wants, instinctual needs, and what reality provides. Omnipotence is an illusion of good-enough matching nurtured in the initial merged relationship between infant and mothering-one. This illusion is necessary for the baby's growing sense of I-ness, or sense of self in that through it the baby learns of her own body and her own basic desires and needs. Having those needs/

---

70. Ibid., 205.

wants met early on allows her later in life to be able to take care of her own needs and be in relationship with others in mutually giving and caring ways. Over time, the mothering-one starts to introduce gradual failure of adaptation, not immediately responding to the baby's cries or leaving the child in the care of another, which introduces a degree of frustration, as the child's desires are not seamlessly fulfilled. This opposition slowly disillusions the growing child's illusion of omnipotence. By introducing frustration, the child is introduced to her own desires as belonging to her as the mothering-one slowly allows the child to begin to come into relationship with the external world outside, not inside the growing child.

However, the good-enough mother, a term coined by Winnicott, does not slowly disappoint this illusion without leaving behind objects for the baby to play with, objects that can be taken up, cuddled with, held, and bitten.[71] Most important to this process are these objects, found by the baby that are considered in themselves a paradox, as they are at the same time both *found*, as they were placed in the environment by the caregiver for the baby, and *created*, in that the baby bestows these objects with subjective meaning.[72] The baby, living through minor failures within the care-giving environment, is met with a tolerable level of frustration and upon finding these objects left about is able to find a way to live through and work out this inevitable disappointment and frustration by imbuing these objects with her own subjectivity or subjective experience of the world; her anger, disappointment, fear, and love. Further, Winnicott says these objects stand for the unity experienced between the mother and child in the first stages of the child's life due to the mother's attunement and preoccupation with the child's needs. These objects are actual objects, blankies and teddy bears that are adopted by the infant and remain under her control. They can be cuddled and mutilated, withstanding the infant's love and aggression. They must have, in a sense, aesthetic value, or be seen to have a quality and reality of their own.[73]

The teddy bear lying around for the one-year-old, is found by her and created with a life of its own, holding for the baby both part of the baby's own subjective experience of the mothering one and parts of others', including her caregiver's, subjective experiences of the baby as well. The teddy bear can simultaneously be held and taken care of by the baby, sung to, cuddled, wrapped in a blanket and toted around in a stroller, and, at

71. Winnicott, *Playing and Reality*, 13–14.

72. Winnicott, *Psychoanalytic Explorations*, 204; Winnicott, *Playing and Reality*, 1–34.

73. Winnicott, *Playing and Reality*, 7.

the same time, thrown across the room in a fit of rage, surviving all the while. These objects, though they are not in actuality the mothering-one or even part of the mother, they represent the baby-mother unity. Winnicott asserts that there is no such thing as an infant at the early stage of development, only a nursing couple or an infant-care dyad.[74] It is in the infant's relationship with these objects that she is able to work out her love and her hate of the caregiver and her inevitable disappointments at the failures of her environment. In their survival, these objects allow the mothering-one to live outside of the baby, beyond the baby's omnipotent control. Ultimately, through reality testing, these objects allow the baby to establish a sense of her external world.[75]

While these objects are symbolic in nature, meaning the teddy bear is not actually the mother but rather symbolizes the mother-child relationship, their symbolic value is not as important in the beginning as their actuality. "The paradox is that the environment is at the same time part of the infant and at the same time it isn't."[76] However, at the initiative of the baby leading play through her own creativity and engagement with the symbols being taken seriously and reflected back in play by the care-giver and her environment, she is gradually enabled to recognize the symbolic value of these objects. When the child tenderly cares for her doll, dressing her up, and taking her to school so that she, the mommy, can then go to work, the actual mother is there reflecting back such thoughtful care giving. When the child later, just before bedtime, takes the doll and chucks her across the room, the mother once again is there to witness the act of aggression and talk with the child about her anger at the impending separation from the mother at bedtime. Throughout development, it is this kind of reflecting back that enables the child to develop a sense of her own emotions as she learns to claim her subjective experience of her mother and later her world.

When objects of transition become symbols with which the baby plays in order to distinguish and accept difference and similarity, the baby or child now, and later the adult, is able to distinguish between reality and fantasy, between inner and outer objects and is able to use the objects as a means for constructing her sense of self and other. That interaction Winnicott calls object relating wherein the child (or adult) is best described as an isolate meaning the child has yet to experience a shared reality with other subjects outside of the child's subjective experience of them. In this interaction, the subject relates to objects as bundles of projections, part of the child's self

74. Winnicott, *Psychoanalytic Explorations*, 54.

75. Winnicott, *Playing and Reality*, 3–4.

76. Winnicott, *Psychoanalytic Explorations*, 580.

and the child's affective experiences of others.[77] However, one is eventually able to move from object relating to object usage, when objects become part of a shared reality and thus have an independent existence of their own, outside of the baby.[78] As the baby transitions from object-relating to object-usage the baby is afforded the time and space to discover her self, that is her subjectivity in the doll and her world, that is the doll as an object existing outside her subjectivity.[79] In the same paradoxical move, the growing child both finds and creates her very self through the use of objects in the space of play.[80] These objects are the child's first symbols.

The transition is made from being merged with the mothering one to being in relationship with her as an emerging self eventually toward being in relationship with the mothering one as someone outside and separate from the baby. In healthy development, these transitional objects will gradually become decathected, or discharged of emotional energy, as the infant and child is able to be in relation with others in the external world of shared reality. These objects do not go away, do not die, are not replaced, are not mourned, but rather they lay the groundwork so to speak, for the experience of one's whole cultural field.[81] The ability to create, have relationships, and eventually live a shared culture rests upon these early transitional objects and more importantly, the space to use and play with these objects.

Winnicott and Location of Cultural Experience

Winnicott goes on to explain the potential space created between the mother and the baby as the space of play. He calls it potential because though it is experienced as a potential separation between mother and baby, separating me from not-me, rather than being experienced as emptiness or separation the space is filled with play and the use of symbols—all that eventually, in adulthood, adds up to cultural life.[82] Winnicott reminds us, however, "reality-acceptance is never completed, that no human being is free from the strain of relating inner and outer reality, and that relief from this strain is provided by an intermediated area of experience which is not challenged (arts, religion, etc.). (cf. Riviere, 1936). This intermediate area is in direct

---

77. Winnicott, *Playing and Reality*, 118.

78. Ibid., 118–19.

79. Ibid., 4.

80. Winnicott, *Maturational Processes*, 179–92.

81. Winnicott, *Playing and Reality*, 7.

82. Winnicott, *Maturational Processes*, 147.

continuity with the play area of the small child who is 'lost' in play."[83] This third area of living is not inside the individual nor necessarily outside in the world of shared reality, but, rather, is in the space in-between inside and outside, negating the very idea of their separation as it allows the individual to play and make sense of her inner and external worlds with basic trust in the foundation of her environment holding her through her love and aggression, growth and maturation of her independent self. In this space of play the self is found and created, *not* manufactured.[84]

To be able to live in this space or be allowed this space provides the foundation of creative living. Ann Ulanov says, "The purpose of playing, aside from the sheer fun of it, amounts to finding and creating oneself and bringing alive the symbols that picture both a reality beyond the self and our experiences of uniting with it."[85] However, living creatively is different from producing creative products.[86] One may be capable of producing a creative product out of necessity or compulsion rather than out of freedom and genuine creativity.

Winnicott reminds us that, "Culture and its values are the direct extensions of transitional phenomena and their values."[87] Similar to the child's development through the transitional space with the transitional objects, the adult experiences this phenomenon within culture. Culture for the adult is both found and created, and as Ulanov says, "he receives it as something of value existing outside of himself that can nourish his soul when it reflects both life's mystery and his responses to that mystery."[88] Also similarly, culture (or its aspects) can be relegated to a subjective experience remaining merely a bundle of projections of the subject's individual inner experience. Until these objects are related to and shared with others, becoming part of a mutual reality, they do not have an existence on their own outside of the individual.[89]

83. Winnicott, *Through Paediatrics to Psycho-Analysis*, 241.

84. Winnicott, *Maturational Processes*, 179–92.

85. Ulanov, *Finding Space*, 13.

86. Ulanov, in "Madness and Creativity" class lecture, Fall, 2010.

87. Ulanov and Ulanov, *Religion and the Unconscious*, 162.

88. Ibid., 163.

89. Winnicott, *Playing and Reality*, 118–19.

The Deuteronomic Covenant as Symbol and the Space
Created Therein as Location of Cultural Experience

Winnicott's theories of the transitional object and location of the cultural experience provide a helpful model to understand the events articulated in Israel's history as it is reported in 2 Kgs 22–23. The text narrates the "finding" of *seper-hatorah* in the temple during the time in Israel's history when, for the first time in a century, the nation to which Israel served as a vassal, was crumbling before their eyes. The story of Josiah, as it is told, instituted a political mandate to pledge allegiance to the book discovered. A religious effort was born with the hope of preserving the nation from the same fate experienced by the Northern Kingdom, or, in an effort to explain the impending destruction. Echoing Horsley's words above, the religious symbol was constructed and, in Winnicott's words, was "found" as a way to relate to the impending political-economic issues.

As Weinfeld contends, Israel transformed a political document, the vassal treaty with Assyria, into a religious document. Thus, rather than serving a king, Israel served Adonai. As he says, "On the whole the Deuteronomic code constitutes a manual for the king and the people. Sacred matters are dealt with here insofar as they touch the religious-social aspect of national life."[90] Weinfeld argues that Deuteronomy is, in a way, an educational manual meant to instruct the king and his people in social, political, and religious life. He highlights the prominent use of the verb *lmd*, meaning to learn, throughout Deuteronomy, which is absent from the rest of the Tetrateuch (Genesis, Exodus, Leviticus, Numbers). Then he goes further to emphasize that the Torah is defined as all wisdom and understanding (4:6), and comprised of the divine will.[91] According to Weinfeld, it was during the period of Josiah that the process of canonization of Scripture, the revelation of Adonai embodied in the written word of a book, was commenced.[92] As he states, "The primary impetus for the crystallization of the sacred Scripture, however, was the sanctification of the book of Deuteronomy, and it was this impulse that changed the religion of Israel into the faith of the Book."[93]

The Deuteronomic Covenant became an object invested with meaning by and for Israel. It came to function, as a symbol for Israel during Israel's many transitions and enabled Israel to establish an identity amongst the landscape of the ancient Near East and under the disintegrating presence of

---

90. Weinfeld, *Deuteronomy 1–11*, 55.

91. Ibid., 55–56.

92. Ibid., 84.

93. Ibid.

Assyria. The formation of the Deuteronomic Covenant, fashioned after the Hittite Loyalty oaths of the fourteenth and thirteenth centuries BCE and the Vassal-Treaties of Esarhaddon in the seventh century BCE, provided Israel an object through which to work out and construct a sense of external and internal reality, during the latter years of Monarchy on the brink of destruction, through exile, and into the time of temple restoration. The Covenant was one of Israel's first symbols in that it was both found and created by Israel. It symbolized Israel's relationship with Adonai and Israel's identity as a nation amidst the ANE. Through the process of constructing the national narrative or history, spoken about now as the DH, with the use of the Covenant, Israel's emerging identity was both created and found in relation to the earliest layer of the book of the Covenant. This analysis is to not merely equate the value of Deuteronomy with that of a transitional object. To do so would be a gross reduction. However, I believe Winnicott's theories widen the space for those of us in biblical scholarship to see a new way into the development of Covenantal themes throughout the canon.

As discussed above, we know from Wiseman, Weinfeld, Levinson, and others that the Deuteronomic Covenant was likely fashioned after Assyrian Vassal Treaties and/or Hittite loyalty oaths. Scholars D. J. Wiseman, Moshe Weinfeld, Paul E Dion, Eckart Otto, and Thomas Römer have laid the groundwork here. Careful analyses paralleling the similarities have provided us with an examination of the infiltration of Assyrian militaristic and nationalistic ideology within the instructions of the Covenant. In the Deuteronomic Covenant, Adonai, the Hebrew Deity, takes on the characteristics of the Assyrian Suzerain king or Deity and Adonai becomes the suzerain of the Israelites subjugating them, as they had been subjugated by Esarhaddon, as Adonai's vassal. As was pointed out earlier, this type of literature was common to the whole of the ancient Near East.[94] It is regarding this point exactly, that Winnicott's theories provide a helpful way of understanding the movement within these texts.

Looking at the VTE and other vassal treaties of the time period as aspects of the larger ancient Near Eastern culture of which the Israelites were a part, we can analyze how Israel utilized these objects, within Winnicott's notion of the intermediate space. Within the space between Israel and Assyria, to whom Israel was a vassal for a large portion of her existence, Israel gathered the things of the culture, objects meant for oppression, and utilized them, imbued them with a cultural subjectivity, working with them and reforming them in order to find and create Israel's own unique identity. During the eighth century, after the fall of the Northern Kingdom in 722

---

94. Wiseman, *Vassal-Treaties of Esarhaddon*, 3.

and before the Judean exile, the scribes in Judah formulated the beginnings of what would later become the book of Deuteronomy. During this time, the texts parallel the VTE formula and lack some of the constringency of the later redactions; i.e., monotheism and election.

It has been argued that the earliest form of Deuteronomy, the Assyrian or the preexilic version can be read in Deut 6:4–5 and parts of Chapters 12–26 and 28. To summarize again, the themes echoed in this earliest version which show resonance with the VTE include love of God, fear of the Divine lord, exclusiveness of oath swearing by name of Lord, educating the next generation in the way of the treaty, cult centralization, and an initial layer of blessings and curses found in chapter 28.[95] These themes however, become more and more rigid during the Exile and concepts such as monotheism and exclusive election begin to surface toward the end of the Babylonian Exile into the Persian period. The symbol of the Covenant regressed to a place of symbolic equation where the Covenant no longer pointed to Adonai but was, in a sense, equated with Adonai.

During exile the nationalistic ideology or "royal propaganda" of the first Deuteronomistic writings from the seventh century had to be explained in light of the Babylonian Exile. The construction of the first layers of the DH recorded in Deuteronomy through 2 Kings began to surface as a form of crisis literature explaining the Exile as a logical consequence for Covenantal disobedience.[96] As Römer explains, "at this stage there is no real interest to explore the future, all efforts are concentrated on explaining the present by describing or constructing the past."[97] So what we read in this layer is a fastening to a particular way of restructuring time and familial relationships. The former objects now destroyed, (temple, priestly structures, monarchy, etc.) new forms of being as articulated within the Covenant, begin to surface.

Finally, the postexilic redaction of the Deuteronomic Covenant, which includes an ideology of separation from the people of the land—i.e., former Judeans, caused class wars between the exilic elites and those who remained in the land upon the Exile.[98] The idea of election becomes rigidified to the point where now the foreigner, meaning now the people of the land who remained in the land upon Exile, and their cultic symbols are to be completely

---

95. Zehnder, "Building on Stone?," 341–74.

96. Römer, *So-Called Deuteronomistic History*, 113, 163.

97. Ibid., 163.

98. Deuteronomy 7 and 9:1–6 and Ezra–Nehemiah. For a counter argument to this, read Middlemas "Going beyond the Myth of the Empty Land," 174–94.

eradicated and intermarriage is strictly prohibited.[99] Further, rather than a mere intolerant monolatry articulated in the Assyrian and Neo-Babylonian additions of Deuteronomy, the new ideology of monotheism surfaces.

In the Winnicottian sense, the Deuteronomic Covenant, fashioned after the Hittite Loyalty oaths and the VTE, throughout exile was worked over, articulated and rearticulated as Israel sought to make sense of its circumstances, the horror of the many exiles, in particular, the Babylonian Exile, and the nature of her changing relationship with God. Josiah "found" *Seper-hatorah*. Though, in a sense, it was waiting to be found as the surrounding culture(s) had already left components of it lying around. In a paradoxical move Josiah (or the priest, or the scribes, or the lay people— either way, an influential community) found and created *seper-hatorah*, investing the found book with the continuity back to Moses, thus imbuing it with ultimate authority as God in their midst. The Book of the Covenant is then imbued with communal subjectivity, working out the resounding environmental traumas of the many exiles previously experienced and the looming Babylonian Exile. *Seper-hatorah* is taken up and re-imagined. In it, the curses previously provided found in the VTE are reinterpreted in light of the shifting economic and political climate of seventh century Judah. A layer of blessings is added to the treaty, ensuring simultaneous destruction *and* renewal. Israel's relationship with Adonai is re-imagined. Adonai becomes Israel's Suzerain. In addition, Israel is re-imagined. Having once been promised safe entry into and residence in the land of Canaan, exile and destruction are foretold as inevitable consequences of disobedience. In the following chapter the discussion will continue regarding the ramifications of trauma upon what was described above as object-usage.

---

99. Deuteronomy 7:1–26 and its closest parallels with Ezra 9.

4

Refiguring the Divine, Communal Self, and Constructed Other in Exile

> When the boundaries of inside and outside have been breached, it is only in between that it is possible for anything to be shown.
>
> —DAVOINE AND GUADILLIÉRE,
> *HISTORY BEYOND TRAUMA*[1]

WE TURN OUR FOCUS now, to the impact of exile upon the Deuteronomistic narrative and the dominant ideological lens through which the *History* of Israel is purported within the Hebrew canon. The historical reality of the many exiles and perhaps most prominently the Babylonian Exile was a defining and influential moment within the construction of the biblical Hebrew social and religious identity. Daniel Smith-Christopher asserts, "the specific Babylonian Exile must be appreciated as both a historical human disaster and a disaster that gave rise to a variety of social and religious responses with significant social and religious consequences."[2] An exilic trope, that is, the foreshadowing and final judgment of the collapse of first the Northern Kingdom and then the utter decimation of the Southern Kingdom runs throughout the dominant history as it is told throughout Joshua–Kings. Dana Fewell argues, "The transition that colors the whole of the Hebrew Scriptures is the Babylonian Exile. It is presupposed. It is narrated. It is forecasted. It is remembered. It is re-enacted. It is the grief, the trauma, that Israel works through again and again in its literature."[3]

1. Davoine and Guadilliére, *History beyond Trauma*, 59.

2. Smith-Christopher, *Biblical Theology of Exile*, 6.

3. Fewell, "Imagination, Method, and Murder," 135. She is agreeing here with

Similarly, Smith-Christopher maintains that "the ancient Hebrew 'theology of exile' arose from the experiences and events of exile (spanning from the time of Assyrian exile into the time of the Persian empire), and therefore any modern 'theology of exile' must carefully recall their context, as well as our own context, for any theological reflection on the biblical experience."[4] He also reminds us that, "irrespective of the very real differences between the political and ideological regimes from before 587 BCE until, and after, 164 BCE, we must always attend to the stubborn similarities of ancient imperial designs toward power and control over wealth, territory, and human resources. On this, there appears to have been little diversity in practice and results."[5]

It is crucial not only to recall the sociological context of those who were exiled but also to attend to the psychological context of these particular groups. By this I mean attending to how traumatized individuals and communities recount traumatic events and the histories that surround such events. While Smith-Christopher briefly references the literature of trauma and refugee studies, I add a new lens by engaging with psychoanalytic literature, theory, and practice with more detail and attention, while expanding upon some of his arguments. Most biblical scholars interested in analyzing texts that have been potentially affected by trauma do so through the field of trauma studies. The theorists employed are largely Judith Herman, Kathy Caruth, Kai Erikson, et al. I do not find these theories as helpful as those that employ a psychoanalytically nuanced model. The difference being the latter de-stigmatizes trauma, rather than labeling it and seeking to "heal" the trauma, it goes into the trauma through a different route. Psychoanalysts recognize that trauma, more often than not, cannot be talked *about* but can be known through its symptoms, which interrupt daily living and make themselves known in the analytic space or in the daily life of the patient. The "goal" is not to bring the trauma into "narrative" which is, simply put, Herman, Caruth and Erikson's model, but rather to engage with the patients' experience of it through the analyst's own messiness and mistakes or reveries and affect, that which gets arranged in the analytic space from the patient's unconscious or from the patient's unconscious to the analyst's unconscious.[6] If there is a "goal," the goal would be to be able to help the patient find and create symbols with which she can relate to and use to work out her loss,

---

information gathered from private communications with David Jobling.

4. Smith-Christopher, "Reassessing the Historical and Sociological Impact," 73. Parenthetical comments are my own.

5. Ibid., 53–54.

6. Ulanov, *Spiritual Aspects of Clinical Work*, 362–65.

aggression, anger, and mourning, and be brought into relationship with her trauma that has inevitably influenced her own psychic disposition. Psychoanalysis is less focused on a cure than on creating a dialectical relationship between conscious and unconscious, or enabling a process within the patient wherein she can observe the ways in which her "illness," at the hands of her trauma, may actually indicate her path to aliveness and creativity.[7]

I use the psychoanalytic literature of Melanie Klein and Donald Winnicott, from an Object Relations perspective to draw connections between their understanding of the developing baby in relation to her earliest objects and the process of symbol formation that either enables growth toward a shared life with others in the world or inhibits growth keeping the individual locked within a merely subjectively perceived world. My engagement with Jungian theory is here most directly focused on the individual process of symbol formation and how this process can stall becoming stagnant or enmeshed, or worse persecutory. The way I use psychoanalytic theory as a lens through which to analyze the historical events of ancient Israel and literary nuances of the dominant historical narrative draws a parallel between the theories that discuss the development of the child's sense of self and subjective being in relation to her care-giver and the external world, including objective others with their own subjective experiences, to a nascent community's developing identity in the context of others from whom they adopt and adapt symbols and structures. This chapter will continue this parallel but will expand and develop the parallel to discuss the role of symbol formation, pertinent for community development, and how the process of symbol formation can stall out, or collapse, within individual and communal development.

Keeping with my method that utilizes the psychoanalytic theories of Donald Winnicott and Carl Jung on symbols as a lens through which to analyze the historical and literary nuances of the Deuteronomic Covenant and the book of Job, the present chapter duly notes the historical, archeological, and literary arguments for the existence (or absence) of a politicized or socialized historical narrative that arose out of the exile(s) that is infused throughout most of the Hebrew Bible, introduced above as the Deuteronomistic History (DH). I investigate the politicized construction of this history, both formative for and further traumatizing of the postexilic community, through the lens of Object Relations theorists Donald Winnicott and his predecessor Melanie Klein and Carl Jung and contemporary Jungians. Thus, rather than arguing for or against archeological evidence for Israel's many exiles beginning with the Northern exile in 722 BCE at the

---

7. Ulanov, *Madness and Creativity*, 70.

hands of the Assyrians, the first Southern exile beginning in 596 BCE and culminating in the destruction of the temple in 586 BCE, and the prolonged foreign influence of Persia throughout the fifth and into the fourth century, I propose a theory for the literary existence of a dominant exilic trope. This trope constellated a national history described above as the Deuteronomistic History (DH), and served as a basis for Covenant Religion. Recognized as a history of Israel through the lens of exile this story was a product of symbolic failure. In this history, the Covenant, and its many tenets, became or perhaps remained equated with God rather than serving as a bridge toward the God of the Covenant and toward other experiences, including the traumatic experience of exile.

Israel in Exile

The first step is to give a thorough picture of the historical and literary nuances of the exilic trope, which I argue is formulated within the DH.

> **Deuteronomy 28:15:** Thus it shall be *if you do not obey the voice of Adonai your God, keeping and doing all of his commandments and his statutes* which I am commanding you today. *Then all these curses will come upon you and they will overtake you.*

> **Deuteronomy 28:25:** Adonai *will give you to be beaten* before your enemies by one way you will go out toward them and by seven ways you will flee before them and you will be an object of trembling for every kingdom on earth.

> **Deuteronomy 28:45:** *All these curses will come over you and will overtake you* and they will overtake you *until you will be exterminated for you did not hear/obey the voice of Adonai your God keeping his commandments,* his ordinances, which he commanded you.

> **2 Kings 17:5–7:** Then the king of Assyria invaded all the land and came to Samaria; for three years he besieged it. In the ninth year of Hoshea the king of Assyria captured Samaria; he carried the Israelites away to Assyria. He placed them in Halah, on the Habor, the river of Gozan, and in the cities of Medes. *This occurred because the people of Israel had sinned against the Lord their God,* who had brought them up out of the land of Egypt from under the hand of Pharaoh king of Egypt.

> **2 Kings 22:13:** Go, inquire of Adonai on account of me and on account of the people and on account of all of Judah concerning

the words of the book, this one found, *because great is the rage of Adonai which has been kindled against us according to that which our ancestors did not obey according to this book*, doing according to all that is written in it concerning us.

2 Kings 24:20: *Because of Jerusalem and Judah, Adonai's anger was against them and Adonai threw them out of his presence.*

2 Kings 25:8–12: In the fifth month, on the seventh day of the month—which was the nineteenth year of King Nebuchadnezzar, king of Babylon—Nebuzaradan, the captain of the bodyguard, a servant of the king of Babylon, came to Jerusalem. He burned the house of Adonai, the king's house, and all the houses of Jerusalem; every great house he burned down. All the army of the Chaldeans who were with the captain of the guard broke down the walls around Jerusalem. Nebuzaradan the captain of the guard carried into exile the rest of the people who were left in the city and the deserters who had defected to the king of Babylon—all the rest of the population. But the captain of the guard left some of the poorest people of the land to be vinedressers and tillers of the soil.

The atrocious events of exile, both in the North and South, are always recorded in the DH with reflective disclaimers, as can be read in the sample of texts above. While recounting the awful events, the narrators of the DH qualified their history with specific phrases and nuances that made a decidedly evaluative judgment. Phrases such as, *this occurred because the people of Israel had sinned against the Lord their God*, and, *because great is the rage of Adonai which has been kindled against us according to that which our ancestors did not obey according to this book*, reflect this evaluative judgment. According to the DH, the Exile, no matter which exile is being referenced, occurred because of Israel's disobedience to the covenant or to the voice of Adonai inscribed within the covenant.[8]

Reading the Hebrew Bible through the lens of exile has important implications for the reorientation that inevitably occurs in one's exegetical stance whether the exegete is a scholar, clinician, clergy, or layperson. This reorientation draws attention to individual and communal psychological wholeness and to the stories that reflectively narrate past experiences. Thus, historical narratives can be analyzed for what they leave out and how they are qualified, providing readers today clues as to how certain symbols in an ancient community functioned to construct identity.

---

8. Israel in this context is an ideological term including both the northern and southern tribes.

Like the field of DH studies, there exists a great deal of controversy over the Babylonian Exile and the use of terms such as preexilic, exilic, and postexilic Israel.[9] The questions that arise when trying to define exile in ancient Israel include: What is one referencing when discussing Israel before and after exile, or cumulative exiles? What and who comprises Israel? Furthermore, which exile is the referent? While I do not deny the concept of "exilic" time periods may be an ideological construction, based on archeological evidence there is not doubt that there were indeed exiles and most prominently, a Babylonian Exile. The makers of history, elite though they may have been, created a narrative that dominates the Hebrew Bible and thus, it is worthy of significant attention.

Exile, here, refers to the conglomerate experiences of the many exiles undergone by the Israelite community of the North and the Judean community of the South. The first of the exiles referred within the canon in 2 Kings 17:7–41 describes the capture of Samaria by the king of Assyria in 722 BCE. Archeological findings, which have been recently reinterpreted, attest to some level of devastation within the Northern kingdom, primarily in the regions of Galilee and the Northern Transjordan.[10] Along with destruction and devastation, other Northern sites experienced momentary occupation gaps when the occupants were exiled to Assyria and no other ethnic group was sent to repopulate the plundered areas, Assyrian or otherwise. Though these archeological findings are being reinterpreted and even contested by some it remains a fact that Northern Israel experienced a major reorganization of power and privilege in the land once their own.[11]

Due to the western campaigns of Tiglath-pileser in 743–742 BCE the kingdom of Damascus was decimated and led to mass deportations and thus a significant reduction of the size of the Israelite state.[12] However, remains from the hill country of Ephraim and Manasseh reveal less destruction and indicate some efforts of rebuilding.[13] There were even a few

9. Cf Torrey, "Exile and the Restoration," in *Ezra Studies*, 285–88; Albright, *Archaeology of Palestine*, 141–42; Blenkinsopp, "Bible, Archaeology and Politics"; Stern, "Babylonian Gap"; Knoppers, "In Search of Postexilic Israel," 152; Carroll, "Exile! What Exile?"; Davies, "Exile? What Exile? Whose Exile?," 128–38, Smith-Christopher "Reassessing the Historical and Sociological Impact," 7 ; Smith-Christopher, *Biblical Theology of Exile*, 6; Kelle, "Interdisciplinary Approach to the Exile," 7.

10. Stern, "Babylonian Gap"; and Knoppers, "In Search of Postexilic Israel," 181–206.

11. Knoppers, "In Search of Postexilic Israel," 170–72.

12. Ibid., 170.

13. Knoppers, based on his interpretation of the data presented by Arav, "Bethsaida Excavations: Preliminary Report, 1994–96."

locations that remained untouched and continuously populated.[14] Knoppers concludes, based on his survey and interpretation of the archeological data that while there is evidence for an average decline in population during the late eighth century BCE in the North, the result is not as clear-cut as once thought.[15] While depopulation occurred, it occurred in the midst of mixed ethnic, social, and religious environs. Upon the campaigns of Shalmaneser V (727–722 BCE) and Sargon II (722–705 BCE), who finally overthrew the Israelite state and transformed Samaria into an Assyrian province, there occurred some form of influx of foreigners who seem to have settled into the local population.

Due to the fact that the depopulation of Israelites was coupled with a repopulation by foreigners the North enjoyed a slow rise in strength and prosperity during the seventh century BCE even after it was taken over by Assyria. The locals held on to their practices, as is evinced in surviving material remains from this time period.[16] While the Northern community never regained the autonomy once enjoyed, it maintained its material culture and seems to have made a quicker recovery after the Assyrian campaigns against Samaria than Judah did after the invasions of Babylonia in the sixth century.[17] However, while the North may have enjoyed some political and economic stability, even after Assyrian invasion, there is no denying the influence of foreign presence upon the reconstruction of the *identity* of the Northern community.[18]

The Babylonian invasion of Judah in the sixth century, on the other hand, took a much greater toll.[19] Archeological evidence has revealed phenomenal damage upon the economic infrastructure of Judah, as well as physical destruction of Judah's fortifications and major buildings.[20] While Samaria grew in strength during the years of the Babylonian Exile, Judea was utterly decimated, the temple, palace, and surrounding city were destroyed, and the makers and sustainers of Israelite public culture, the scribes and priests—the ruling elite, were deported off of their land.[21] This juxtaposition may account for why there was such tension and controversy between

14. Knoppers, "In Search of Postexilic Israel," 170.

15. Ibid.

16. Ibid.

17. Ibid., based on evidence from Stern, *Archaeology of the Land of the Bible*, 49–51.

18. See Finkelstein's latest book, *Forgotten Kingdom*.

19. See Oded, *Early History of the Babylonian Exile*; Smith-Christopher, *Religion of the Landless*, 29–31; and Kuhrt, *Ancient Near East*, 532–34.

20. Knoppers, "In Search of Postexilic Israel," 171.

21. See Oded, *Mass Deportations and Deportees*, for more on the influence of deportation upon demographics within the ANE.

the Samarian and Judean communities recorded in biblical texts such as trito-Isaiah (Isaiah 55–65) and Ezra–Nehemiah.

Jill Middlemas gives a provocative argument reassessing the scholarly construction of the exilic/postexilic time period in her article "Going Beyond the Myth of the Empty Land: A Reassessment of the Early Persian Period."[22] She asserts that given the reality of the multitude of exiles Israel experienced in the course of its monarchical history one should not consider the time after the first temple was destroyed at the hands of Babylon in 586 as the exilic period (174–94). She goes on to challenge the scholarly assumption of the repatriation of Judah at the instigation of Cyrus given the fact that the extra biblical evidence used for proof (the Cyrus Cylinder), has been critically challenged and the fact that the only strong biblical evidence is found in Deutero-Isaiah. She points out that Haggai or Zechariah, two other prophets dated to this time period reflect a different ideological position, less contentious and despairing than Ezra–Nehemiah or Deutero-Isaiah (176). Ultimately her work calls for a "reassessment of conceptions about the end of the period," arguing that rather than a division within the Israelite community between repatriates and non-repatriates, it is possible there was a push toward unity within the community seeking to create an identity of ancient Israel during this period.[23] Her argument comes from her close read of Haggai and Zechariah 1–8 in contrast to other literature of this same time period, Ezra–Nehemiah. She proffers the term "templeless period" rather than exilic period, believing the history to have been creatively reconstructed from Judea rather than Babylonia and thus reflecting the ideological perspective of the Judeans rather than the exiles in Babylonia. She reassesses the literature along these lines. Middlemas asserts, "There are three types of themes into which the literary deposit fits quite comfortably: literature of grief with no clear positive outlook such as the communal laments in the Psalter, the book of Lamentations and the Deuteronomistic History; prophecies that straddle the themes of judgment and hope like those of Jeremiah and Ezekiel; and literature that perceives a new divine action and urges the restoration of the community and a renewal of covenant loyalty like that of Deutero-Isaiah, Ezekiel 40–48, Haggai, Zechariah 1–8 and the Holiness Code."[24]

While I would challenge Middlemas' assumptions of the coherency of such delineated categories, and am not fully convinced by her argument of such unity within repatriate Judah, I do agree with her reformulation of

---

22. Middlemas, "Going beyond the Myth of the Empty Land."

23. Ibid., 189.

24. Ibid., 187.

the repository of literature of the templeless period, in part. I argue in the next section of this book, that Job is another example of literature during the templeless period but provides a fourth category. This fourth category is a bit more developed than the literature of grief read in Lamentations, Lament Psalms and the Deuteronomistic History. Rather than remaining hopeless, providing no "positive outlook" as Middlemas suggests of these former three, jumping immediately into literature of hope or propaganda for restoration and renewal, there is another voice that begins to emerge during this temple-less period. The voice of Individuated religion that maintains ambivalence and aggression, tells a different kind of historical narrative.

While the Exile was, no doubt, a profound moment in the life of Ju-dea, as it remains the reference point of the ancient Israelite history, there are virtually no biblical archives describing life in exile—neither from the perspective in Babylonia or in Judea. A question emerges out of the ar-cheological evidence and scholarly arguments regarding the exiles. If the North enjoyed greater stability and even grew in strength during the years of the Babylonian Exile, why is the dominant history told through Judah's lens? Why does the DH contain a strong exilic trope, narrating history through the lens of exile? While one cannot ever know for sure, one prob-able cause has to do with the severity of the Babylonian Exile and Judah's psychological response therein.

Using object relations theorists Klein and Winnicott, and Jung and contemporary Jungian's, I analyze the historical evidence just given and the DH's literary proclivity to evaluate and judge the events of the Exile in a par-ticular way. I thus provide a theoretical background for how the trauma of cumulative exiles co-opts the dominant historical narrative of Israel by col-lapsing the symbol of the Covenant. The Covenant, both found and created by ancient Israel, enabled Israel to define who they were amongst the warring superpowers of the eighth–seventh centuries. However, due to the experi-ence of repetitive exiles and internal divisions within the two communities (North and South) the symbol that once provided the space to establish a sense of identity, rigidified. The distinction between the inner reality, a com-munal understanding of Israel and Israel's relation to Adonai for the sake of Israel's future, and outer realities, the social and political reality in the Fertile Crescent, after the trauma of the Babylonian Exile merged into the traumatic experience itself. Thus, the Covenant and the God of the Covenant, were equated with this traumatic experience. I suggest, this equation caused Cov-enant Religion to concretize an image of God that demanded right action and obedience as a prerequisite for protection and salvation.

Symbolic Failure in Light of
Object Relations Theory

What began in the beginning as a symbolic object that enabled Israel to find and create a national identity in the shadow of Assyria became *equated* with the trauma itself as a result of the Babylonian Exile.[25] As Klein says in light of the Babylonian Exile, " . . . almost all of the old symbol systems (temple, Davidic dynasty, land, covenant and priesthood) had been rendered useless. Almost all of the old institutions no longer functioned. What kind of future was possible for a people which traced its unique election to a god who had just lost a war to other deities?" While I do not agree with Klein's analysis that the concept of election was developed before the Exile, this quotation captures the sense of symbolic failure experienced externally as a result of the Babylonian Exile. This symbol, *seper-hatorah*, found and created by Israel, at one time enabling Israel a sense of autonomy wherein space was created to formulate a communal identity in relation to the surrounding nations, became an object of internal and perhaps, at least in fantasy, external torture.[26] In Exile, *seper-hatorah,* functioned to place blame upon the Israelites themselves, figuring the divine as the trespassed and thus angry vassal lord who heaped out consequences for Israel's disobedience. Then, in postexilic Israel, the Covenant was fashioned to demand eradication of any hint of otherness within the Israelite community, including Judeans themselves who had not been exiled, in order to protect and secure future restoration and blessing.[27]

Melanie Klein on Symbolic Equation

Melanie Klein, psychoanalytic forerunner and later, a colleague of Donald Winnicott, explains how the process of symbol formation is necessary for ego development in the young child. In the earliest stages of ego development, Klein suggests symbol formation begins first through symbolic equation. Through symbolic equation, the breast is the mother, from the perception of the developing infant. In the act of nursing and cuddling, the child identifies with this good object, the warm and nourishing breast—that is the mother, by taking into her own self, introjecting, the nurturing and good characteristics of this mother. Through this identification and taking in of the good characteristics, the child's growing ego begins to develop around

---

25. Klein, *Israel in Exile*, 5.

26. Here I am referring to the creation of the conquest narratives in Joshua.

27. Read Ezra 9 as an example.

these internalized images, or what Klein calls part-objects as the good and nurturing breast is part of the external love object, the actual mothering one.[28] The ability of the infant to identify with the good characteristics of the mother, experienced as the breast in the earliest moments of life, lays the basis for other helpful identifications.[29] The introjected part-object enables the growing infant to experience frustration when her needs are not immediately met, without losing the image of the good inside. Evidence of early identification with the loving and nurturing aspects of the mothering-one is seen in the play of the small child when she imitates her mother and carries an empathetic and nurturing attitude toward other younger children.[30] If the baby is able to introject good and loving characteristics the child will eventually grow to see her own self as good and loving. This stage, which is possible through one's fantasy, is necessary for all future symbol formation and for developing a relationship to one's internal and external worlds.

However, not only are there nurturing and loving experiences early on in development, but also, there is felt within the child, aggression and hate toward her mother and later her father. Klein, following Freud, believes the root of this aggressiveness and hate lies within the death instinct, existing in all human beings from the time of birth. Internal aggression comes from the child's own death instinct, and the fear of this death instinct, which Klein, following Freud, believes children have from the first moment of life. This fear is the seed of the super-ego. As Klein explains, the child, "perceives his anxiety arising from his aggressive instincts as fear of an external object, both because he has made that object their outward goal, and because he has projected them on to it so that they seem to be initiated against himself . . ."[31] These feelings of aggression and hate are directed toward the child's earliest objects—her parents or caregivers—due to the child's frustration with the breast that does not always provide warm milk exactly when the child is ready or the rivalry felt with the father who seems to take the mother's attention away from the baby. The feelings that arise are frightening for the child and the child's developing ego, thus they are projected, or put upon the mother, in the earliest moments of life, and later upon the father and other external figures.

Through projection the infant and growing child achieves another kind of identification, similar yet different from identification that results

28. Klein, *Envy and Gratitude*, 251–52.

29. Ibid., 251.

30. Ibid.

31. Klein, *Love, Guilt and Reparation*, 250. Cf Winnicott, *Through Paediatrics to Psycho-Analysis*, 216.

from introjection. The child projects her own aggressive and hateful instinct into the mothering one and, in a sense, creates a bad object, the "bad-breast." Part of the mother is felt to be bad and persecutory, due to the child's inability to hold her own aggressive instincts in fear of them spoiling the good object inside, or good-breast experienced as mother. The tendency of the infantile ego to split impulses and objects into good and bad, loving and hating, is a primal activity of the ego and in fact, is never entirely given up but remains a life-long process in and out of which one moves.[32]

This process of introjecting the good and loving characteristics of the good part-object mother and the projecting of aggressive and hateful instincts of the child upon the "bad" part-object mother, is described as the paranoid-schizoid position. This early position in ego development in which persecutory anxiety leads the child to split her own impulses into good and bad in order to protect her love from her hate and her loved object from the dangerous object is supported through symbolic equation. The infant identifies the good aspects with the good-breast and the bad aspects with the bad-breast without initially realizing both of these aspects are introjected from and projected upon the same mother. By splitting, the individual preserves the child's belief in the good object, the loving and nurturing mother, and his capacity to love it.[33] Splitting protects the young child's ego from being overwhelmed by the fear of being destroyed by a hostile external world and his own inner hostility. As Klein says, "If the interplay between introjection and projection is not dominated by hostility or over-dependence, and is well balanced, the inner world is enriched and the relations with the external world are improved."[34]

Persecutory anxiety, aggressive impulses, and splitting, are natural processes of ego development enabled through symbolic formation. In normal development these processes however, diminish through a growing integration of the ego.[35] When these processes diminish, the person is able to bring together the contradictory impulses within her own ego, thus leading to a greater synthesis of good and bad for her own self and in her understanding of the external world.[36] In normal development, symbolic equation, possible through the process of identification described above, gives way to symbol formation.[37] As Klein says, "A sufficient quantity of anxiety is the necessary

32. Klein, *Envy and Gratitude*, 253.

33. Ibid., 253.

34. Ibid.

35. Ibid., 255.

36. Ibid.

37. Klein, *Love, Guilt and Reparation*, 220.

basis for an abundance of symbol-formation and of phantasy; an adequate capacity on the part of the ego to tolerate anxiety is essential if anxiety is to be satisfactorily worked over, if this basic phase is to have a favourable issue and if the development of the ego is to be successful."[38] Once the child is able to form other symbols through fantasy, that symbolize the mother and the mother's body though are not in actuality the mother, the child is able to work through, in fantasy, the process of adapting to reality.

However, if the child is unable to be in touch with fantasy life that Klein believes is our inner life, our internal reality, then one is unable to form symbols and unable to play. If one is unable to form symbols, unable to play, due to overwhelming persecutory anxiety or actual traumatic events, than one is incapable of expressing her inner reality. In this case, either her aggression will remain projected upon external objects while maintaining only the good inside or her aggression will overwhelm her interior life, inhibiting an establishment of the good within the child's own ego. In other words, one's ego will remain split failing to integrate the good (loving instincts) and the bad (aggressive instincts). Since, in the beginning, symbols are equated with the objects they symbolize, the child's own aggressive anxiety can overwhelm and frighten her if she experiences her aggression as capable of annihilating her love object or vice versa, fear that her love object (the empty breast) will annihilate her.[39]

The child gradually realizes her own aggressive impulses and emotions that have been directed toward the mothering one and gradually the good and bad mother are one mother containing both part-objects (good and bad breasts) previously experienced as separate. When this happens the child is able to take back her own aggressive and loving instincts integrating these ambivalent energies through her developing ego, her conscious identity. The mother grows whole and the child grows whole. Having previously lashed out in aggression toward the annihilating object, the child feels guilt for damaging (in fantasy) the love object and now seeks to repair the damage done in fantasy to this object, related to now as a whole object.

Klein refers to this process as the depressive position, the position after the paranoid-schizoid position, being characterized by depressive anxiety, anxiety arising from the feeling of guilt once the child realizes the bad-object she sought to damage was part of the same internalized good and loving object.[40] In this position the child seeks to make reparation with the whole mother or mothering one and thus take back the previously split

38. Ibid., 221.

39. Klein, *Envy and Gratitude*, 5–12.

40. Klein, *Love, Guilt, and Reparation*, 271–75.

good and bad into her own ego.[41] It is considered the depressive position not because the child is actually depressed or melancholy, but because the child has come into contact with external reality as separate from her own aggressive impulses. For Klein, this has to do with the death and life instincts, which she believes are part of the person's psychic composition from day one. The death instinct is active early on during the paranoid-schizoid position and is felt as aggressive impulses coming from the part-object mothering-one, which are in actuality projected impulses of the child's own ego upon that mothering-one. The depressive position is the position when the infant slowly begins to integrate her own aggressive instincts back into her ego, integrating the life and death instincts, beginning to see her self and her caregiver as complex whole people that contain ambivalence, love and hate.[42]

It is through this process of making reparation, that is—seeking to repair that which she has in fantasy maimed, and having her reparation accepted and reflected back upon by the caregiver that the child is able to establish and maintain an active and meaningful fantasy life. However, if the child is unable to maintain this ambivalence or fears that the aggressive instincts projected upon the mothering-one are life-threatening, or the child fears her own aggressive instincts will kill her love object, then the child may be unable to access her own fantasy life. In this case, the child will not be able to reach the depressive position or will regress back into the paranoid-schizoid position where symbolic equation rules, and there get stuck. If the child fears the mothering-one will actually kill her, fears her self to be too bad to receive the mothering-one's love, or fears that her love within will be damaged by her own hate, the child is unable to symbolize, unable to play and work out her own aggressive instincts and offer reparation, and thus unable to experience an integrated and whole ego, a movement toward relating to the outside world. She remains frozen in anxiety and guilt.

For Klein, similar to Winnicott, symbols are the medium upon which an individual is able to release her aggression felt toward the object that she has earlier identified with and taken in as the good and loving object. Thus, symbol formation is crucial for ego development. It is through the process of symbol formation the growing individual is able to understand her love-object or caregiver in reality—as she grows to understand both she and her caregiver contain good and bad, love, and aggression. Previously, the two were split, and the caregiver became the placeholder for the child's own aggressive energy unacknowledged or integrated. At this stage, the caregiver

41. Ibid., 265.
42. Ibid., 262–89.

was felt to be a persecutor, as a result of the child's own frustrated desires and her aggression as a consequence.

Klein suggests that it is through play one releases and acts out one's aggression coming from the death instinct.[43] In play symbols become symbols in their own right to be used and manipulated through the work of fantasy, rather than being wholly equated, as in symbolic equation, with one's primary love object. This play, or serious internal work with the symbols formed and used, enables the child to take back the aggression into her own ego, realizing her own good and bad emotions and impulses. In play, the child can give her doll a time out for hitting her teddy bear, a way of working out the child's own aggression (by being able to have one of the toys hit another) toward her mothering one or her brother or friend for hurting her or thwarting her desires. She is also able to work through her guilt feelings in the act of giving the doll a time out. Or the child can kill her dolls through play, and make them come back to life, acting out some impulse or desire she experiences in fantasy toward her mother or her sibling. Through symbolization in play the child can reclaim her own aggression, learn to tolerate the annihilating anxiety, and can begin to make reparation. Without recognizing aggression and love belong together those objects felt to be persecuting within the first position, the paranoid-schizoid position, remain so and the good, not well enough established internally, is subject to the wrath of the child's destructive aggression.

Without the capacity for fantasy and symbol formation the child remains helpless to defend herself against the bad projected out upon the love object felt to be directed toward her, or helpless to defend the good within and, others externally, against her own aggression and hate. As Klein says, "not only does symbolism come to be the foundation of all phantasy and sublimation but, more than that, it is the basis of the subject's relation to the outside world and to reality in general."[44]

Before symbol formation there is aggression, and before aggression there is anxiety that comes from the death instinct. It is necessary for the growing individual's ego to be able to tolerate some level of anxiety. Anxiety stems from felt persecution coming from the outside world and, for Klein, the death instinct from inside the child projected upon her outside objects. This persecution includes the child's own aggression she has exported upon her caregiver/love-object and, in part, the caregiver's own actual aggression. The first step to symbolization however, is being able to tolerate the anxiety produced from feeling this persecuting energy and being able to sublimate

43. Klein, *Envy and Gratitude*, 137–38.
44. Klein, *Love, Guilt, and Reparation*, 221.

the energy into forming symbols upon which she can retaliate. For instance, in the example above, the doll who is in timeout symbolizes the child who experiences her own impulses to hit, kick, or bite the mothering one who has frustrated the child. The child is able to tolerate the anxiety of this persecuting energy coming from inside the child, but projected upon the mothering one by both acting out the aggressive act of hitting (the teddy bear) and then placing the doll in timeout—expressing both the persecutory (the earliest position when the child experienced the mothering one as bad and good, annihilating and loving) and depressive anxieties (the root of the next position when the child realizes the part-object she attacked in order to protect herself is only part of her whole love object). It is through this kind of serious work, known as play, the child gradually comes to realize and own her own aggression, take it back in forming a more whole ego that contains the good and the bad, enabling her the ability to be in relationship with the reality of the external world. However, in some cases the growing child's ego is not able to tolerate this initial anxiety produced in part by the child's own death instinct. In these cases, the child's own aggressive energy has nowhere to go, no symbols are formed wherein the child may work out her own feelings and relations to her external world. The energy remains locked up within the child.

In normal development, repression is used to deal with conflicts.[45] However, another mechanism used to deal with conflicts is flight from reality. "Much more than would appear on the surface, the child resents the unpleasantness of reality and tries to adapt it to his phantasies and not his phantasies to reality."[46] The play life of a child is made up of his impulses and desires, working them over, performing them and fulfilling them in playful imaginative plots.[47] Observing a child throughout life, watching how he plays with his animals, dolls, or action figures, retelling experiences from the day or working out family dynamics, reveals the seriousness of such work. Sometimes however, children can seem as though they are comforting themselves, or not seeming upset by situations that are actually upsetting (losing a parent or sibling, being the subject of abuse or incest, experiencing the separation of his parents, etc.), giving the impression that they are better off than they are in reality. Again, here the role of fantasy is used to assuage the child's anxiety and unhappiness.[48] Except that in this case, the child tries to adapt the traumatic reality to his fantasy rather

45. Klein, *Love, Guilt, and Reparation*, 180.

46. Ibid.

47. Ibid.

48. Ibid., 181.

than the opposite. An example of this is when a child blames the vulnerable object within his play characters for the dire circumstances of the play sequence. Or worse, the child is unable to play with toys at all. His silence may be interpreted as "getting over it" or being resilient, while internally he becomes the object and subject of a devastating persecutory anxiety. As an example, relevant to the topic at hand, to be discussed in detail below, a community can construct a narrative that assuages the horrible pain of national trauma by finding a way to blame themselves for the devastating loss and destruction of their culture. Fear, as the result of a trauma, can lead to a greater repression before the way for sublimation is opened. Thus, there is no channel through which to work the traumatic situation over because symbolization is inhibited and is fixed, or stuck, at this point. The result, according to Klein, is an installation of a cruel super-ego, stuck in the primitive paranoid-schizoid phase, splitting bad and good and punishing himself for the bad that overwhelms the good in his own ego.[49]

In other words, even in normal development it is possible that the intrusion of trauma *at any stage* could lead to a negative repression, a repression without sublimation. Sublimation is possible through symbol formation. When sublimation is inhibited so, too, is symbol formation. When symbol formation is inhibited the individual, child or adult, loses access to her rage, aggression, and disappointment - all natural responses to trauma. The individual then, rather than being able to work out her anger at the actual traumatic event or toward a real perpetrator, in a sense, loses access to reality. The space between inner fantasy and outer reality are blurred. Stories may get created that provide a cognitive way of explaining external circumstances, such as the history of Israel told through the lens of Exile as it was foreshadowed, came to fruition, and then attributed to the evil kings and Israel's neglect to keep the Covenant. However, these stories are anything but symbolic because they work to make reality (the devastating loss of land and religious, political, and economic structure) fit a fantasy (they got what they deserved—they did not uphold their end of the Covenant, were too religiously promiscuous, and thus deserved the wrath of Adonai), rather than the other way around. The other way around would have allowed for the pain of exile to make its way into the texts and the disillusionment of Covenant Religion to be addressed rather than silenced. In exile, the stories of Israel's coming into being as a nation, inscribed during the eighth–sixth centuries, become necessary for survival. Through a Kleinian lens, the stories were equated with the God of the Covenant and the actual horrific

---

49. Ibid., 183. Fairbairn, *Psychoanalytic Studies of the Personality*, 82—136; Klein, "Notes on Some Schizoid Mechanisms (1946)," in *Envy and Gratitude*, 1–24.

event of the Exile was explained as punishment coming from Adonai. While living in Babylonia, the constructors of history found a way to make sense of the Exile by finding the blame within the community.[50] If the community would be faithful to the Covenant, according to Covenant Religion, there would remain a promise (a hope) of salvation and restoration.

A more recent example of this can be seen in the construction of American history.[51] The history books used when I was in grade school nearly erased the vicious reality of the systematic removal and relocation of native populations and the inhumane removal and use of African peoples in the founding of our nation. Merely blips on a page, these atrocious realities only haunted the pages that highlighted instead America's struggle for liberation and democracy in the shadow of the aristocratic and authoritarian British Empire. Illuminating other historical events that led to American independence overshadowed the insalubrious aspects of our history. Growing up in the South, for instance, the events of the civil war were taught with a decidedly Southern spin commemorating the confederacy while all but ignoring the horrendous reality of slavery. Nowadays of course, more light has been shed on these unsavory moments of America's history. Entire disciplines have emerged as protest in response to dominant culture's portrayal of history.[52] These discourses have emerged, as voices from the margins,[53] within the field of biblical studies as well, but few have fully analyzed the construction of history within the Hebrew canon. Sugirtharajah in his book, *Voices form the Margin: Interpreting the Bible in the Third World*, provides both a thorough introduction to the postcolonial/subaltern method and a compilation of essays expressing a wide range of its application within the field of biblical studies. However, this method in general and the essays in this book are mostly from an ideological perspective. What I am attempting to do is to deconstruct the accepted notion of history that is so often used in juxtaposition to ideology. In my opinion, history *is* ideology as events (that actually do take place—even horrific events such as abuse, holocaust, war, etc.) are immediately and continually interpreted through the lens of the observer who inevitably has social and/or political stake in their interpretation whether it is the community who underwent the trauma and is trying to ensure their own safety and survival, or the community who is responsible for the event and seeks to distance themselves from the harm-

50. See Houck-Loomis, "Good God?!?," for more on this concept.

51. See Bender, *Rethinking American History in a Global Age*.

52. Postcolonial criticism, which only emerged in the 1990s. Barry, *Beginning Theory*, 185.

53. Sugirtharajah, *Voices from the Margin*.

ful choices and thus consequences of their political system. This does not minimize the actual horrific events that happened, but rather, it recognizes when these events become "history" they have already been interpreted through an individual or community's lens and agenda.[54] Thus the question still remains, what happens to the (hi)story when the symbols fail?

Winnicott and Symbolic Failure

Winnicott explains, "In health, when the infant achieves fusion [with the mother], the frustrating aspect of object behavior has value in educating the infant in respect of the existence of a not-me world. Adaptation failures have value in so far as the infant can hate the object . . . can retain the idea of the object as potentially satisfying while recognizing its failure to behave satisfactorily."[55] The object referred to in this quote is the mothering-one or the primary love object, the one the infant is fused with early on if there is enough adaptation on the part of the environment, on behalf of the "good-enough" mother.[56] Being merged with the mothering-one is essential in the beginning, in order for the developing child to exist and go on existing in her own body and in relation to her developing self and eventually to others.

Eventually, in order for the infant to discover her own self outside of her unity with the mothering-one, the illusion of omnipotence wherein the baby experienced all her needs and wants automatically and almost autonomously met, must be pulled back ever so slightly introducing frustration. However, the good-enough mother does not introduce frustration without laying around objects for the baby to play with and relate to. Explained in chapter 3, these objects symbolize the merged unity between mothering-one and baby and the baby's feelings about this relationship and toward her mothering-one. They are subjectively related to allowing the baby to work out, in fantasy, her aggressive impulses due to the frustration experienced at the opposition introduced by the environment and the mothering-one. In this frustration, a sense of ambivalence arises in the child. Opposition is felt and met with aggressive impulses or her life-force potential urgently prodding her to get her needs and desires met. Ambivalence arises as the child experiences frustration toward the one whom has introduced momentary pain while also holding on to this same one as good and loved. Eventually the aggressive impulses lead the child to pick up the objects laid about that represent the unity experienced between the child and her mothering-one

54. Kim has published a book close to this titled, *Decolonizing Josiah*.

55. Winnicott, *Maturational Processes*, 181; parenthetical comments are my own.

56. Winnicott, *Psycho-Analytic Explorations*, 254.

and her own feelings of frustration, her subjective experience toward this unity, urge her to destroy these objects. It is at this moment in development the child is able to use the objects that have previously been subjectively related to. During this stage, the child is able to destroy the mothering-one in fantasy as she seeks to destroy the objects that have stood for the merged unity between mother and baby.

Winnicott describes this transition as moving from object-relating to object-usage wherein the objects previously subjectively related to (subjective-objects) become objects in their own right (objective-objects) outside of the child's subjective experience of them. This is a natural transition allowed by the good-enough environment. The attuned care-giver has provided objects for which the baby can relate and is then able to withstand or survive the baby's aggressive impulses toward the objects provided that stand for the mother-baby unity and the baby's feelings about that unit. This enables the baby to use the objects and using the objects allows the baby to place them, and therefore her mother, outside of her subjective experience. It is through aggression the baby is able to establish external reality and live in a world of shared reality with others.

However, if the play space, the space for working out one's internal reality in relation to the external world, is not created or is impinged upon either by the caregiver or the environment, Winnicott explains the child can be robbed of her ability to find and create herself and her ability to live creatively, precisely because her ambivalent feelings go unnoticed or are shamed. Impingement can come from the mothering-one herself, introducing too much opposition early on or from external environmental factors such as war-torn ghettos, displacement, poverty, or any other circumstance (such as exile) that robs the caregivers themselves of the ability to live creatively. Impingement can also come from external circumstances that directly destroy the symbols of one's culture or objects used in the serious work of play.

What can happen in dire circumstances when the frustration within this transitional space is too great is that these symbolic objects get stuck or become fetish objects creating behaviors that lead to addiction rather than transition.[57] When there is inadequate space provided by the environment or the growing child is robbed of her ability to find and create herself, behaviors such as thievery or addiction develop.[58] In other words, when the space between the object and the thing the object symbolizes collapses,

---

57. Winnicott, "The Concept of Trauma in Relation to the Development of the Individual within the Family," in *Psycho-Analytic Explorations*, 130–36.

58. Winnicott, "Ego Integration in Child Development (1962)" 52.

then the object becomes equated with the thing it once symbolized and the individual must have it in order to keep functioning. While symbolic equation (Klein) and the creation of subjective objects (Winnicott) are the beginning of symbol formation, one can get stuck at the stage of symbolic relating and fail to gain the ability to use objects that would enable the child to establish external reality. In some cases, the symbols become literal rather than symbolic and what is literalized is the child's subjective perspective that the objects hold for the child. In healthy development aggression intervenes and allows symbolic objects (transitional objects) to be used in relation to grappling with one's external world. When one is thrust back into the earlier phase of object relating wherein objects are related to subjectively rather than used by the child allowing her to be in relationship with external reality, the object is rigidified, literalized, and concretized. The doll is the mother and thus cannot be played with for fear that she may be destroyed. The doll remains necessary for relating to the external world. Rather than the doll withstanding one's destruction and love the object is idealized and protected, related to subjectively, and thus cannot survive the child's aggressive impulses.

Klein and Winnicott illuminate the necessity of aggression and destructive energy as a means by which the individual develops ego strength and a consolidated personality. With a stronger ego, one is able to maintain ambivalence, the simultaneous feelings of love and hate toward others. With a consolidated personality comes the ability to live with others who are different, not-me, and the ability to accept other's differences without feeling threatened or feeling the need to merge with them in order to be in relationship.[59]

Klein and Winnicott also both warn that trauma (or impingement) can interrupt this process, which causes the individual to internalize aggression or inhibits the individual's ego from linking the aggressive and erotic impulses.[60] Klein suggests in the individual this plays out in trying to match reality with her internal fantasy, rather than using fantasy to work out her aggressive and erotic energies. Winnicott indicates this inhibits the ability to integrate aggressive impulses within the individual, disallowing her the ability to place objects outside of her subjective experience of them. In individuals who have suffered severe trauma the trauma takes up the internal fantasy life and the victim remains the victim rather than being able to be the perpetrator, i.e., to access her own natural aggressive impulses, her

59. Cf Klein, *Envy and Gratitude*, 4–5 and Winnicott, *Playing and Reality*, 124.

60. Cf Klein, *Love, Guilt and Reparation*, 250–53; Winnicott, *Maturational Processes*, 127; and Winnicott, *Playing and Reality*, 95.

anger toward the actual harm done. In acute cases, children may not be able to play with toys at all because the reenactment would, in a sense, reify the trauma and the child might be punished again in fantasy.[61]

Winnicott describes how aggressive impulses may fail to get linked up with one's erotic impulses due to an excess of opposition early on in development. When one's natural aggressive impulses are not integrated, one is not able to relate to the external world and her objects, rather than being symbols, are fixed or believed to be the actual objects they were meant to symbolize, they remain subjectively related to. When one's symbols become fixed or remain subjectively related to, the object is not placed in the external world and thus cannot be used to help the individual transition from subjectively to objectively relating to others and to the world.[62] If the early environment cannot withstand the aggressive impulses of the growing child and the (fantastical) destruction of the objects that stand in for the caregiver, the child must hold on to the objects, believing these objects to be the actual caregiver rather than merely standing in for the caregiver. An external reality never gets established in contrast to the child's inner reality.

We can analyze now the Covenant as an object for Israel during transition. During Israel's transition from a nascent village community to burgeoning city-state and then collapse of city-state autonomy and eventual loss of land and community structure, this object that enabled the Israelites to find their particularity and uniqueness in the midst of the larger Near Eastern context and provided structure for them to survive after years of Assyrian domination, ceased from being a symbol due to the trauma of the Exile under Babylonian domination. When the object ceased from being a symbol the space between the Covenant and that which the Covenant symbolized (Israel's national identity and relationship with Adonai) collapsed. The object found and created by Israel and used for transition from a nascent village community to a burgeoning city-state, subjectively related to during Israel's time of growth, remained equated with Israel's own bundle of projections, Israel's subjective experience.

As stated above, one of the similarities Deuteronomy 28 shares with the VTE is the emphasis on self-blame for the exile or national collapse. In essence, Israel adopted a self-blaming system from the objects found and created lying around in culture. Upon the devastation of the Exile this self-blaming system was elevated to a national history maintained in Covenant Religion, articulated in the Deuteronomistic History. This history provided

---

61. Klein, *Love, Guilt and Reparation*, 128–38.

62. Winnicott, *Through Paediatrics to Psycho-Analysis*, 242.

a reason for the unspeakable events of exile, the reason being Israel's disobedience to the Covenant.

In this way Israel could no longer retain their initial ideas of their community and God articulated in the Assyrian layer of Deuteronomy, described above as royal propaganda that promised Israel protection from the surrounding enemies and a future in the land of Canaan. The hope for renewal, provided during the late seventh century at the initial formulation of the Covenant and the story of its being found, collapsed. The Covenant, rather than creating a way into relationship with Adonai God, placed an unseemly amount of blame on Israel for disobeying *seper-hatorah.* In the national narrative maintained in the dominant Covenant Religion, only realignment with and perfect obedience to *seper-hatorah* would give Israel any hope for renewal. The ramifications of this trauma are seen in the narrowing and rigidifying aspects of later redactions of Deuteronomy and the construction of a historical narrative.

Winnicott explains the intermediate stage in development when the person's experience in relation to the good or satisfying object is the refusal of it; this refusal, or what has been described as destruction on the part of one's aggressive impulses, is part of placing it outside of one's internal world. Being able to refuse, that is destroy, objects and yet watch them survive, is what puts something outside of the child, allows the child, and later the adult, to experience another's objective existence as an other subject in one's own right.

This intermediate area, the transitional space between inner and outer, between self and other, is the area of communication. However, when the objects like one's ideologies, values, or ethics are actually destroyed and do not survive the transition through the intermediate area between living subjectively related to the world to objectively related, the space collapses and the objects within that space are not seen as external. These objects are taken back up into the self and are needed in order for survival. There is a regression back to symbolic equation or the earliest stage at which illusion defined the area of object relating. While this initial stage was essential for symbolic formation regressing back to this stage due to traumatic events at a later stage of development inhibits a subject or subjects from relating to other subjects in their own right in a world of shared reality. At this point, creativity and communication cease and there is no room to move around.

In the final Babylonian Exile, after living through a century of exiles, Israel was robbed of all objects—places of worship, institutions, music, and land. What were left were the words of *seper-hatorah* loosely fashioned just before exile. The only objects at Israel's disposal during the trauma of the Exile were the words of the Covenant written on Israel's heart. The community of Israel, relating to the Covenant is unable to use the Covenant as a symbol because the intermediate area of communication allowing for otherness and difference has collapsed.

It is my view that this theory provides us another lens to view the changing nature of the Covenant and its History throughout and beyond exile. During the traumatic experience of the Babylonian Exile this object, the Covenant, the one thing left after Babylonia ransacked Judah, ceased to carry its symbolic value because that which the symbol mediated, Israel's growing national and religious identity and Israel's relationship with Adonai, was seemingly destroyed. Exile created a massive impingement upon Israel's physical and psychological environment effecting their development as a national and religious community. The Covenant that originally created space for a developing Israelite identity during seventh century BCE in later sixth and fifth centuries threatened to collapse the space by becoming literal in its meaning. As a result, a literal interpretation of the Covenant shaped the construction of history. This further split Israel from Israel's own community by blaming the Northern kings and later blaming the Judeans who, during the exile, were forced to remain in the land and chose to marry foreign women who worshiped foreign gods.

This may explain why the DH blames the Northern kings and kingdom and reads as though it is told through the eyes of the South. Rather than due to the fact that the Southern Kingdom lasted longer than the Northern kingdom, I would argue that the Southern bias in the DH is a result of the severity of the Babylonian Exile that proved to be much more devastating than the earlier Assyrian exile in the North. While the North was able to remain somewhat stable due to its slow repopulation and the fact that it was not utterly demolished but maintained some economic stability and strength, the environment remained good-enough for Israel to maintain a sense of autonomy. However, as a result of the Babylonian Exile the South was utterly destroyed. While it is likely not the case that all of Judah's inhabitants were exiled, leaving the land empty of Hebrew inhabitants, it is true that the majority of the political and religious elite were killed or taken into captivity.

Römer explains, "The exile becomes during the Persian period a new foundation myth for the 'real Israel.'"[63] If trauma becomes one's reference point, the objects at one's disposal during that time lose their symbolic value and become equated with inner fantasy rather than allowing one to place external reality outside of the subjective experience. These objects then hinder growth and differentiation, an experience of self and other,

---

63. Römer, *So-Called Deuteronomistic History*, 164.

and an experience of pain and mourning in the face of devastating events. As many scholars will argue, much of the Hebrew canon was written and shaped during Exile and it was likely during the Hasmonean period that the Hebrew canon became a formalized entity, a standardized corpus of strictly Hebrew texts, in order to compete with the standardized Greek texts used for education during the Hellenistic period.[64] Thus what is reflected upon within the Torah and the Prophets, the first manuscripts during the Hellenistic period that closely resemble the later Masoretic text (MT) tradition, is the history of Israel in light of Israel's Covenant with Adonai, told through the lens of Exile.

Symbolic Failure and Cultural Complexes

Jung and contemporary Jungians, provide a theory of psychological complexes, personal and cultural, that will help illuminate how the Covenant, in losing its symbolic function, becomes a host for a cultural complex amongst exilic Israel, which then gets inscribed as history. The term complex has almost become a colloquial saying. When describing one's dread of failure one might jokingly say, "What can I say, it's my inferiority complex!" Jung first posited his growing theory of autonomous psychic complexes in 1905 following the research for his dissertation, *On The Psychology and Pathology of So-Called Occult Phenomena,* written in 1902 and his subsequent work at the Burghölzi Hospital. Working under Eugen Bleuler, at Burghölzi Hospital, Jung revamped the word association test, at the time used by Wilhelm Wundt, adding a number of additional measures for assessment including the use of a galvanic skin response, cardio-pulmonary function, establishment of a control group or base norms of response within different cohorts of people to show a fuller picture of the actual human bodily response.[65] Jung's innovations to the test led to new discoveries of the psychological and physiological interconnection. Through a series of word stimuli Jung measured time response in connection with physiological (pulse, galvanic skin response, etc.) and found evidence that a "complex" existed with autonomy, outside of the conscious awareness or direction of the individual. Through analyzing the word stimuli that elicited a significant fluctuation in response time Jung maintained something of the individual's psychic life, though remaining unconscious to the individual, was being autonomously presented.[66] Through his findings Jung

64. Carr, *Introduction to the Old Testament*, 256.

65. Hogenson, "Archetypes," 39.

66. Jung, *Structure and Dynamics of the Psyche*, ¶201.

argued that it was the "feeling tone that defined the complex, not just the associative references and cognitive delay in response."[67]

Jung then defined a complex as an emotionally charged group of ideas and images incompatible with one's normal conscious perspective.[68] A feeling-toned complex, according to Jung is,

> the image of a certain psychic situation which is strongly accentuated emotionally and is, moreover, incompatible with the habitual attitude of consciousness. This image has a powerful inner coherence, it has its own wholeness and, in addition, a relatively high degree of autonomy, so that it is subject to the control of the conscious mind to only a limited extent, and therefore behaves like an animated foreign body in the sphere of consciousness.[69]

As he pointed out, there is a wide acceptance of the colloquial concept of a complex. What is less known however, is that we do not have complexes in as much as complexes *have us*.[70] Complexes disturb any theories about the unity of consciousness in that they seem to possess a life of their own entering consciousness autonomously, seemingly from out of nowhere, subverting one's best attempts to present one's self in a particular way. Jung understood complexes as splinter psyches, "The aetiology of their origin is frequently a so-called trauma, an emotional shock or some such thing, that splits off a bit of the psyche."[71] Any internal conflict, any rupture of one's consciously identified self creates a split wherein one maintains one's conscious perspective of self and the other half of her self, unable to be integrated as a result of cognitive dissonance, falls into the realm of the unconscious. Jung contended that complexes are more or less unconscious, which "guarantees them all the more freedom of action."[72] He warns that, "In such cases their powers of assimilation become especially pronounced, since unconsciousness helps the complex to assimilate even the ego, the result being a momentary and unconscious alteration of personality known as identification with the complex."[73]

Ibid.

67.. Hogenson, "Archetypes," 39.

68. Jung, *Structure and Dynamics of the Psyche*, ¶200.

69. Ibid., ¶201.

70. Ibid., ¶200.

71. Ibid., ¶204.

72. Ibid.

73. Ibid.

A major way complexes "alter" us is we fall under their power. We become indentified with our own complex, and are barely, if at all, conscious of that fact. Identification with the complex is another cause of symbolic failure. Without knowledge that one is in the grip of a complex, she believes the complex is reality. Thus, how one images her reality or makes sense of it through story, is within the perspective of the complex rather than outside of it or in relationship with it. However, one can work to become aware of the complex, through directed conscious attention. Awareness of a complex allows the complex itself to offer a method wherein one can begin to gain awareness of where one's symbols no longer function as a bridge toward where the symbols point.[74] When this happens, the space between self and other, or in the case of ancient Israel, between the Covenant and Israel as a community, between the Covenant and Adonai, or the Covenant and the experience of Exile, collapses and the symbol of the Covenant is equated with what before it pointed to; i.e., Adonai God and the community of Israel amongst the landscape of the ancient Near East.

Jung maintained, "Complexes are in truth the living units of the unconscious psyche, and it is only through them that we are able to deduce its existence and its constitution."[75] If we want to know about the unconscious, we must get to know the complexes that have us in their grip. When we are identified with the complex we cannot see it, we are blinded by it in that we are in it and absorbed by it. As Jung says, "Complexes are very much a part of the psychic constitution, which is the most absolutely prejudiced thing in every individual."[76] Consciousness, in an effort to maintain its sense of unity, claims the complex as its own activity seeking to make the complex unreal, a "ridiculous nothing, that we are positively ashamed of . . . and do everything possible to conceal."[77] In so doing however, we deny its reality, silence the pain at the root and ripen the soil for an outbreak of a neurosis. As Jung said, "From this moment the complex establishes itself on the conscious surface; it can no longer be circumvented and proceeds to assimilate the ego-consciousness step by step, just as, previously, the ego-consciousness tried to assimilate it. This eventually leads to a neurotic dissociation of the personality."[78]

Jung's theory of the complex is not limited to the individual but applicable to the collective as well. Just as the method of ascertaining the contents

74. Ibid., ¶210.

75. Ibid.

76. Ibid., ¶213.

77. Ibid., ¶207.

78. Ibid.

of one's personal unconscious on its own terms comes via the personal complex, so too, the way to ascertain the contents of a cultural unconscious comes via a cultural complex. In Jung's structure of the psyche he holds that there exists not only the personal, but also the collective unconscious. Jung defines the collective unconscious as:

> part of the psyche which can be negatively distinguished from a personal unconscious by the fact that it does not, like the latter, owe its existence to personal experience and consequently is not a personal acquisition. While the personal unconscious is made up essentially of contents which have at one time been conscious but which have disappeared from consciousness through having been forgotten or repressed, the contents of the collective unconscious have never been in consciousness, and therefore have never been individually acquired, but owe their existence exclusively to heredity. Whereas the personal unconscious consists for the most part of *complexes*, the content of the collective unconscious is made up essentially of *archetypes*.[79]

Jung argued that the collective unconscious is a "second psychic system of a collective, universal, and impersonal nature which is identical in all individuals . . . is inherited . . . and consists of pre-existent forms, the archetypes, which can only become conscious secondarily and which give definite form to certain psychic contents."[80] Jung's theory of the collective unconscious was met with suspicion and misunderstanding but remains today as one of the basic tenets of Jungian analytical psychology. Contemporary Jungians have taken up Jung's theory of the collective unconscious and as a result, his theory of the archetypes, and expanded them to include a cultural unconscious and cultural archetypes.[81] They argue that while there is a certain layer of the psyche that is indeed inherited (we all dream, make symbols, must deal with our instincts, etc.), there is another inherited layer that is not identical in all individuals but rather quite different, that is, for each grouping—whether tribe, society, cult or community—shared and influenced by one's historical-social-cultural location.

Thomas Singer and Samuel L. Kimbles were the first to apply Jung's complex theory to the life of groups and nations arguing that "cultural complexes exist within the psyche of the collective as a whole and the individual

79. Jung, *Archetypes and the Collective Unconscious*, ¶88.

80. Ibid., ¶90.

81. Singer and Kimbles, "Emerging Theory of Cultural Complexes"; Henderson, "The Cultural Unconscious."

members of the group."[82] They explain that cultural complexes "mostly have to do with trauma, discrimination, feelings of oppression and inferiority at the hands of another offending group—although the 'offending groups' can just as frequently feel discriminated against and unfairly treated."[83] Just as a complex works within the individual, so powerfully affecting the individual that his entire physiology changes or is ignited in a very specific and routine response, similarly, a cultural complex can affect the individual or an entire group when triggered.

Singer and Kimbles build upon Joseph Henderson's contribution of the *cultural unconscious*. Henderson defines the cultural unconscious as:

> an area of historical memory that lies between the collective unconscious and the manifest pattern of the culture. It may include both these modalities, conscious and unconscious, but it has some kind of identity arising from the archetypes of the collective unconscious, which assists in the formation of myth and ritual and also promotes the process of development in individuals.[84]

Henderson locates the cultural unconscious at the group level of the unconscious, within the collective unconscious of a particular culture. Thus, the cultural unconscious manifests in the space between personal and political. History or *historical narratives* are then, in Singer's and Kimbles' assessment, organized by cultural complexes and are in themselves a living, dynamic field.[85]

Cultural complexes arise out of the "cultural unconscious in its interaction with both the archetypal and personal realms of the psyche."[86] Singer and Kimbles refer to cultural complexes as the components containing an abundance of information and misinformation about groups and structures of society that form an inner sociology.[87] In Jung's understanding of the unconscious there is a personal as well as group level. He terms the group level of the unconscious the collective unconscious that can be known or studied by analyzing individual material or mythology. He says, "from the collective unconscious, as a timeless and universal psyche, we should expect reactions to universal and constant conditions, whether psychological, physiological, or physical . . . (It) appears to consist of mythological motifs or primordial

82. Singer and Kimbles, "Emerging Theory of Cultural Complexes", 177.

83. Ibid., 178.

84. Henderson, "The Cultural Unconscious," 182.

85. Ibid., 184.

86. Ibid., 185.

87. Ibid.

images, for which reason the myths of all nations are its real exponent . . . We can therefore study the collective unconscious in two ways, either in mythology or in the analysis of the individual."[88] While cultural complexes are not the same as a cultural identity they are inevitably informed by or can even become an identity. As they say, "Groups emerging out of long periods of oppression struggle to define new psychological and political identities by incorporating sometimes long submerged traditions, which can easily become confused with potent cultural complexes that have accrued over centuries of trauma."[89]

In the case of ancient Israel during the Persian era, after living under a long period of oppression, and in many ways still living under oppression at the hands of the Persians, the community struggled to define its political identity by incorporating the Covenantal narrative that was, in part, adopted from the VTE as discussed above. In wrestling to make sense of the incomprehensible experiences of destruction and deportation this national identity gets confused with a very potent cultural complex that accrued over centuries of trauma. The Persian period redactions of Deuteronomy and the DH emphasize monotheism and election (ex: Deut 7//Ezra 9; Deut. 12: 2–7; Deut. 23:1–9).[90] Texts that call for a strict separation from other nations, including Judeans and Samarians or "people of the land," the rural population, who remained and intermarried during the time of the Babylonian Exile, also belong to this period.

Römer suggests that the Persian editors of the "history" add a new ending to the story "which clearly indicates the acceptance of a Diaspora situation."[91] As Römer points out the ending of the story (2 Kgs 25:27–30), that highlights Jehoichin's release and rehabilitation as he is welcomed at the Kings table the rest of his days, mirrors the literary conventions in other 'Diaspora novels' such as Esther, Joseph (Gen. 37–45) and the book of Daniel. In each of these stories the exiled one is released and made second to the king, clothed with the symbol of new garments indicating a change in status.[92] These stories privilege the exilic experience, which has led scholars to argue that the very notion of an "exilic" period is, in itself, an ideological construction of the Judean elites that becomes inscribed as the dominant history of ancient Israel.

---

88. Jung, *Structure and Dynamics of the Psyche*, ¶¶324–25.

89. Ibid., 185.

90. Person, *The Deuteronomic School*; Römer, *So-Called Deuteronomistic History*, 165–69.

91. Römer, *So-Called Deuteronomistic History*, 177.

92. Ibid., 177.

John Perry (1914–1988), a Jungian psychiatrist,[93] explains that the ramifications of a complex upon the ego act in a bipolar fashion. When a complex is ignited the ego splits in two, one part of the ego aligning with the unconscious affect of the complex and the other part of the ego aligning with the external object through which the complex has become ignited.[94] The affect-ego is the part of the ego that gets taken over by the complex. As explained above, Jung describes this as an example of the autonomy of the psyche—that it exists and is not entirely under the control of consciousness. Affect-ego is Jung's definition for when a complex is activated and the energy given to the complex causes a reduction of energy in the ego. Jung explains, "Where the realm of complexes begins the freedom of the ego comes to an end, for complexes are psychic agencies whose deepest nature is still unfathomed."[95] When this happens, we do not have a complex but rather the complex *has* us. Perry explains that the other part of the ego or bipolar pair is projected onto the person with whom one is caught in the complex and they, in turn, become an "affect-object." What occurs is a highly charged interaction between the individual whose complex is triggered and the individual who triggered the complex, as the latter becomes the container for the former's negative (or positive) projections. The inner world is projected into one's outer world by way of the unconscious and it is through this kind of external mirroring of the internal world that one becomes conscious of one's unconscious contents.[96] Singer and Kimbles bring Perry's definitions into their discussion of the cultural complex to describe what happens when a cultural identity is taken over by the affect of the cultural complex "built up over centuries of repetitive traumatic experiences."[97]

Cultural complexes act like individual complexes in that they are autonomous, repetitive, products of the unconscious that resist consciousness, and will collect experiences that confirm their historical viewpoint.[98] Additionally, cultural complexes "tend to be bipolar, so that when they are activated the group ego or the individual ego of a group member becomes identified with one part of the unconscious cultural complex, while the other part is projected out onto the suitable hook of another group or one of its members."[99] Most poignant for the current argument, "cultural com-

93. O'Callaghan, "Conversation with John Weir Perry," 3.

94. Perry, "Emotions and Object Relations," 1–12.

95. Jung, *Structure and Dynamics of the Psyche*, ¶216.

96. Perry, "Emotions and Object Relations," 7.

97. Singer and Kimbles, "Emerging Theory of Cultural Complexes," 186.

98. Ibid.

99. Ibid.

plexes can provide those caught in their potent web of stories and emotions with a simplistic certainty about the group's place in the world in the face of otherwise conflicting and ambiguous uncertainties."[100]

The Covenant narrative formulated in Deuteronomy and through-out the DH over the course of Israel's many exiles and general oppression throughout the seventh–fourth centuries BCE provides a web of stories and emotions with a simplistic certainty about the group's place in the world. Israel is pictured in the construction of Covenant Religion articu-lated throughout Deuteronomy and the DH as deserving of the atrocity of the Babylonian Exile due to Israel's unfaithfulness to the Covenant. This self-blaming system was adopted from Assyrian vassal treaty language and incorporated into a national narrative by way of a cultural complex amassed through the prolonged trauma of exile.

Kimbles describes how a cultural complex functioning at the level of the cultural unconscious "implies levels of meaning that bind individuals to each other and provide a sense of coherence, producing continuity for the group. The cultural complexes are nucleating centers that allow for a continuous movement of affect and images, leading to narrative and rituals passed from generation to generation."[101] One of the most prolific phrases in the Hebrew canon reads as some iteration of the *Shema* (Deut 6):

> Hear, O Israel: Adonai is our God, Adonai alone (1) . . . Keep these words that I am commanding you today in your heart. Recite them to your children and talk about them when you are at home and when you are away, when you lie down and when you rise (6–7) . . . When your children ask you in time to come, 'What is the meaning of the decrees and the statutes and the ordinances that the Lord our God has commanded you?' Then you shall say to your children, 'we were Pharaoh's slaves in Egypt, but the Lord brought us out of Egypt with a mighty hand (20–21) . . . *If we diligently observe this entire command-ment before the Lord our God, as he has commanded us, we will be in the right* (25).

These words, which are reiterated throughout the dominant history providing an explanation for the events of the Exile and used to exhort community renewal or eventual restoration of the homeland, act as hinges that, through affect and images, create a Covenantal narrative backed by ritual passed down through the generations. The dominant narrative of the Covenant mandates Israel's complete obedience to it and threatens Israel

100. Ibid.
101. Ibid., 188.

with images of exile, torture, and decimation should they neglect it. While the Covenant served to bind Israel together and provided a sense of coherence and continuity during exile and upon return, it also served to unduly blame Israel and damage relations between those who were exiled and those who remained in the land as evidenced in trito-Isaiah,[102] and Ezra–Nehemiah.[103] In the formulation provided by Perry above, Israel's affect-ego is absorbed by Covenantal Religion and the affect-object, as it is inscribed in the history, is first the rebellious northern kings who sinned in the sight of Adonai, then the southern King, Manasseh, upon whom the blame of the Babylonian Exile rests (2 Kgs 21:10–15; 22:14–17; 23:26–27; 24:1–4), and later the 'am ha'eretz, the rural population who remained in the land during the Exile (Isaiah 58, Ezra 9). The affect-object in the Hebrew canon morphs into anyone who does not follow Covenantal Religion.

The Archetypal World of Trauma

In order to investigate further how a cultural complex can lead to traumatizing responses within a group, I use Jungian analyst Donald Kalsched, along with Singer's and Kimbles' amplification of Kalsched's theoretical paradigm of "archetypal defenses of the personal spirit," to further analyze the adoption and adaptation of the Covenant narrative within postexilic Israel. Kalsched's work investigates how an individual constructs life-saving defenses that enable and even assure survival of her human spirit when she is threatened by the annihilating blow of trauma.[104]

Kalsched gleans a noticeable pattern in bright, sensitive individuals wherein they seemingly plateau and stagnate after an initial period of growth and improvement. These individuals, he says, share a commonality. Each was forced, in some way, to become prematurely self-sufficient sometime during early childhood. As a result, these individuals severed authentic relations with their parents or caregivers and proceeded to take care of themselves throughout their developing years. A tough outer façade developed as a result, lending the impression that they were strong and independent, when all the while underneath they were wrought with shame at their secret dependence. While these individuals adapted early on, becoming their own caretakers in the absence of any external caretaker or protection from an abusive caretaker, they appear resilient externally while internally they

---

102. Third Isaiah, Isaiah 55–65.

103. This point is challenged by Middlemas, *The Templeless Age.*

104. Kalsched, *Inner World of Trauma*, 1.

remain hopelessly dependent upon the shaming inner figures that mirror their early object relations who proved unreliable.

These individuals, Kalsched explains, were in the "grip of an internal figure who jealously cut them off from the outer world, while at the same time attacked them with merciless self-criticism and abuse."[105] This inner figure proved to be so powerful, it led Kalsched to describe it as a *daimon*. Not only was the figure powerful but it was duplex: it carried both an attacking, sabotaging inner force but also a kind of guardian angel quality who would act in a soothing way toward the inner childlike part of the self, protecting and hiding it in a shameful way, from the outside world.[106] The duplex nature was a persecutor and a protector. Kalsched explains that these duplex images make up an *archetypal self-care system* that play both protective and persecutory roles, punishing the inner child or protecting it depending on whether the inner child is felt to be "bad" or "good."[107] As mentioned above, archetypes, as psychic structures, are best understood as a frame that one fills with content based on her personal and cultural experiences. Thus, the archetype is, in a sense, good and evil, potentially containing the positive side of the archetype as well as the negative. An example would be the mother archetype that can be experienced in images of the nurturing, mother-earth and images of the wicked-witch mother, attacking and eating her children.[108] Kalsched surmises that this system is a "universal inner system in the psyche whose role seems to be the defense and preservation of an inviolable personal spirit at the core of an individual's true self."[109]

This self-care system can be attacked by its own psychic autoimmune reaction. Kalsched explains the psyche has, in a sense, a self-care system. Similar to Klein and Winnicott, as articulated above, Kalsched understands that the developing individual is constantly taking in and throwing together (*symbolic*) through introjection and symbolic formation and throwing out or apart (*diabolic*) through projection or differentiation,[110] in a movement toward psychic integration and ego maturation.[111] Similar to the body's immune system, the psyche operates on the threshold of inner and outer worlds, between conscious and unconscious. "Strong currents of affect

105. Ibid., 12.

106. Ibid.

107. Ibid.

108. Jung, *Archetypes and the Collective Unconscious*, ¶¶155–60.

109. Ibid., 12.

110. Kalsched, *Inner World of Trauma*, 17.

111. Ibid., 14–9; Freud, *Outline of Psycho-Analysis*, 77–80; Klein, *Love, Guilt and Reparation*, 346–47.

reaching the psyche from the outside world or from the body must be metabolized by symbolic processes, rendered into language, and integrated into the narrative "identity" of the developing child."[112] Kalsched, however, proposes that in response to a trauma, in the case of some individuals, something goes wrong in this natural immune response and what would in normal development be thrown out or differentiated through the work of aggression (rejecting the frustrating object) is instead taken in and identified with as the child's own internal object. For instance, in the case of an abusive father, the child introjects the father's aggression into her inner world and identifies with it. She comes to hate her neediness and weakness (mirroring the father's aggression toward her) rather than being able to hate or at least acknowledge the actual harm done by the actual external object, the father.[113] Simultaneously, the abusive aspect taken in, links up with the archetypal defense operating internally as the *daimon-protector*. Therefore, it is not trauma alone that accounts for this kind of psychic splitting of the good and bad where the introjected object is simultaneously the persecutor and the protector. Instead, the interior psychic life of the individual identifies in some way with the archetypal dimension of the aggressor and in order to protect herself she introjects both the aggressor and the protector. Kalsched explains how "archetypal inner objects are numinous, overwhelming, and mythological. They exist in the psyche as antinomies or opposites, which gradually come together in the unconscious as dual unities, which are alternately blissful or terrifying."[114] The individual has very little access to effective aggression because her true self has gone into hiding behind the protection of the *daimon* figure, which is simultaneously protective and torturing.[115] This process, while self-attacking and in this way described as a psychic autoimmune response, aids in preserving the individual's ego from being annihilated all together.

Singer uses Kalsched's model and expands it from the inner world of trauma to the *group* world of trauma emphasizing the archetypal defenses of the *group* spirit.[116] He suggests:

> The traumatized group may develop a cohort of Protector/Persecutor leaders who function like the Daimones in the individual psyche where archetypal defenses are employed to protect the wounded spirit—whether it be of the group or the individual or

112. Kalsched, *Inner World of Trauma*, 17.

113. Houck-Loomis, "When Fast-Held God Images."

114. Kalshed, *Inner World of Trauma*, 18.

115. Singer and Kimbles, "Emerging Theory of Cultural Complexes," 190.

116. Ibid.

both. In other words, the traumatized group spirit may well be subject to the same nurturing protection and/or violent torture at the hands of its Daimones leaders. All the group's defenses are mobilized in the name of a self-care system which is designed to protect the injured divine child of the group identity, as well as to protect the group "ego" from a terrifying sense of imminent annihilation.[117]

The group mobilizes events, creates stories, perhaps even constructs a history that serves to protect its identity, even if that story, and the leaders elected to uphold the constructed narrative, are further traumatizing. This is a case of the traumatized becoming the traumatizing one(s). The community creates its own structure, or narrative, to keep in place a way of protecting their group identity, even if this structure becomes the persecuting agent.

Reflecting back again upon the Deuteronomic Covenant, formulated by a community who lived under a century of oppression at the hands of Assyria, Egypt and Babylonia, we can analyze the formulation of such rhetoric within the covenant that blames Israel and creates a god who lashes out in anger at Israel's disobedience. In Deuteronomy 28 it is clearly articulated for Israel, that if Israel does not obey Adonai's Covenant then Israel will be subject to disproportionate suffering (vv. 15–68). Deuteronomy 30:1 assures Israel of the blessings *and the curses* that will come upon them that they should recall *when* in exile. It is the blessings and curses that will remind Israel to turn back to God. The language of the Covenant simultaneously blames and comforts Israel, shaming Israel for her disobedience but promising her eventual restoration based on her renewed obedience. Josiah, upon having the book of the Covenant read to him, tells of Adonai's great wrath that burns against Israel because of generational disobedience (2 Kgs 22:13) and Hilda prophecies the evil Adonai will bring upon all the inhabitants of Judah because of their disobedience (2 Kgs 22:15–17). Later, during the Persian Period Ezra becomes this protector/persecutor leader who functioned as a *daimon* within the group psyche of Israel who upheld the belief that their utter destruction was as a result of generational disobedience to the Covenant and thus against Adonai, rather than the result of the surrounding national and political circumstances—superpowers vying for control of the Fertile Crescent.

117. Ibid., 191.

History through the Lens of Trauma

When working within the realm of trauma, traditionally accepted notions of *history* must be redefined. Gayatri Chakravorty Spivak, a forerunner in subaltern/post-colonial studies, highlights the problem well by explaining how the available sources for writing a subaltern[118] history are typically only those sources of the elite/colonizers.[119] Meaning, the artifacts used to help retell or even recreate historical events are artifacts of the elite. The artifacts of the non-elite often do not survive. This is true of the construction of the history of ancient Israel. As explained in chapter 3, Deuteronomy and other aspects of the DH were adopted from the VTE. The interesting and complicated aspect of any history of Israel, especially given the reality of its oppression and exile(s) is determining who it is that is writing the history; from what perspective is it written? The controversy regarding the Exile seems to circle around the issue of whether or not the Exile was as traumatic as has been postulated, or whether one should think of the Exile as prominent within the entire Hebrew community given it perhaps only effected a small, elite, portion of the community. I contend that these arguments are missing the mark. The issue at root here is not whether or not the Exile was as invasive and devastating as some contend but rather how the historical narrative that is constructed by the elite class (during exile) became the dominant historical narrative.

Spivak helps us understand the challenge, on one level, as he sheds light on the subaltern's use of dominant culture's sources (Israel's adaptation of the VTE), which are inevitably oppressive to the marginalized culture. However, another aspect must be considered when trying to understand any literary product of exile. While those in exile were certainly a marginalized culture within Babylon, and it may be argued in the ANE as they were living in the shadow of Assyria, Egypt, and Babylonia nearly their entire existence, those responsible for constructing the history were, nevertheless, the elites within Israel. Thus, the community responsible for constructing the dominant historical narrative inhabited a dual identity, the elite (within Israelite society) and the marginalized (amongst the greater ANE and especially in Babylonia). This distinction is helpful when considering Kalsched's notion of the duplex image of the *Daimon* protector/persecutor and Singer's and Kimbles' elaboration of his concept for the group spirit as the *Daimon* protector/persecutor, which is embodied in the group's leaders and narratives about the traumatized community's cultural identity.

---

118. A social group who is socially, politically, and geographically outside of the hegemonic power structure of the colony.

119. Spivak, "Subaltern Studies," 7–12.

The person or community affected by such intolerable experiences dissociates or cuts off the emotional response to the intolerable experience as best they can in order to enable a functional external life. This dissociation does not occur without grave internal consequences. While the external life may appear normally equilibrated with mainstream society, the internal life of the individual or group takes an enormous toll. Kalsched reminds us that, "the memory of one's life has holes in it—a full narrative history cannot be told by the person whose life has been interrupted by trauma."[120]

David Janzen surmises that the national historical narrative, congealed within what I have called Covenant Religion (what he calls the master narrative), is interrupted or subverted by trauma. In his book, *The Violent Gift: Trauma's Subversion of The Deuteronomistic History's Narrative* he provides ample examples throughout Deuteronomy, Joshua, Judges, Samuel, and Kings where "trauma erupts into the narrative to subvert or undermine this explanation of trauma and the linguistic concepts on which the explanation depends."[121] He argues that trauma interrupts the master narrative's attempts to explain the reason for exile by challenging the assumptions therein and negating the language used, "putting this speech on trial and rendering it ambiguous, making any certainty in explanation impossible."[122] I agree with Janzen on many levels of his argument but he almost seems to personify trauma as he regularly refers throughout his argument to "trauma's subversion" or "trauma's intrusion." However, trauma is active and is used to describe a moment or several cumulative moments that have had great psychological and sociological effect on people—individuals and communities. What Janzen is getting at, and perhaps why he fumbles over the terminology, is the fact that trauma is not known, represented, or understood directly. He rightly contends that trauma cannot be integrated into explanatory narratives that make sense to sufferers and thus refers to the "trauma narrative" as an anti or non-narrative which cannot be literarily traced throughout the canon but can be noticed in the gaps, literary mishaps, or historical intrusions/contradictions throughout the master narrative.[123]

Weinfeld asserts, "It is the consciousness of sin on the part of the Israelites from the conquest to the Exile that motivated the writing of the Deuteronomic historiography."[124] I believe it is the growing consciousness that the consequences of such proposed "sin" were so grossly overdone that

---

120. Kalsched, *Inner World of Trauma*.
121. Janzen, *Violent Gift*, 59.
122. Ibid., 60.
123. Ibid.
124. Weinfeld, *Deuteronomy*, 59.

some within the Israelite community were motivated to create a different kind of narrative, or an alternative history, in contrast to Covenant Religion's *history*. This other history is not told directly, but metaphorically and symbolically, offering another way to engage the trauma of exile and perhaps even re-enlivening the symbol of the Covenant, which experienced symbolic collapse through the events of the Babylonian Exile. This is the lens through which we will now turn to read Job.

Part 2

Individuated Religion

History, Ideology, and the Symbol of Job

> Nowadays the ancient magical belief in hereditary trans-
> mission unto the seventh generation seeks the backing of
> genetics instead of teaching us how to put into a story the
> foreclosed parts of history.
>
> —DAVOINE AND GUADILLIÉRE[1]

THE BOOK OF JOB contains a story of the foreclosed parts of Israel's history. The story maintained makes way for a new symbol outside the dominant Deuteronomic Covenantal tradition upheld throughout the national historical narrative reported in the DH. The character of Job and the God imaged within the book emerge as new symbols in the Hebrew canon due to the story's engagement with, yet resistance of, the dominant historical perspective read in the DH. These symbols point back to Adonai who is beyond the conditionality of Covenant Religion that found a way to justify the horror of the Exile by blaming a disobedient Israel.

Jung and Winnicott both describe a symbol as something that emerges in the space between or from outside of one's consciousness that enables the individual or community to make meaning and to experience both differentiation and unity within and with others. Jung understands symbols as images that orient one to a new way of seeing one's self, bringing one's left-out bits into consciousness. The symbol points to something beyond one's egoistic perspective and acts as an orienting device on the journey of psychological development, which requires one to move away from, even

---

1. Davoine and Guadilliére, *History beyond Trauma*, 55.

sacrifice, the ego's orientation. Winnicott understands an object, which arises or is found at the initial realization of the separation between self and other, as a symbol, symbolizing the union of two separate and distinct entities. Transitional objects, the bear or blanket, are the baby's first symbols; later, for the adult, they are the things of culture like art and religion. In both theories, symbols simultaneously help an individual differentiate from others and allow for greater unity and connectedness with others experienced as separate and unique from the individual subject. At the same time, symbols can allow individuals to reflect upon and make meaning out of painful experiences.

The book of Job arises as a symbol precisely because of the narrator's willingness to situate the drama in the midst of the gap opened up by trauma, the trauma of Job's allegorical suffering of evil. The narrator does not quickly justify Job's circumstances by presenting only one voice, that of the dominantly held Deuteronomistic claims—reward as a consequence for obedience and conversely punishment as a consequence of disobedience—though this is the view Job's friends uphold, and urge Job to uphold, throughout the book. Rather, the narrator of Job exploits a particular vocabulary and writing technique that pointedly reveals the other side of this developing national narrative. In the narrator's portrayal of the main protagonist and his seemingly contradictory character between the prosaic and poetic sections of the book, along with the intriguing response of God at the end of the book, new symbols begin to emerge. The character of Job and the God imaged within the story emerge as symbols that contain aggression, desire, anger, and passion, and relentlessly sit in the frightening gap opened up by the dissolution of the concretized symbol of the Covenant.

5

The Book of Job as a Symbolic History

What is there, when there is no meaning? Only nonsense
or madness . . . but . . . nothing will deliver you from disorder and meaninglessness, since this is the other half of the
world.

—CARL G. JUNG[1]

FOLLOWING THE METHOD PROPOSED throughout this work that uses the
psychoanalytic theories of Carl Jung and Donald Winnicott on symbols as
a lens through which to analyze the historical and literary nuances of the
Deuteronomic Covenant and the book of Job it is necessary to start at the
place from which I read Job, methodologically and critically. I will continue
articulating the psychoanalytic theoretical background that informs a nuanced read of this text in historical relationship with the Deuteronomic
Covenant and the history of Israel formulated throughout the years living
in exile. Thus far it has been shown that the dominate historical and ideological bent of the Hebrew canon follows from the instructions and consequences from actions in compliance with or against those instructions laid
out in the book of Deuteronomy and expounded upon through Joshua—2
Kings. Given the known but perhaps *unthought*[2] of tragedy of a community
built upon exile and oppression culminating in the horrific event of the
Babylonian Exile and destruction of the Jerusalem temple, ancient Israel
can be understood through the lens of what cultural critic Ann Cvetkovich

---

1. Jung, *Red Book*, 235.

2. Freud, "Mourning and Melancholia," regarding the unconscious aspect of loss
when one's love-object dies. Bollas describes the *unthought known* as the experience
that is known within the psyche or body but is not thought about thus not integrated or
even approachable, *Shadow of the Object.*

describes as a trauma culture. Cvetkovich's project in her book, *An Archive of Feelings*, seeks to "seize authority over trauma discourses from medical and scientific discourse in order to place it back in the hands of those who make culture, as well as to forge new models for how affective life can serve as the foundation for public culture."[3] Cvetkovich deconstructs the medical notion of trauma in an effort to depathologize it and thus allow individuals and communities of trauma to inform national culture rather than be relegated to the clinics, Analysts' offices or prescribed drugs. As she says, "I am compelled by historical understandings of trauma as a way of describing how we live, and especially how we live affectively . . . This trauma archive offers new approaches to national History and requires acknowledgment of affective experience as a mode of participation in public life."[4] In this way, she sees how trauma "digs itself in at the level of the everyday, and in the incommensurability of large-scale events and the ongoing material details of experience."[5] Trauma archives, "demand models that can explain the links between trauma and everyday experience, the intergenerational transmission from past to present, and the cultural memory of trauma as central to the formation of identities and publics,"[6] The Book of Job can be read in light of Cvetkovich's definition of an archive of public culture, a trauma narrative that contains the underside of the dominant history, embodying a new symbolic expression of the history of trauma experienced in exile causing a rupture in the construction of the national narrative as it becomes the hinge between "systemic structure of exploitation and oppression and the felt experience of them."[7]

Dating the final redacted and authored book of Job to the postexilic period of the Israelite community sometime between the sixth—third centuries BCE, one way to read the book of Job is as a *symbolic history* of ancient Israel, a history that counters the so-called Deuteronomistic History reported within the books of Joshua—Kings, also compiled and redacted during this same time period. This symbolic history is symbolic because it enabled differentiation from the stated national history formulated in the historical books, and while it does not recount actual historical events, it is a history in that it includes enough references to the national history and the traumatic affect of the Exile for the community of Israel, by whom and for whom this story was originally written, to recognize its subtleties.

3. Cvetkovich, *Archive of Feelings*, 20.

4. Ibid., 38.

5. Ibid., 20.

6. Ibid., 39.

7. Ibid.,12.

Additionally, it is a symbolic history in that Job's story, due to his access to and expression of anger and aggression at the confrontation of an experience with evil, spans the chasm of time, speaking to the depths of human experience even today.

This chapter presents a way of reading Job as a symbolic history through the lens of psychoanalytic theory developed to better understand the somatic and psychological ramifications of trauma upon individuals and communities. It presents this methodology in conversation with cultural critic Ann Cvetkovich, French psychoanalysts Françoise Davoine and Jean-Max Guadilliére, analytical psychiatrist Carl Jung, and Jungian analyst Ann Ulanov all of whom challenge and redefine the medical notion of trauma, broadening the category and de-stigmatizing trauma as an illness, upholding a prospective and synthetic view of madness. What this broadening allows for is space. The space opened up is between the national narrative formulated in Covenant Religion and the trauma of the Exile that ruptured and rigidified this narrative. It is within the space between the national narrative and the reality of the horrific experience of Exile a new symbol arises. This new symbol, the character of Job and the God imaged within the book, creates an opening that affectively *re*members the evil of the trauma by plunging right into the disillusioning gap between the dominant historical and ideological perspective held during the exilic period of Israel and the devastating affective experience of having land seized, houses of worship destroyed, and community deported. The following Chapter will engage critical biblical scholarship more deeply, highlighting the arguments of dating and the history of interpretation, while providing a literary analysis of the text.

The goal behind analyzing the historical and literary nuances within the book of Job through the lens of psychoanalytic theory is to show how Job can be read as a symbolic history of Israel. This symbolic history is the history that was erased affectively, rather than practically or physically, from the dominant history of Israel presented in the historical books of the Hebrew canon as discussed in the previous section of this work. As it has been shown, the Babylonian Exile and temple destruction of 586 BCE is the reference point for the dominant historical narrative throughout the Hebrew canon, and *seper-hatorah* is, in part, an adaptation of the VTE, under whom Israel served as a vassal for decades. Therefore, I am not denying that the event of the Babylonian Exile, and the cumulative exiles of the Hebrew people, plays a most prominent role in the biblical history of Israel. Rather, what I am suggesting is that while the event itself is perhaps the ultimate reference point of the dominant historical narrative the utter inexplicable reality of the event, the affective experience of the trauma, and the ambivalent response toward the established national-religious dogma wanders as a ghost haunting the pages therein.[8]

Job stands in the Hebrew canon as a critique of the dominant history deconstructing the theology presented within the Deuteronomistic History.[9] The book of Job presents an alternative, yet not conclusive or totalizing, history of Israel's experience during the Babylonian Exile and the way in which the postexilic community, including those that were exiled and those that remained in the land, wrestled to make sense of their necessarily shifting identity as it was simultaneously being articulated and shaped within the Deuteronomic Covenant. It is the crux of this argument that the book of Job provides a schema from which postexilic Israel and those who read Job today might begin to reference, picture, and perhaps even integrate or live in relationship with, traumatic events of the past and present. By engaging in the collective experience of evil done to Israel, drawing from the particular experience of a community in some ways defined by its inferior relationship to the superpowers throughout the ancient Near East, the story of Job, as an archive of public culture,[10] allows for the trauma of the Exile to become part of the fabric of Israel's life and story in a way contrary to the conventional Covenantal tradition as articulated in the first half of this work.

John Rogerson has argued, in *Prophets and Poets: A Companion to the Prophetic Books of the Old Testament*, that Jonah ought to be interpreted allegorically, as a symbol of the Israelite people in Exile, having been written after the Exile around the fifth century BCE.[11] He interprets the message of the book, and the character of Jonah specifically, symbolically. In the story, Nineveh, the capital of the nation who oppressed Israel for decades is the nation who actually listens to the prophet who comes to call them to repentance. Israel however, remained deaf to the message of the prophets and thus suffered the events of the exile. Reading this story from the location of exile, after the events of the exile had taken place, it can be read as a paradox. "God sent his people into exile because they would not repent. The response that he hoped for from his own people was made in extravagant terms by a people who owed him nothing at all."[12] The view proffered here is that Job may be interpreted allegorically as the symbol of the Israelite people after the Babylonian Exile struggling to make sense of the meaning of such

8. Gordon, *Ghostly Matters*.

9. Rowley, *Job*, 18; Gordis, *Book of Job*, 125–51; Wolfers, *Deep Things out of Darkness*; Ticciati, *Job and the Disruption of Identity*.

10. Cvetkovich, *Archive of Feelings*, 1.

11. Rogerson, "Jonah."

12. Ibid., 241.

devastation. Similarly, yet in a different tone than Jonah, which carries one of irony and paradox, the book of Job utilizes the symbols relevant to the culture it was originally addressing but offers another interpretation of the events of exile. Rather than maintaining the master narrative, that of the Covenant, wherein Job would ultimately be found guilty for his refusal to uphold the instructions of the Torah, the character of Job arises as a symbol within the book of Job. Job as symbol provides a new narrative that acknowledges the importance of the Covenant but ultimately argues Israel's God is not the Covenant itself but beyond the treaty's constructed identity of both Adonai and Israel.

According to Winnicott's notion of a symbol, the story of Job functions, in a way, as a transitional object. The story symbolizes the union of two separate, though previously merged entities—Israel and Adonai—at the "point in time and space of the initiation of their separateness," the time when Israel began to understand itself as a people outside of its once merged identity with Adonai of the Covenant.[13] The events of the Babylonian Exile, compiled upon the previous exiles within the northern and southern Kingdoms, forced Israel to construct a national narrative, a history that gave reason for these atrocious events. The book of Job, rather than giving a reason that somehow denied Israel's traumatic rupture with the nationally constructed God of the Covenant and neglected to acknowledge the objective reality of God outside of Israel's construction, recognized the rupture and worked to symbolize the unity of Israel with Adonai outside of the Covenant's constringency's. According to Jung's notion of a symbol, the book of Job arose as a symbol as a means of transformation, converting and channeling the energy locked up within the confines of the exilic and postexilic rigidification of the Covenant into a new understanding and experience of Israel in relation to Adonai. The new interpretation offered in the book of Job provides a different narrative, a counter-story wherein Israel's identity as a nation, in relation to other nations and to the Divine, is re-envisioned.[14]

David Wolfers, after twenty years of research and work on the book of Job, published his book, *Deep Things out of Darkness*, wherein he argues similarly that Job ought to be read as an allegorical figure. However, he argues that Job represents the people of Judah and their King Hezekiah during the Assyrian conquests.[15] He believes this comes out of a very conscious and conscientious literary decision on the part of the narrator and unless one reads from this angle one is bound to miss the book of Job's most profound

---

13. Winnicott, *Playing and Reality*, 130.

14. Nelson, *Damaged Identities, Narrative Repair*, 106–49.

15. Wolfers, *Deep Things out of Darkness*, 15.

messages. He argues it is the "veiled story of national disaster, the rupture of Covenants between the tribal desert God and His chosen people, and the trial of faith of Israel in exile which is the true theme of the book, while the superficial layer, treating of personal disaster, betrayal and temptation, is merely an exceptionally effective and compelling disguise and vehicle."[16] Wolfers' approach takes seriously the allusions and intertextual references throughout the book to the terms of the Covenants articulated in Exodus, Leviticus and most pronounced though most disguised, *Deuteronomy* and posits that the author's purpose was ultimately to reconfigure the relationship between Israel and God showing how the Covenants had been unilaterally abrogated by Adonai and transgressed by the people of Israel, leaving them inoperative. He concludes that the purpose of the book of Job is to show how each party (Israel and God) understood each other's transgressions in light of the events of the Assyrian conquests (in the eighth century BCE), which disrupted the notions of truth upheld in the Covenant.

Ultimately, Wolfers' conclusion comes close to the present argument. Regarding the author of the book of Job Wolfers contends, "He therefore wrote this book to point the way to a different form of relationship between man and god, one no longer dependent on reward and punishment, recip-rocal rights and duties, but relying on an internalized god, devotion to righ-teousness of necessity in the teeth of the 'living God who denied me (Job) justice, the Almighty Who embittered my soul.'"[17] The difference between our two approaches lies in the interpretation of how Job utilizes the Deu-teronomic Covenant, our methodological approaches for how we analyze this, and in our final conclusions.

Wolfers' proposes the author's intent was to thoroughly deconstruct the notion of the Covenant as it was rendered in the eighth century believ-ing it useless upon Israel's decimation at the hands of Assyria. Where he argues the book of Job shifts the religion of Israel from that of Covenant to "internalized god," I proffer that while this shift may be read within the book of Job, the proposition of an Individuated religion is not in place of Cov-enant Religion but can only ultimately be understood in relationship and in tandem with it. A point of departure between Wolfer's theory and my own is that I do not believe the Deuteronomic Covenant was fully operative within the eighth century. Not until later, perhaps even as late as the sixth century, was the Covenant understood as a ceremonial as well as a national narrative. My use of Winnicott and Jung helps to elucidate how symbols, while arising spontaneously from outside of consciousness, ultimately function to unify

16. Ibid., 15.
17. Ibid., 17.

(the individual, the community, the individual with the community, etc.) not to replace or set the individual over and above the collective but to help the individual or community experience greater unity in their differentiation, or as Jung says, their individuation.

Reading Job symbolically does not deny the importance and reality of the Covenant within the biblical history of Israel but rather frees the Covenant up from the confines placed upon it due to the unacknowledged trauma of the Exile. An example of this is found in the final Chapter of the book of Job. After Job's encounter with Adonai within the final stanzas of the poetic core, Job is ultimately recognized by God for Job's willingness to speak of the pain and injustice he experienced. It is my view that his expressed and named anger at God's silence in the face of such evil, and his refusal to accept the blame that Covenant Religion (via Job's friends) sought to export upon him is the action the author(s) of the book of Job indicate receives God's attention. Job 42:7 reads, "After Adonai spoke these words to Job, Adonai said to Eliphaz the Temanite: My wrath has been kindled against you and against your two friends; for you have not spoken to me that which has been established by my servant Job." Job established (or spoke according to the NRSV) a new way into relationship with the God of the Covenant and ultimately a new formation of the Covenant.

To assert that the author of Job, "Freed the Lord to move from His exclusive partnership with His chosen people towards that universality which has left Him in the Western world as the One Sole God, with no rival in the heavens or on the earth"[18] seems too simplistic and perhaps even anachronistic. Instead, rather than assuming authorial intent, my approach to the book of Job does not assume one particular outcome or purpose but rather, it wonders about the unconscious content Job, as a character in the Hebrew canon, holds, not only for postexilic Israel but for the history of Israel as a whole and investigates some possible interpretations of this content. The possible interpretations are derived from the similar approach of reading Job allegorically and symbolically as the nation of Israel, and even lead to some similar conclusions, particularly that the book "contains religious innovations as momentous as the Ten Commandments."[19] However, while hints of the religious innovations the book offers can be gleaned they are in no way totalizing. Rather, I suggest these innovations provide psychic equilibrium to the ever-concretizing narrative of Covenant Religion during the exilic and postexilic periods of Israel.

18. Wolfers, *Deep Things out of Darkness*, 16.
19. Ibid., 17.

Analyzing the historical and literary nuances through a psychoanalytic lens allows for a greater understanding of the role this history plays in relationship to the Deuteronomistic History, in general, and the Covenant, more specifically. Winnicott explains that after object relating, the initial stage of symbolic formation, there is object usage. In order for the child and, later, the adult, to establish externality, one must be able to use the objects initially related to through one's projections when one was still merged with her other (primary love object for the baby, one's new idea or lover or creation for the adult). Object usage indicates the object is real, part of shared reality, and not only a bundle of projections.[20] When one is able to use the objects previously related to only through one's own projections, one has come to be able to accept the object's existence outside of herself, having been there all the time (i.e.; not merely created by the individual). Winnicott describes the sequence in development as, "First there is object-relating, then in the end there is object-use; in between, however, is the most difficult thing, perhaps, in human development . . . This thing that there is in between relating and use is the subject's placing of the object outside the area of the subject's omnipotent control; that is, the subject's perception of the object as an external phenomenon, not as a projective entity, in fact recognition of it as an entity in its own right."[21] This change from object relating to object usage requires that the subject destroy the object. Destruction in this case happens only in fantasy, in the imagination of the subject, for it is in the very survival of the object that the object is placed outside of subjective relating and into the world of external reality, a reality shared by others.[22] The ability for the individual to imagine destroying the objects that previously stood for the merged unity between subject and object (baby and mothering-one) is a step toward maturation and differentiation, in Winnicott's words it is a step toward independence.[23]

What I designate as Individuated Religion is religion that enables a community to challenge the former symbols of the dominant religion, transgressing its norms, and including the other side of experience—the somatic and affective experiences that enable greater access to what lies in the unconscious, that which is awaiting integration personally and socially. Individuated Religion, which I propose is proffered in the symbol of Job, does not replace the Covenant but rather revitalizes the Covenant, rendering it ṵin, in the sense of Israel's ability to use it rather than relate

, *Playing and Reality*, 118.

Maturational Processes, 90–92.

to it as a bundle of Israel's own projections or rather than be afraid of it or blamed by it. In the book of Job, the Covenant survives Job's destruction of it and, more importantly, it survives because Adonai survives Job's destruction evidenced in the author's decision to have God show up and confront Job face-to-face and affirm what Job established about God in Job's protest throughout the poetic core. It is in Job's ability to destroy the Covenant, poetically imaged in the core of the book, his refusal to accept Covenant Religion's stated demands of perfection and obedience as a prerequisite for salvation, that allows the Covenant to live outside of Job (and thus Israel's) projection. By projection I mean that in the dominant historical narrative the Covenant holds Israel's subjective experience of Adonai, important and crucial for their developing identity, as a people of God and in relation to their surrounding others, but eventually potentially destructive as Israel equated its actions as a nation with the events of Exile leading to an interpretation of God's wrath upon them as a nation.

As Winnicott says, being able to use an object rather than merely relating to it is the simultaneous process wherein, "The subject destroys the object because the object is placed outside the area of omnipotent control [and] it is the destruction of the object that places the object outside the area of the subject's omnipotent control," that makes the object real.[24] The symbolic history told in the story of Job allows for Israel's aggression and anger in response to the Exile to surface, which essentially destroys (in fantasy) the Covenant. This makes the Covenant real in the sense of it and Adonai living outside of Israel's omnipotent control. The Covenant is not replaced by individualized religion, as Wolfers proffers, but Individuated Religion, as a new symbol arising in the character of Job allows the Covenant to function as a symbol once again, pointing Israel toAdonai, and toward an identity that integrates the experiences of the Exile rather than casts them off or deems them as their own fault.

Symbolic History: An Introduction

The concept of symbolic history is not one that is readily employed, and requires some definition. By symbolic history I mean a story, that is born out of a community, something that is, in the Winnicottian sense, both found and created together, and that, in fact, requires an Other to acknowledge and even experience what it is that is being created in the space between. The story that emerges points to the Real[25] as something that is

24. Ibid., 121.

25. Lacan, *Language of the Self*, 143. Winnicott, *Maturational Processes*, 187.

true but has been cut off or annihilated from the conscious reality of an individual or community. Françoise Davoine and Jean-Max Guadilliére, in their compelling book *History beyond Trauma*, describe how psychoanalysis is one of the few arts in this century wherein madness has found a path to make itself known.[26] Through the intentionality and peculiarity of the set-up and container of analysis it allows the analyst to "come into contact with, and to exist in, the patient's zones of non-existence."[27] What is woven together between analyst and patient is an unknown text and it is from this place "madness speaks to itself—shows outside of temporality what no one wants to know anything about and what is not inscribed as past."[28] Thus, the story or perhaps merely the affect that arises in the room between patient and analyst, drawing on, in particular, the analyst's own affective response, is the very crisis, the disaster area, the point at which the "social fabric creases or tears," the moment when the patient exhibits an erratic or untimely social link precisely because the crisis has not been known, has been completely eradicated, or cut-off.

This, in essence, is a model for understanding Job. In light of the third and fourth methodological assumptions laid out in Chapter 2 regarding the third space, the space between biblical scholarship and psychoanalytic theory and the space between the text and scholar made possible by way of engaging the shadow of the national history, the reader of Job, in a way, functions as the analyst, not in order to make interpretations but to serve as an Other, an Other who can be a witness to the eradicated, cut-off trauma of ancient Israel. Part of the vocation of the biblical scholar is to be this other, this other who witnesses the cut-out experiences of Israel by engaging deeply with the text, listening for what the text is saying affectively rather than concretely through its detailed logic or story, listening for the fourth[29] or the shadow bits which then creates space between one's self and the text. Similarly, as it is part of the vocation of the analyst to hear the painful suffering experienced by her analysand, suffering that presents itself not verbally or in the narrative, but rather through behavior, the so-called madness of the patient, so too, it is part of the vocation of the one who calls these texts sacred—to see the suffering within the texts (silenced voices, marginalized stories, pain etched in poetry) that is not spoken about directly but that connects affectively to the suffering of others.

---

26. Davoine and Guadilliére, *History beyond Trauma*, 12.

27. Ibid.

28. Ibid., 13.

29. See chapter 2 and chapter 9 for a fuller definition of the fourth.

The story being told in Job, which is only experienced affectively in relation to the text as it is read and engaged polyphonically, for its many voices
and many perspectives, ushers the reader into one's own and another's madness. The story of Job then, can serve as a "social link instead of nothing."[30]
Where there might be nothing, there is literature, a story that is itself messy
and unkempt with multiple voices and perspectives in dialogue throughout.
The existence of this literature within the Hebrew Bible is Israel's own social
link and ours as readers of this text.

A symbolic history then, becomes the "improbable other, of what
official history has marginalized or trivialized . . . details that have been
unclaimed."[31] It is the suspension of a particular time or place that allows
history to arrive between the space of one and another. This one and another can be thought of as a dyad, as Davoine and Guadilliére speak of it coming from the psychoanalytic world, though it need not be relegated to this
concept. As discussed in chapter 2, the space between two entities, whether
it is between two disciplines, between two texts or between the scholar and
the text, opens up a space to critically analyze the biblical text. The space
between one and another can be between one community's experience of
an event and another community's experience, or between a community
and one who witnesses an event, or between multiple interpretations of a
singular event within one particular community. The space could be, the
singular other holding the place of the plural other within a narrated history, as is often used grammatically within Hebrew.[32] Or the space between
could arrive between two competing histories.

Davoine and Guadilliére's work seeks to, "bring into existence zones
of nonexistence wiped out by a powerful blow that actually took place. But
whatever the measures chosen for erasing facts and people from memory,
the erasures, even when perfectly programmed, only set in motion a memory that does not forget and that is seeking to be inscribed."[33] It is noteworthy
that there are very few details of the Babylonian Exile, or for that matter,
the previous exiles within ancient Israel. There exists in the Hebrew Bible

---

30. Davoine and Guadilliére, *History beyond Trauma*, quoting J. Revel, (2001)
"Qu'est-ce qu'un cas?"

31. Davoine and Guadilliére, *History beyond Trauma*, 11.

32. An example of this is in Deuteronomy 28 throughout the blessings and curses,
though the people of Adonai Elohim are being addressed collectively as a community
by Moses, it is the second person singular "you" pronominal suffix being employed.
Thus, while the community will be blessed collectively or cursed collectively, the blessings and curses will touch each individual as well. This helps make the link toward being able to read individual characters such as Job, symbolical as collective community.

33. Davoine and Guadilliére, *History beyond Trauma*, xxvii.

lament literature, primarily found in Lamentations and Psalms, mourning the atrocities of 722 and 586 BCE. However, aside from 2 Kings 25: 8–30 there is no other account of the actual devastating events of the Babylonian Exile and no historical account of life in Babylonia or Judea during the Exile made it into the dominant historical narrative that was later canonized. It seems the atrocity of the Exile is in itself a zone of nonexistence. The Deuteronomistic History almost seems to erase facts and people from memory or, at the very least, paints certain kings who supposedly fraternized with the "enemies" or defiled and desecrated the sanctuaries and temple with foreign gods in a horrible light, even if this was mandated by their vassal nation,[34] finding a way to blame these "evil kings" for the events of the Exile. However, there does exist within the Hebrew canon, counter-texts that even with the "perfectly programmed" Deuteronomistic History, "set in motion a memory that does not forget and that is seeking to be inscribed."[35]

What I am suggesting here is that a counter-text, or what has been referred to as the counter-narrative of Job promoting an Individuated religion, allows for the unknown story to slowly begin its formulation, not by trumping Covenant Religion but merely by existing, and often existing affectively, linking affect with experience, in the context of the narrated story of Job's own flaws. Davoine and Guadilliére point out that the most important detail in the clinical paradigm they are presenting is that the mutative agent within the analysis comes through the flaws of the analyst as opposed to the analyst offering the right interpretation.[36] What counter-texts, such as Job, within the Bible offer is a conversation with the tradition, a conversation that is often flawed in some way—whether the protagonist or the literary composition—and it is through this messiness that something new arises. In the protagonist's flaws (Job's refusal to abide by his friends' helpful suggestions based on the stated Covenantal mandate) and/or the "flaws" of the literary composition (a poetic core that vastly contradicts its prosaic frame, an issue that, to this day, baffles form-critics), a new perspective emerges, that can "talk" to the tradition (Covenant Religion) about the unknown, unprocessed, unformulated event of the Exile. Davoine and Guadilliére expound upon Lynn Hunt's views. Hunt, a historian of the French Revolution, speaking on history and psychoanalysis says that:

> the two disciplines were made to encounter one another . . . (but the difficulty stems from) the incommensurability between the historical approach based on the analysis of social forces and

34. Albertz, *A History of Israelite Religion*, 146–86.

35. Davoine and Guadilliére, *History beyond Trauma*, 11.

36. Ibid., xxi.

the clinical approach that is so quickly reduced to the individual
scale. Between the 'tyranny of the social and that of the individual,' the outcome, as always, cannot be found in dichotomy . . .
Where it occurs is in the gap opened up by those patients who
rightly lament they have no self . . . no individuality. They teach
us that this absence of boundaries is the source of their ability
to bear witness to the stories that have been erased from history,
the history of breakdowns in the social link (c. Rousseau 1762),
whose disaster they reveal at the price of their own identity.[37]

Thus, it is in the gap opened up between the individual and the collective
experience, the self and the other, that we can glean, from the stories of individuals (whether actual or fictionally narrated), foreclosed parts of history
(including a nation's history) otherwise inaccessible.

Psychiatrists Bessel A. van der Kolk and Onno van der Hart state in
their article *The Intrusive Past: The Flexibility of Memory and the Engraving of
Trauma*, "Memory is everything. Once flexibility is introduced, the traumatic
memory starts losing its power over current experience."[38] They argue, based
on Pierre Janet's theory of dissociation, that psychic flexibility is introduced
by the act of remembering and then reimaging the traumatic memory. In a
sense, bridging the gap between the traumatic experience and present-day reality so that the traumatic memory no longer interrupts or maims one's ability
to function in daily life. This vein of thought that Judith Herman articulates
step-by-step in her book, *Trauma and Recovery*, builds upon an earlier psychological theory of trauma born out of the conflict between Jean-Martin
Charcot, Pierre Janet, and Sigmund Freud.[39] One way in which Herman,
van der Kolk and van der Hart suggest memory recovery and assimilation
happens is through the process of symbolization, that is, affect now pointed
to and expressed or represented by words.[40] Van der Kolk and van der Hart
suggest symbolization enables one to express memories and thoughts linguistically and they argue that this is the way one maintains narrative memory.
Thus, in the process of being able to or perhaps *coerced*, due to the therapeutic
agenda, to tell the traumatic story over and over again supposedly, one slowly
integrates one's cognitive and affective experiences of the event. Thus, one's
repetitious behavior or memory intrusions will slowly rescind, as she is able
to formulate the traumatic experience symbolically.

---

37. Ibid., xxi–xxii.

38. Van der Kolk and van der Hart, "The Intrusive Past," 178.

39. Herman, "Forgotten History," 7–32.

40. Van der Kolk and van der Hart, "Intrusive Past," 176.

Having the capacity to symbolize, to find a bridge between internal and external, as I have argued throughout this work, does indeed allow one to transition and experience something beyond or outside of one's self that connects to an inner and an outer reality. However, what happens when one is unable to symbolize or symbolic failure occurs? What I suggest is that making a causal relationship out of the historical reality of a traumatic event concretized what was once a symbol. While the Deuteronomic Covenant does not explicitly recount the events of the Exile it does repeat the equation, "you failed to keep the Covenant of Adonai by following other gods, therefore you will be exiled and utterly decimated." The outcome of the Exile (the historical reality—Israel destroyed and some percentage of Israel's elites deported from their land) is narrated as the consequence for disobedience of the instructions inscribed in the Covenant. Therefore, the prominent narrative that works to construct an Israelite identity, the Deuteronomic Covenant, by inscribing fault for the events of the Exile actually serves a traumatizing function, collapsing the space between the symbol and what the symbol symbolizes, or points toward. As discussed in chapter 4, a symbol ceases from being a symbol when the space between self and object/symbol collapses and the realm of fantasy and imagination is suffocated. By placing the blame within the suffering community, the historical narrative constructed throughout the exilic and postexilic redactions of the Deuteronomic Covenant collapses the space through which Israel could have brought the trauma into their lived experience rather than having to cut it off as an experience that happened to them due to some evil, external or internal.

The works of trauma theorists such as Kathy Caruth, Judith Herman, van der Kolk and van der Hart, useful and important in the field of trauma studies, have the potential of glossing over a population of people who are simply unable to symbolize or to cognitively adapt psychic flexibility in order to bring the traumatic memory into consciousness so that it can be transformed into narrative memory. Their theories have the potential to suffocate the realm of fantasy by mandating the need to bring traumatic experience into narrative memory. What if some stories are simply erased and the only way to begin to access them are through fantasy, other forms of story telling outside of verbal narrative, or affectively and in the messy work of transference. What Davoine, Guadilliére, and Cvetkovich suggest is that sometimes healing does not occur due to the work of an attuned analyst, through the just-right interpretation or through the patient narratively repeating the historical event of the trauma, but rather healing comes slowly and unexpectedly through the willingness of the analyst, scholar, or interpreter to step into the muck and mess of the trauma of which she is also a part. Sometimes the story resists being known and will never be known directly but only affectively.

As Ann Ulanov says, "To approach madness in the more customary way, through clinical terms for disorders of mental distress, puts it at a distance and removes us from the scene, as if madness happens only to the other guy."[41] She rightly reminds us that madness is part of the human condition and cannot be cut out of our own experience, thrust upon another group or person apart from one's self.[42] Madness is simply the other half of life a part of the "country we share."[43] To locate madness outside of ourselves in another person or group perpetuates the cycle, broadens the chasm between two people, two communities, two nations, two religious groups or positions within a group. Madness is externalized and located in another due to one's own sense of the good, or what Jung in *The Red Book* calls the ruling principle. The ruling principle is what one considers the all knowing, all good way of living, the projected ideal, what one strives for or to live by. It is the idealized mantra of one's own life.

For postexilic Israel, it was the internal conflicts between the people of the land who remained in Judah during the Exile and the returnees from Babylonia during the Persian period given sanctions, by Cyrus, to rebuild the temple of Jerusalem. The returnees' ruling principle differed from those who were left behind or remained in the land after 586 BCE, each group upheld a different sense of the good and exported upon the other bad left out from their guiding principle, that which frustrates and is perverse, that which is considered evil. These conflicts can be read throughout the canon and one position is dominantly held indicating the canon's own ruling principle.[44] The dominant position aligns itself with the Covenant in the strictest sense, as can be read in Nehemiah 9, a national Covenantal confession professed upon the rebuilding of the temple. In this national confession, the escape from Egypt is recited yet again, as it is all throughout Deuteronomy, but this time explicit reference is made connecting the Exile with the exodus experience considering the Exile as the return to slavery and in fact, continued slavery, even during post-exile, in their own land at the hands of foreign nations from the days of Assyria into the time of the

---

41. Ulanov, *Madness and Creativity*, 8.

42. Ibid., 8.

43. Ibid., 9.

44. Ezra 4; 9; 10; Nehemiah 4; 5; 10; 13:3, 23–31; Trito-Isaiah. The canon's own ruling principle is, of course, a result of those who held the prominent positions of power in Israelite society, the Levite priests, descendents of Judah and Benjamin. However, as mentioned at the end of the last Chapter this issue is not so cut and dry. The ones who held the power were also a marginalized and traumatized group.

Persians who allowed them back into their own land, though not without cost. As Römer postulates,

> "An important number of biblical texts from the Persian period establish a sharp distinction between the Golah, as elite community, and the 'people of the land', the rural population which had remained in Palestine during the Babylonian occupation. This Golah perspective can be detected in some late additions in the Deuteronomistic History as well as in certain passages in the books of Jeremiah and Ezekiel which probably also underwent, at least partially, Deuteronomistic editing. The returned elite from Babylon considered itself as the 'real Israel', which therefore excluded the entire non-exiled population."[45]

The work of Ann Cvetkovich challenges the traditional notion of historical memory or narrative, what she refers to as archives. Her claim that "trauma raises questions about what counts as an archive is thus connected to a further claim that trauma also raises questions about what counts as a public culture."[46] Her goal is to suggest how, "affect, including the affects associated with trauma, serves as the foundation for the formation of public cultures."[47] She suggests that trauma cultures, "public cultures that form in and around trauma,"[48] are actually doing the work of therapy collapsing the distinctions between private or individualized and collective and political.[49] Hers is not in an effort to get the trauma into some normative conceptualization but instead to embody the trauma in the public sphere, allowing it to remain raw, messy, and affectively experienced. This resonates with Davoine and Guadilliére's work although their work is primarily within the analytical office. Both theoretical approaches are attempting to analyze the space between individual and community, private and corporate experiences of trauma and offering madness or the affective experience as an archive or witness of an erased experience without reducing trauma to an illness or category of "other" waiting to be healed or cured.

In my opinion trauma theorists such as Judith Herman, van der Kolk and van der Hart coming from the medical community and taken up in literary critical theory by scholars such as Kathy Caruth may be employed a

---

45. Römer, *So-Called Deuteronomistic History*, 169. See also Davies, *In Search of 'Ancient Israel'*, 75–93; Stulman, "Encroachment in Deuteronomy"; Clines, *Theme of the Pentateuch*.

46. Cvetkovich, *Archive of Feelings*, 10.

47. Ibid.

48. Ibid., 9.

49. Ibid., 10.

bit reductively as the solution is not always as simple as getting the patient to narrate the trauma in order to transform traumatic memory into narrative memory. This could in fact have harmful consequences and even be re-traumatizing. In fact, Herman does account for this and cautions that timing in the therapeutic space, concerning when the tough material is broached and how far one goes within one session, is essential.[50] I find the work of Davoine and Guadilliére, Cvetkovich, Jung, and Ulanov more compelling as they confront the *unthought known* (known unconsciously, felt affectively, but lacking conscious reflection or thought) through the messy transferential relationship on the side of the analyst or the affective experience of public culture, or the madness in his or her own self rather than focusing only on the madness of the patient. In the case of ancient Israel, it is primarily a written history that serves as the means by which Israel is able to engage the trauma of the Babylonian Exile as they work to access the symbols that once were crushed (harps laid down by the waters of Babylon, the temple demolished, Jerusalem/land seized, God of the Covenant—silent) but in doing so present another history, counter to the dominant history, full of aggression and desire.

Cvetkovich's theoretical approach explores "how trauma can be a foundation for creating counterpublic spheres rather than evacuating them."[51] She too, critiques medicalized trauma theory offering the alternative idea that trauma itself creates cultures and communities wherein the mutative agent is not found within cognitive solutions or hierarchical therapeutic techniques but is found within the collective witness and affective experiences of trauma shared publically.[52] Jung would not disagree here though his theoretical approach is not strictly within the realm of trauma *per se*. He would agree that the mutative agent is not found in a particular solution to a problem, whether it be bringing repressed material into consciousness or accessing the archetypal drama within which one is caught, but gaining some access to cut off parts of one's self that can be found within culture at large, what Cvetkovitch would call public cultures, and integrating those parts.[53]

Fançoise Davoine and Jean-Max Gaudilliére discuss the preverbal memories of, or affectively formed responses to, trauma that surface in the analytic space as they once did on stage in the Middle Ages. They radically venture to glean from the world of madness using madness as a theoretical paradigm rather than as an illness to be subdued, medicated, or

50. Herman, *Trauma and Recovery*, 176–95.

51. Cvetkovich, *Archive of Feelings*, 15.

52. Ibid., 7–13.

53. Jung, *Structure and Dynamics of the Psyche*, ¶¶131–93.

silenced. Using as a model, the "Fool's Theater," which began in France at
the end of the Middle Ages to cope with and tell a world-ending message
after the plague and the Hundred Years War had wreaked havoc on their
land and people, Davoine and Gaudilliére analyze the role of the jester, or
Mother Fool/ Mother Crazy and the subjects, the fools who carried out the
message of the story through their nonverbal actions. They describe that
throughout the course of the play the fools would drag into center stage the
court officials, kings, and royalty—the tyrants of the day who would need
to answer for their misdeeds. These officials, dressed in royal garb, once
brought upon stage were asked the questions on everyone's mind, called
to account for the atrocities experienced by the plebeian class. The royalty
were stripped of their royal clothing showing underneath the Fools clothes,
symbolically communicating that they were simply fools, like everyone
else, dressed in king's clothing.

> This state of being "out of one's mind," coming from the border-
> lands of discourse, did, to be sure, concern the human, but it was
> understood that it could be captured or tamed only through fic-
> tions, oral or written. The madman, the fool, the jester, ancestors
> of the clown Auguste, descendants of the ancient know-how of
> the oral tradition used carnivalesque and unseemly gestures to
> show what cannot be said. They were the heirs of the indigenous
> spirits, of the pagan festivals and trances in which they could
> bring the ancient deities to life (Nagy 1996) with the suspicious
> blessing of the Church. They were the historiones (actors or
> historians?) who relate unofficial history by means of gesticula-
> tions and who, by virtue of being "out of their minds," they were
> deconstructing constituted discourses.[54]

They describe how the "canonical form of these plays was simultaneously
political and therapeutic."[55]

The book of Job, which many have argued is more accurately read
as a play or fictional book recounting a dialogical narrative between the
polyphonous voices of postexilic Israel, could also be read in light of this
articulation of the "Fool's Theater" of the Middle Ages as a canonical piece
of literature that was and is simultaneously political and therapeutic. There
is a dominant trend in the history of scholarship regarding the book of Job
to view Job as a book that portends to be written in a far away place and a
far away time but in actuality was written very late in the history of ancient
Israel. This fictional archaism gives the book a different kind of authority.

54. Davoine and Guadilliére, *History beyond Trauma*, 8.
55. Ibid., 8.

One could argue it was created as intentionally subversive to the dominant history being written during exile, as an 'older' authority. Davoine and Gua-dilliére make the link between the stage of follies in the Fool's Theater and the analytic space, the space where "slowly and painfully, something of this knowledge comes to be shared."[56] They describe the role of the analyst as an active player on the stage of the theater of madness that has entered her office. The one who is shown to be mad is but the very analyst herself, and it is in her submission to this role that enables the truth, which has previously been distorted, to materialize in the space between analyst and patient.[57] Similarly, as the scholar or reader engages with the book of Job, it is not until the scholar or reader submits to her own role in the play, that the truth may begin to materialize. This methodological paradigm of madness as an inroad to truth allows us to submit to the deconstructive work the book of Job is about. The questions remain, what is being deconstructed? How does the book of Job offer a new view of truth? Is it Truth or a truth?

Now our task is to bring these theoretical approaches into dialogue in order to set the methodological foundation for engaging the book of Job. As previously discussed, central to Jung's method is the role of the third, the image or symbol that emerges between conscious and unconscious re-alities.[58] The third he describes as the transcendent function, a noun and a verb, something that emerges from the dialectical relationship between conscious and unconscious, and serves as a regulating principle between the two which are bound in a compensatory relationship.[59] The third emerges through one's engagement with one's inferior function, what Jung terms 'the fourth', as opposed to one's ruling principle. The fourth presents another side of reality, the side left out, relegated to the shadows, demonized or shamed into hiding. When one begins to engage this part of self or community, one begins to know more of one's self or one's social group or community and is thus able to be in greater relationship with others in their own right rather than as mere projections of one's unintegrated parts. Ultimately one is able to be in deeper relationship with what is utterly unknown, stepping into the mystery rather than masking it with projections. Davoine and Guadil-liére call this unknown space the gap and suggest, "this gap that opens up is precisely that place into which there slips a transference that can name the pain—demonstrated, perhaps even not felt—on behalf of the other."[60] Cvet-

56. Davoine and Guadilliére, *History beyond Trauma*, 11.

57. Ibid. Winnicott, *Playing and Reality*, 97–106.

58. Ulanov, *Spiritual Aspects of Clinical Work*, 321–32.

59. Jung, *Structure and Dynamics of the Psyche*, ¶¶131–93.

60. Ibid., 49.

kovich might refer to this space as the existence of multiple expressions, multiple experiences of everyday trauma that queers the "rigid binarisms of gendered distinctions between private and public trauma or between sexual and national trauma that can often be reproduced even in feminist work that seeks to transcend the separate spheres paradigm."[61] Ann and Berry Ulanov speak of this space as the gap where "our seeing enters a zone of communication that challenges common sense. Subject and object blur in their indwelling. We feel our own *I* to be there with a *not-I*. What we see mediates to us things we do not see, but in such a way that what we know, we experience immediately, without intervention."[62]

The Ulanovs describe the gap as the place where symbols arise from outside of one's knowing. In a beautiful clinical example one of Ann Ulanov's patients likens his fear of the gap to:

> leaving a 'picture postcard world' to travel across a rope bridge to some perilous other side. Halfway across, he froze. He knew he would not go back. The postcard was his former life- too small for living, good only for sending a fixed message of a frozen 'ideal.' There was no room to breathe and to be himself. Yet when he looked ahead, there was nothing before him, only a brown barren desert—no inhabitants, no green spots, no water, not even roads. He froze there on his bridge, stopped, and dared to look down. The gap beneath him only widened, deepened into impenetrable depths. He could not move for fear of falling.[63]

When we are able to traverse this path, standing in the gap, resting there as opposed to racing across or turning the other way to avoid the pain she suggests we do three things, "We let it happen. We see what happens. We reflect upon what happened."[64] This, in essence, is the symbolic gift of Job in the canon. As a story it lets Israel, and readers today, spend time in the gap of not knowing, the gap where trauma thrusts us but also allows us to sit in and see what arises and then calls us to reflect upon what happened, through the allegorical trauma of Job.

Davoine and Guadilliére argue, "there are circumstances in which awareness is altered not by brain damage but by the damage that wrecks the dimension of otherness to the point of one's paradoxically becoming the subject of the other's suffering, especially when this other is unable to

---

61. Cvetkovich, *Archive of Feelings*, 33.

62. Ulanov and Ulanov, *Healing Imagination*, 25.

63. Ibid., 20.

64. Ibid.

feel anything."[65] In Job, we read a man wrecked. All that defines a person in ancient Israelite society—land, possessions, status among the religious elites, progeny—have been devastatingly erased, prosaically over the course of what seems to be less than a week. The narrative function of Job as it stands within the Hebrew canon without a specific time stamp or exact location or any actual historical evidence opens up the possibility that Job exists as a story about someone else (or other community).

Bringing Cvetkovitch, Davoine and Guadilliére, Ulanov and Jung into dialogue it is my view that the book of Job ought to be engaged methodologically as a literary tale, a symbolic expression, that stands between the affectively erased experience of the trauma of exile and the logically explained reasons for the Babylonian Exile purported within the dominant historical narrative of the Covenant tradition. Job remains as an archive of a trauma culture,[66] a fool's theater or a gap wherein a transference might come.[67] Or, Job serves the inferior function within Israel's dominant history, the story (of the Exile) known but not affectively integrated, enabling, in Jungian terms, room for the transcendent function both within the written text and in the experience of the reader or reading community. In other words, the book of Job serves a compensatory function in relation to the dominant history, referred to now as the Deuteronomistic History (DH), and in this way, creates space between Covenant Religion and the Covenant by engaging with the unconscious affective experience of the Exile. This space is possible and is maintained through the transcendent function, the union of conscious and unconscious contents.

Additionally, I suggest Job serves a vital function in relation to the DH as his plight inevitably elicits an affective reading or response from the reader enabling a felt experience of Exile to surface providing a new image or symbol to touch the everyday, bring the everyday experiences of trauma into view. In this way, something transcends within the text itself, a new perspective is felt, read, and understood, and something transcends within the reader of the text as the text touches the everyday experience of the reader. Job becomes an interlocutor of the national narrative as he not only takes part in the dialogue or conversation that emerges throughout the book amongst the host of characters, but as the protagonist who is given the majority of lines within the dialogue and is portrayed as the

---

65. Davoine and Guadilliére, *History beyond Trauma*, 49.

66. "'Trauma cultures'—as cultures that form in and around trauma." Cvetkovitch, *Archive of Feelings*, 9.

67. Davoine and Guadilliére, *History beyond Trauma*, 9–10.

"man in the middle of the line in a minstrel show who questions the end men[68] and acts as a leader."[69]

The stage is now set for us to read the book of Job as a symbolic history of ancient Israel. The character of Job stands as the interlocutor, whose story moves its reader into the gap opened up, and thus into the reader's own gap between conscious living and unconscious reality, between the known story and the affectively erased reality of that story. Job's story, the *tam* and *yashar* man who becomes the divine chess piece or the object of horror upon which to gaze, in a sense loses its subjectivity, and stands to bear witness to all the people who suffer that fate and to their stories that have been erased from history. Through Job, the exiled Israelites and surviving generations of the Judeans were able to regain a foothold in history, "not reducible to adaptation or social conformity" (Deuteronomic Covenant/ Covenant Religion).[70] There was a community or part of the larger community who did not simply accept the History being told by the dominant social narrative, did not accept the blame given them nor necessarily seek an enemy outside Israel. The counter-stories that remain throughout the canon, Job being one of them, remain as the "inscription of a dissociate truth, an 'unthought known,' known through impressions that have been split off and the awakening of a subject of history . . . This is even the condition of the emergence of the subject of desire."[71] What is at stake is not simply a repressed history, lying in the unconscious,[72] or a dissociated history as trauma theorists who use Pierre Janet's model of the psyche suggest,[73] but rather an erased history, "reduced to nothing, and yet inevitably existing . . . A cut out unconscious."[74]

As Davoine and Guadilliére explain, it is the very dimension of otherness, the trustworthiness of another and as a result one's own individual subjectivity, that gets injured during trauma or traumatic events.[75] I would expound on this and say that relegating trauma to a medical category further ostracizes one's dimension of otherness, one's ability to access the raw material, the subjectively experienced pain of the trauma that medical diagnoses seek to medicate whether through narrative therapy or through

---

68. The end men are the actors at the end of the row or line who banter back and forth with the interlocutor.

69. Merriam-Webster online dictionary, http://www.merriam-webster.com/diction ary/interlocutor/.

70. Davoine and Guadilliére, *History beyond Trauma*, 47.

71. Ibid.

72. Freud, *Beyond the Pleasure Principle*.

73. Janet, *Psychological Healing*, 660–63.

74. Davoine and Guadilliére, *History beyond Trauma*, 47.

75. Ibid., 51.

actual medication. Such classification denies the right for one to exist as a subject in and of herself, with her own lived experience of trauma and how that trauma may manifest itself within the larger culture, however unkempt or disruptive it may be. Perhaps the work of both the analyst and the biblical scholar as with the reader of literatures is to help air the symbolic that has gone into hiding, or failed to maintain its symbolic value due to the violence of trauma.

As a symbolic history, Job offers a hinge into the mystery of evil, his personal experience with evil—both that which he suffered and his own transgression of the Covenant by refusing to take the blame—dropped him into the experience of the collective, the larger story of Israel's experience in Exile and the felt injustice Israel suffered but could not articulate.[76] Rather than in the traditional and colloquial ways that read the book of Job as a book about theodicy, providence, or retribution theology, I contend that the book of Job though relevant to these later theological and existential concerns, contains a history inscribed as a drama. The drama allows for the symbol, that which orders and names the exilic experience, "which provides a third other as a locus of trust,"[77] that is not evoked in the later redactions of the DH. As Davoine and Gaudilliére state,

> when the symbolic cannot be evoked in the face of absurdity *(exile and destruction of Jerusalem temple)* and denial *(Deuteronomistic History's portrayal of the Exile, denying its utter absurdity by creating "logical" reasons for its occurrence)* one has to make do with two dimensions of logical stop-gap: it is better to assume that one is oneself the cause of an inexplicable event *(as in the case of Covenant Religion, Israel blaming Israel's own past deeds)* or to unload it onto the other *(this could be blaming the Northern Kings, blaming Assyria/Egypt/Babylonia, or in the book of Job—Job's friends blaming Job rather than allowing the horror of the experience to challenge their own worldview)*, than to confront an event without a reason. This is one of the most effective survival strategies in the face of the uncanny, the strange and disturbing field of the Real.[78]

Rather than the book of Job taking one of the two sides of the logical stop-gap—assuming the blame or unloading the blame onto others—it arises in relation to the dominant history as a third other precisely by resting in the unknown, providing a hinge into the mystery of evil. "Meditating on

76. Ulanov, *Unshuttered Heart*, 135–55.

77. Davoine and Guadilliére, *History beyond Trauma*, 72.

78. Ibid. Parenthetical comments my own.

the evil we do and that is done to us, we go on struggling for more justice, greater clarity, and push through to the inevitable mix of order with disorder, good and evil in all things."[79]

The story of Job, a fictional poetic narrative, tells a story about a blameless and upright man who seemingly becomes checkmate in a divine game of chess. Though Job is considered Adonai's blameless and upright servant unlike any others on the earth, the one who fears Elohim and turns from evil (1:7), all that he has, his many possessions, including herds of animals, and his children and eventually his health are taken from him without warning. Though the prose introduction is significantly shorter than the poetry, two chapters with a total of thirty-five verses compared to thirty-nine chapters of poetic dialogue, it serves a decisive function for the book. The introduction positions the reader to read from a particular location, from the third-person omniscient perspective.

As readers, we have been given insider information. We know that God seemingly values Job and particularly Job's *tam* or *tummah/timmah* (blamelessness/completion or integrity) and yet, God is readily enticed or incited by *hassatan's* taunt that Job only fears Adonai because of Job's grandiose compensation (*hinnäm*); i.e., his wealth, health, progeny and prosperity. *Hinnäm* means without giving or taking compensation, for nothing or in vain, without cause or undeservedly. *Hassatan* asks Elohim, "Does Job fear Elohim without compensation?" (1:9). Without dramatic build-up Adonai readily invites *hassatan* to take away all of Job's compensations admitting in 2:3 that Adonai had been incited by *hassatan* to swallow him (Job) up in vain or without cause (*hinnäm*). So *hassatan* pushes Adonai further suggesting not only Job's possessions, but also his very life must be threatened in order truly to test Job's faithfulness. Adonai allows *hassatan* to afflict Job's body as long as *hassatan* saves Job's life. *Hassatan* proceeds to strike Job's body with terrible itchy sores from head to toe (2:7). However, the prologue ensures us that in "all of this Job did not sin . . . with his lips" (2:10). The drama unfolds. Within the prologue the reader is poised with information not privy to the faithful servant of Adonai who became the target of *hassatan's* aggression. Immediately one feels the curtain has been drawn and a theatrical performance of epic dimension is about to debut.

Based on his review of the history of interpretation and the narrative sequence within the prologue Alan Cooper argues that the reader is given three basic ways of reading the book of Job that largely depend upon which of the three main characters one's empathy ultimately lies.[80] If one's empa-

---

79. Ulanov, *Unshuttered Heart*, 151.

80. Cooper, "Reading and Misreading the Prologue to Job", 73.

thy lies with the *hassatan* one understands there is "predictable causality" in God's "dealings with humanity."[81] If one's empathy lies with Job he argues one will understand Job as a story of causality with no predictability. Finally, Cooper argues, if one's empathy lies with God one will read from the perspective of *hinnäm*, wherein there is no causality or predictability.[82] Cooper admittedly reads from this third perspective but argues the important caution against a reductive unilateral reading that concludes a right or wrong reading of the book. Instead he describes the book of Job like a tangram puzzle that elicits multiple solutions wherein the purpose is not the product but the process, to learn about one's way of handling and responding to its (the text's like the tangram puzzle's) shapes, colors, and forms.[83] Cooper rightfully cautions that it is "only by oversimplifying, harmonizing and ignoring data that the reader can get the book's multiple images into focus . . . (a focus which) is not that of the book's, but of the reader gazing into his or her reflection."[84]

It is my view that this statement is true regarding not only the book of Job but regarding the book of Job in relation to the dominant historical narrative within the Hebrew Bible. It is the very inclusion of the book of Job within the Hebrew canon that serves to open the reader up into other ways of knowing and seeing Self, Other, and the Divine. While it has been argued that there seems to exist a strong current toward a particular theology or ideology within the history, what I have surmised as Covenant Religion coagulated within the dominate historical narrative as told throughout Joshua—Kings, it is precisely the construction of books such as Job, and their inclusion in the texts of the sacred canon, that destroy the ability to create a unilateral image or understanding, one "right" theology or ecclesiology. While the following argument will make the case that the book of Job ought to be read as a symbolic history of Israel, it will be argued that this is only possible through the multi-vocal, polyphonic nature of the book which resists reductive endings, singular interpretations, and seamless closures.[85]

Within the history of scholarship four basic ways of reading the book of Job have been argued.[86] However, what continues to be ignored, avoided or silenced is the struggle of the book to offer the critique of

---

81. Ibid.

82. Ibid. This is a similar interpretive disposition of Ticciati who takes this as a starting place for a new interpretation of Covenant relations between God and humanity.

83. Ibid., 74.

84. Ibid., 75.

85. Newsom, *Book of Job*, 21.

86. Outlined in the following chapter.

an omni-benevolent God. A few scholars and theorists including David Clines and David Burrell on the Bible and theological side and Jung on the psychoanalytic side have raised the notion of an ambivalent God, a God or god-archetype that encompasses both dark and light, and have raised the critique of the book of Job having anything at all to say about the reality of suffering or evil in the world.[87] However, many more have argued that the book of Job is ultimately about Theodicy, that is, the goodness of God in the face of suffering; or about retribution theology. They see the story of Job as a story about inevitable consequences for one's actions. This lines up with the dominant Deuteronomic ideology throughout the historical books and the prophetic writings and much of the wisdom literature of the Hebrew Bible. While the present work inevitably must wrestle with a traditional question—the question of evil and the goodness of God in relation to Israel's own history of exile—it will place the emphasis on the opposite side of the traditional argument. I seek to acknowledge and reckon with the presence and consequences of evil on a personal and collective level, and madness that erupts in the face of evil, especially when the consequences of it are denied or silenced.

Rather than interpreting the epilogue as a testimony to the ultimate goodness of God, I explore the existence and experience of evil within the texts in relation to the dominant history through the symbolic function of the book of Job and in particular, of the character of Job. The character of Job is an interlocutor of the national Covenantal tradition. As an interlocutor, Job hovers over the chasm of evil, evil allegorically done to him with the provision of the Divine, and his own evil as a way of transgressing Covenant Religion. Job's story becomes the hinge upon which readers of Job, past and present, are forced to face the multiple levels of personal, collective, and historic evil.

---

87. Clines, *Job 1–20*; Burrell, *Deconstructing Theodicy*; and Jung, *Psychology and Religion*, ¶¶553–758.

6

The Book of Job

An Historical and Scholary Overview

From antiquity to the present . . . the book of Job has been
a fascination, often a problem, occasionally a scandal and a
danger.

—LEO G. PERDUE AND W. CLARK GILPIN[1]

BEFORE MOVING INTO THE crux of my argument it is first necessary to provide some historical background for the book of Job, its history of interpretation and some historical-critical information. In this chapter I will analyze
a few key literary devices regarding the description, function, and conversations of the main protagonist in the book of Job. I continue the case for
approaching Job as a symbolic history of Israel. Included here is an analysis
of the use and function of the word *tam* employed throughout the book in
various ways to describe Job, Job's self-advocacy juxtaposed between the
prose narrative and poetic center, and the dialogue between God and Job at
the end of the book. The following argument will be placed in the greater
context of the history of interpretation regarding the book of Job building
upon the questions, observations, and interpretations that have come before
while contributing a new angle for the field of Joban scholarship.

A Brief History of Interpretation

As Carol Newsom points out in *The Book of Job: A Contest of Moral Imaginations,* while interpretive perspectives have changed over the course of

1. Perdue and Gilpin, *Voice from the Whirlwind,* 11.

time, the many problematic features of the text itself remain subject to exegetical inquiry.[2] The answers given for these problematic features may differ somewhat given one's particular methodology. For instance, if one approaches the book from an historical-critical lens, one's lens will narrow in to focus on the two distinct genres within the book (prose and poetry) and will hypothesize about the time, place, and authorship seeking to understand who constructed these two distinct literary works and about the history of transmission for how these two sources were eventually brought together.[3] On the other hand, if one methodologically approaches the Bible synchronically, as a unified whole, one may read Job through the lens of a grand narrator, and seek to glean the message of this narrator/author's tone.[4] Another way of reading synchronically is to juxtapose the multiple perspectives presented in the dialogue between Job and the three friends (chapters 4–31, minus 28), Elihu (chapters 32–37), wisdom (chapter 28) and God (chapters 38–41).[5]

Given the universal experience of suffering and the conflicting moral assertions made by the host of characters within Job, the message of Job lends itself to being read ideologically, through the eyes and experience of a particular reader or reading community reading one's self or a community's experience into the character of Job or into any number of the antagonists within the book.[6] Unlike any other book of the Bible perhaps, Job "lends itself to such a degree of personal involvement . . . for it propounds many ideas that are in conflict with one another and in so doing compels the reader to make personal evaluations."[7] There are a number of answers or positions that are repeated at different moments throughout history regardless of any particular methodological bent. The beauty and challenge of the book of Job as it stands in the canon as an archive of culture, to borrow a phrase from Cvetkovich, is the way in which it speaks at the level of the individual inevitably urging one to use one's own life as an interpretive lens for understanding the dilemmas within the book. While this approach is resoundingly ideological, it also takes seriously the historical reality, imagining the time at which it was finally redacted. This approach imagines how this piece of work became a way of telling history that opens up readers today to their own lived experience and to something felt but not articulated

2. Newsom, *Book of Job*, 3.

3. Zuckerman, *Job the Silent*, 3.

4. Habel, *Book of Job*, 24.

5. Newsom's approach in *Book of Job*, utilizing Mikhael Bakhtin's dialogical method.

6. Clines, *Job 1–20*, xxvix.

7. Ibid., xxxii.

about the Israelite experience during the Babylonian Exile. In this way, it is both ideological and historical, each informs the other. There is something utterly transcultural about the story of Job, an innocent man who suffers egregiously, ultimately at the hands of his God, that draws on the reader's sympathies because the reader is forced to consider her own, her community's, or her neighbor's innocent suffering.

However, its interpretive possibilities do not end here. As mentioned in the previous chapter, the book of Job serves the Hebrew canon, offering a symbolic history of Israel wherein the evil experienced over the multiple years of oppression and specifically during the Babylonian Exile is expressed, felt, and brought into the narrative of the Hebrew people. The book of Job exists as another interpretation of the Exile, another way to engage with the pain of loss and devastation. *In Job's story the symbol of the Covenant*, that I argue lost its symbolic value in the dominant narrative of Covenant Religion due to a cultural complex constellated during the Babylonian Exile and inscribed in the dominant history of the canon, *is enlivened and renewed in postexilic Israel*. To reiterate my view, the Covenant became a useful object, in the Winnicottian sense, something that existed outside of Israel's subjective experience of it as attributing the Exile to their disobedience. In the book of Job, Job is gradually able to "use" the Covenant once again as an Other, a not-me object, that allowed the character of Job to have a face-to-face experience with the one whom the Covenant pointed toward. The Covenant, in the book of Job, is dislodged from former projections wherein Israel's shame at being destroyed and exiled was projected upon this national and religious symbol that then became an object blaming them for their wrong behavior. In Job's refusal to take the blame he destroys this symbol as it is constructed within the dominant history and therefore allows the symbol to transcend the shame of the Exile, redefining Israel's relationship with the Divine.

Job in the Pre-Critical Era

Even before the critical era of biblical scholarship four basic arguments regarding the meaning and inclusion of the book of Job within the biblical canon have troubled Rabbis, exegetes, theologians, and scholars alike. From Ambrose (340–397), Maimonides (1135–1204), to Calvin (1509–1564) the dominant message of the book is understood ultimately to be about theodicy, moral retribution, providence and/or the problem of innocent suffering. More often than not these themes are inevitably intertwined. Susan Schreiner suggests the following questions structure the pre-critical interpretations of Job: "Does suffering elevate or alter one's perception of reality? Is there any discernible order in human events? What can one perceive about providence in times when the wicked prosper and the good suffer? What does suffering, particularly inexplicable suffering, mean for one's understanding of history?"[8] These are the same questions that guide much of modern day scholarship on the book of Job as well. While these questions may be disguised in the cloak of historical, literary, or traditio-critical methods, the questions asked by our scholarly and religious ancestors still lie at the root of the inquiry. It is necessary therefore to briefly introduce their arguments, especially given that their arguments touch on the main points of the case laid out in the following chapter.

In Moses Maimonides' *Guide of the Perplexed* (twelfth century CE), he dedicates two chapters to analyzing God's answer to Job in chapters 38–42. Maimonides posits it is in God's response to Job that the "philosophical question of divine providence" is authoritatively answered.[9] Maimonides argues Job is not at fault *per se* but rather simply lacks wisdom about the ways of God. The parabolic message in the book of Job is that following Torah or rabbinic law is not enough, one should seek to acquire the kind of wisdom that comes from God as evidenced through the book and in the character of Job.[10]

Thomas Aquinas (1225–1274) on the other hand argues Job may be wise but in fact, is not blameless.[11] Reading into Job his own ideological perspective, that of professor or wise teacher who wrestles with how he communicates his wisdom to his students and enables students authentically to embody their own questions and struggles gaining a more profound and nuanced intellect, Aquinas argues that Job's problem is not his wisdom but the error of his communication. Believing the story of Job to be an historical reality, Aquinas suggests that the lesson this historical figure teaches is caution against one's potential hubris. While wisdom is beneficial for the student and the teacher, a wisdom tempered with modesty is what is required.[12]

Maimonides concludes that the message of Job regarding the providence of God states that "individual suffering is a matter of chance" and God is indifferent toward undeserved suffering.[13] Aquinas asserts, using the same

---

8. Schreiner, "Why Do the Wicked Live?," 129.

9. Yaffe, "Providence in Medieval Aristotelianism," 111.

10. Ibid., 16. Longman, *Job*.

11. Yaffe, "Providence in Medieval Aristotelianism," 12.

12. Ibid., 118.

13. Ibid., 119. Cooper comes to a somewhat similar conclusion in his own read of

textual evidence (Job 9:22–23 and 21:23–26) that God is not indifferent but rather that all have sinned and therefore all will die (exemplifying some of the early differences in Jewish and Christian perspectives). Aquinas's Job is an Aristotelian philosopher and throughout the book works to convert his friends to understand as he understands, proffering a belief in the resurrection of the soul after death. Aquinas asserts that Job is stunned into silence and therefore forced into repentance at the end of the book arguing Job's sin is not from pride or impurity but from superficiality of thought. According to Aquinas God is providing practical as well as intellectual guidance in the form of divine parables.[14]

John Calvin (1509–1564) defined "Job's suffering in terms of providence" understanding the book of Job to be a story about "suffering, perception and history."[15] Calvin was perhaps building upon the work of the earlier material of Ambrose who believed there to be two prominent themes in the book of Job:

1. Job as a model for how to suffer as suffering builds endurance, perseverance, and character.

2. Job as an example of how suffering enables deeper wisdom.

Ambrose argued, "Only suffering leads to a truer perception of reality, a perception that liberates one from enslavement to that which is illusory and fleeting."[16] Thus, suffering in the book of Job, did not upset Ambrose's understanding of theodicy because the affliction therein was not understood to be an evil act. A similar view was held by Gregory the Great (540 CE–604 CE) who believed suffering carries, in and of itself, a curative power.[17] According to Schreiner, Thomas Aquinas made Job a story about immortality as he argued God's providence/justice should not be relegated to history or earthly matters alone. The problem with Job's friends is that they judge his suffering based on some earthly logic rather than understanding God's justice and providence which is not temporal, bound by time and space, but transcends this earthly reality.[18]

Calvin picks up on Aquinas's argument that the friends restricted God's providence to history but takes his argument a step further to explore

---

Job as his sympathies lie with God, inviting him to read from the perspective of God's *hinnäm*.

14. Aquinas, Exposition 441–42 on Job 39:33–55; ibid., 128.

15. Schreiner, "Why Do the Wicked Live?," 130.

16. Ibid., 132.

17. Ibid., 133.

18. Ibid., 134–35.

"the incomprehensibility of providence (defining) Job's suffering in terms of the hiddenness of God."[19] In this case Job represents some form of spiritual torment caused by the hiddenness of God. Though in much different historical locations (Ambrose in Milan during the fourth century and Calvin in Geneva during the sixteenth century) the two theologians arrive at similar conclusions about the message of the story of Job—the incomprehensibility of providence and suffering in terms of the hiddenness of God. Calvin wrestled between the seemingly opposing sides of God, between God's "visibility and hiddenness, revelation and silence, knowability and incomprehensibility" in order to keep the God of history from receding into "utter inscrutability."[20] Calvin believes Job acts out of hubris—acknowledging the reality of original sin (14:4) but refusing a penitential spirit.

Calvin routinely elevates the biblical David over Job as a man who rightly confessed his sins and asked for forgiveness. Ultimately Calvin's theological interpretation of Job supports his view of the world, that the suffering of Job portrays "a rational, intelligible, and predictable universe where God rewards and punishes according to the Law."[21] While he upheld this notion he simultaneously challenged it acknowledging that this is but one meaning of suffering. The other side of suffering, Calvin proposed, is simply unknowable given the hiddenness of God in this present history. The activity of God is outside of this history and human knowing. While suffering, as a result of sin, is inevitable the larger picture of suffering remains a mystery given the mysteries of God. Thus, one cannot make sweeping statements about retribution theology because one does not know all of God. Given the witness of nature in the world, one can glean truths about God that God's order is at work, even when it is unknown and unseen. In Calvin's view, suffering ultimately changes one's perspective as, "the sufferer perceives truths that the nonsufferer cannot understand."[22]

"Calvin juxtaposes the two realms of nature and history as an opposition between revelation and hiddenness."[23] Based on Calvin's exegesis of the divine speeches at the end of the book, God maintains a level of anonymity and hiddenness. This leads Calvin to a hermeneutical decision that one can never fully understand the wonders of God or God's creation. Given Calvin's own theological disposition he ultimately affirms that God will bring order out of chaos. Precisely due to the witness of nature, that there is, without a

19. Ibid.
20. Ibid., 135.
21. Ibid., 137.
22. Ibid., 142.
23. Ibid., 140.

doubt, a maintained order in all things, so too, God's goodness and order is an inseparable part of God's seemingly hidden providence.[24] Calvin's view, along with Ambrose, and Aquinas justifies suffering by making it some form of a moral pedagogical tool or by making it an aspect of the mystery of God. In my opinion, Maimonides leaves more room for the mystery of evil by not relegating it to the mystery of God. He opens up the possibility that God does not ordain evil and simultaneously that God is, simply put, indifferent to suffering caused by evil.

In pre-critical rabbinic Judaism, Job was often considered to be a Gentile given the description at the beginning of the book, a man from the land of Uz, which was not within Israelite or Judean territory, if it existed at all.[25] According to Judith Baskin much of the rabbinical study of Job was concerned primarily with Job's ethnic origin.[26] There is no rabbinical consensus, whether Job was a gentile, upright and righteous or a blasphemer; or whether Job was a righteous Israelite. Some rabbinical thought was born out of contentious relations with Gentile nations and sought to counter Christian appropriation of the story and character of Job within the book. "For rabbis, who could neither deny divine justice nor explain innocent suffering, the quandary of the Gentile's place in God's creation remained the central exegetical issue of the book of Job."[27]

Joban Studies in the Critical Era

The questions raised and interpretations given by our scholarly and religious ancestors of the pre-critical era give us insight into our work with the text today. One reason for introducing some of their main arguments is to show the continuity of such questions and areas of concern that the book of Job continues to raise for people trans-generationally. This reality speaks volumes about the role of the psyche in the scholarly endeavor of interpretation and exegesis. A brief introduction to the history of scholarship raises these questions, "What role does Job play in relation to the rest of the Hebrew canon?" "Is the question of suffering paradigmatic to the book of Job?" "If so, what do we make of innocent suffering, how is it to be understood?" "Who is the one suffering and how does this one suffer?" "What is the purpose of such suffering, be it allegorical or historical?" And

---

24. Ibid., 141.

25. Baskin, "Rabbinic Interpretations of Job," 101.

26. Ibid., 102.

27. Ibid., 110.

finally, "What is spoken and what remains unspoken in the text and in the years of scholarship?"

The book of Job remains in the canon and resists reductive interpretations. Each of the historical figures mentioned above approached the book of Job from his own particular ideological and sociological location and this location inevitably influenced his particular interpretation. So too, even in the age of "critical" scholarship, any interpretation that purports a hermeneutical objectivity is simply doing an injustice to the authenticity of his or her interpretation.

The reason for providing a broad sweep of the history of scholarship on the book of Job is to illuminate the questions and contentions that still guide current studies of Job. The questions Schreiner suggests that structure the pre-critical interpretations of Job remain the same questions for today. Modern scholarship has acknowledged the presence of polyphonous voices within Job offering multiple perspectives on these basic themes, rather than justifying singular dispositions. They urge readers not to reduce Job to one particular reading but rather to read for what these voices are saying in and of themselves and in relation to or in conversation with one another.[28] However, the questions of the pre-critical era still loom. While modern biblical scholars camouflage these questions in terms of a particular critical or methodological bent, ultimately one is forced to reckon with the meaning of suffering and God's participation in the suffering and how one's understanding of these questions shapes her understanding of history, both as an observer and as a participant.

With the rise of historical-criticism in the nineteenth century, a critical issue regarding the structure and form of the text was raised and that forced the dialogue around the book of Job in a different direction. Attention to the unity and integrity of the book of Job even with its disparate genres, contradicting Joban personalities and a different line-up of characters, shifted the assumption that the book of Job be read as a unified piece of work. This challenge laid the groundwork for an era of historical-critical scholarship whose focus shifted away from gleaning an overall message from the book of Job, pondering its universal problems even if the answers given contested one another, toward a search for understanding the perspectives of the distinctive authors of the prose folk-tale that serves as an *inclusio* or envelope to the differing, perhaps even contradictory, poetic middle section.[29] The questions and propositions raised by the historical-critical era distanced the discussion from the difficult theological or philosophical topics of the prob-

---

28. Cooper, Newsom, Clines, Zuckerman.

29. Budde, *Das Buch Hiob*, xii–xiv; Duhm, *Das Buch Hiob*, vii–viii.

lem of evil, theodicy, and innocent suffering, providing scholars new areas to investigate with somewhat more tangible answers to arrive at contrary to the impossible questions raised previously when the book of Job was read as a unified text. The areas for research focused on the community of origination, comparative literature and the particular ideological or theological nuances within the prose narrative in contrast to the poetic center.

However, investigations into the historicity, authorship, and comparative literatures did not prove conclusive or anything more than conjecture. Dissenters of the historical-critical and traditio or form-critical method upheld the unity of Job, even if recognizing the vastly different genres. The dissenting argument maintained the book ought to be read as a unified piece of work.[30] Unfortunately, in their explanation for how the disparate pieces fit together, Kautzsch and Dhorme did an injustice to the ideological significance of the prose narrative treating it merely as an *inclusio* without paying attention to its own unique teaching, doctrine or ideological perspective.[31] As Dhorme says, "The monument which the author aims at creating is the poem. The Prologue and Epilogue are no more than its entrance and exit."[32] The important question for both the diachronic and synchronic schools of reading became how the two styles, the prose narrative and poetry middle, or the argument set within a narrative,[33] fit together to structure the book. What do the two have to say, if anything, to one another?[34] Dissatisfied with the historical-critical inability to satisfy the quandary into how the book of Job is to be read given the seemingly incongruent parts, since seemingly shrugging off the narrative as peripheral does not seem to account for its existence,[35] and the lack of historical information to provide a comprehensive sketch, more recent commentaries lean, once more, toward a synchronic, final-form reading of the book of Job.[36] This is, ultimately, the perspective taken up in this work. While it may be that the prosaic prologue and epilogue is an earlier folk narrative used to frame the later poetic center, or visa versa, (arguments which will be taken up in the following section) the editors and redactors of the canon

---

30. Kautzsch, *Das sogenannte Volksbuch von Hiob*; and Dhorme, *Commentary on the Book of Job*, lxii.

31. Newsom, *Book of Job*, 5.

32. Dhorme, *Commentary on the Book of Job*, lxv.

33. Clines, *Job 1–20*, xxxv.

34. Newsom, *Book of Job*, 5.

35. Westermann, *Structure of the Book of Job*, 15.

36. Clines, *Job 1–20*.

placed the two together, presumably for important methodological (be it ideological or historical, perhaps both) reasons.

Dating and Genre

Though there is no real consensus among Joban scholars regarding the historical-critical questions I agree with a number of scholars who articulate the following reconstruction. The poetry and prose of Job originate from different points of contact. Whether these points are historically different times, or different communities of authorship within the same time period remains unknown and is relatively tertiary to do hermeneutical and exegetical justice to the book. The two distinct sections include the prose narrative or folktale read in chapters 1–2 and 42:7–17 and the poetic core in chapters 3:1—42:6.[37]

The folktale presents a Job from a far away place in a far away time.[38] It is a story without a timestamp or particular historical location mirroring the kind of narrative set-up given in the ancestral narratives. This particular setting is not actual but rather used as a narratological device.[39] The Job presented in folktale is perhaps the same Job mentioned in Ezekiel 14:14 and 20 which relates Job to Noah and Daniel (three vastly different characters and time periods) in their righteousness which is honored but not ultimately beneficiary for dating purposes. Perdue and Gilpin state that the folk narrative can be regarded as the oldest part of the book, perhaps written and compiled sometime during the Monarchical period of Israel (900 BCE–587 BCE) while the poetry section chapters 3—42:6 (with the exception of chapters 28 and 32–37) may have been written during the period of the Babylonian Exile (587 BCE–538 B.C.E). The two additions, the wisdom insertion in chapter 28 and the Elihu speeches in chapters 32–37, reflect a later *Weltanchauung* likely originating from the Persian period (538 BCE–332 BCE).[40] While, I agree with the latter two assertions I remain ambivalent as to the period from when the prose narrative originated. Literary-Form critic Jan P. Fokkelman dates Job (only reluctantly so since he believes it merely a rough estimation) to the fifth century BCE because ideologically he sounds similar to Qohelet, which has been dated to the third century BCE due to its Mishnah-Hebrew style. However, because Job uses lyrical poetry as in the book of Psalms, which is differentiated from the younger language, he

37. Seow, *Job 1–21*, 27–28.

38. Ibid., 47.

39. Talmud, Baba Batra 15a; Dhorme, *Commentary on the Book of Job*, xv.

40. Perdue and Gilpin, *Voice from the Whirlwind*, 12–13.

does not date the book quite as late as Qohelet.[41] While it is interesting to postulate about the dating of the various sections in the book of Job, given there is no real evidence by which to do so, it is perhaps more helpful simply to consider the final compilation of the book of Job being achieved and archived sometime around the fifth to third century BCE. Attention to the changing social and political climate of Israel during this time period will help give a lens into the impossible problems being addressed in this literary piece particular for its relevance and existence within the Hebrew canon but additionally for its continued relevance for today.

Most scholars believe the book of Job was originally composed in Hebrew though it is arguably one of the most difficult books to translate within the Hebrew canon. There are around 1100 hapax legomenon, words used only once within the Hebrew canon, in the book of Job.[42] Avi Hurvitz suggests that the Hebrew in the prose section reflects a late biblical Hebrew as read in Esther, Chronicles, and Ezra leading to a date no earlier than the Exile.[43] Many scholars agree that at least in the prose section of Job, there exists an archaic sense of the story as a story written long ago in a far away place but that this is perhaps merely illusory. Many explain this illusion as an intentionally archaizing style.[44] For part of my own translation work I had the opportunity of working closely with biblical scholar and philologist C. L. Seow at Princeton Theological Seminary, who recently published the first volume of his commentary on Job. Though I have spent the past several years reading Job in the Hebrew, I do not pretend to be an expert on the language. Thus, the following argument, while working with the nuances of the particular Hebrew nouns and verbs that repeat or lend themselves to a symbolic reading is not a philological or textual argument but rather a broader literary argument.

The book of Job has received a variety of genre identifications including dramatized lament,[45] forensic literature, tragedy, comedy, parody[46] and even apocalyptic literature.[47] There is no other book quite like Job, within the Hebrew canon, encompassing a distinctive prosaic *inclusio* surrounding an almost sardonic poetic core. While portions of Job read like psalms, even if contradicting them (Job 10:1–22 reads as an anti-Psalm 139 for instance or

---

41. Fokkelman, *Book of Job in Form*, 20–21.

42. Longman, *Job*, 27. Cf Wolfers, *Deep Things out of Darkness*, 13–46.

43. Hurvitz, "Dating of the Prose-Tale of Job."

44. Ibid.; Newsom, *Book of Job*; Seow, *Job 1–21*.

45. Westermann, *Structure of the Book of Job*; Fokkelman, *Book of Job in Form*, 4.

46. Dell, *Book of Job*; and Zuckerman, *Job the Silent*.

47. Johnson, *Now My Eye Sees You*; Longman, *Job*, 29.

compare Job 7:17 to Psalm 8:5), other sections carry strong legal tones similar to court scenes or legal documents found in Deuteronomy or Samuel–Kings (Job 12–14, 19, 23, 34). When it is read all together, and particularly in a community, it carries the tone of a theatrical drama, though I believe it does more than this or perhaps it is precisely its theatrical nature that allows for the symbolic. The voices and the agony, the setting and the stage direction give life to this ancient drama and one can see it formulating on the stage of one's mind. There is a great deal of emphasis in these separate poems addressed between the characters, which read as speeches or monologues, and an uncanny emphasis throughout Job on the various characters' words, speech, lips, speaking and/or the narrative choice to keep them silent. The explicit emphasis on words, speech and the act of writing down these words in stone leads me to believe the book of Job is critiquing, analyzing, even deconstructing the stated claims of a dominant historical or communal narrative, read in the Deuteronomistic History, offering an alternative narrative with the intent and desire that this alternative perspective be taken seriously and cut in stone, just as the Covenant was cut.

I agree with Jan Fokkelman that, "the author remains, in his capacity as narrator, the first and last person responsible for the long series of poems."[48] Ultimately, whether the prose section was part of oral tradition or a folk story that was passed down and linked up with the intricate poetry makes little difference to the overall existence and witness of this book within the Hebrew canon. Some one or some community was responsible for editing and adapting the prose narrative in relationship with the poetry and this creativity of the author or authors is what I wish to now examine. Some explorations will be attempted in an effort to imagine what the story might be saying if all the literary pieces originated from the postexilic era. For instance, one hyposthesis is that the "folk tradition" or narrative prose was part of oral tradition, one of the liturgical symbols maintained throughout the Exile along with the ancestral narratives. During Exile this story of a blameless/complete man, upright, living according to the covenant, rigorously so in fact, began to describe the way in which the Exiles felt about their life lived in Israel. It is not hard to imagine Israel reading themselves into this folktale. There was Israel, sitting on an ash heap after the events of Exile, after living rigorously according to the covenant. One explanation is that they indeed did sin and God was punishing them. Another explanation, however, can be read in the protest of Job and the dialogic truth presented in the conversations between all of the characters. The pain they had endured did not match up to whatever sins they presumably committed. One can image the Exiles

---

48. Fokkelman, *Book of Job in Form*, 4.

adopting the narrated character of Job as their own identity and then constructing lament-protest poetry as a response to their circumstances. This is the grounds for the argument laid out in the next chapter.

This will not be examined for the purposes of pinpointing an author or a community from which this text arose specifically but rather for the purposes of reading Job for its symbolic and ideological undertones. How is Israel imaging themselves in community and how is Israel imaging God after exile? While it is true Job can be mined for Israel's theodicy or theology of retribution, the overlooked point is how Israel uses this fictional story as a way of retelling the trauma of the Exile and Israel's polyphonous ideology as a result. In this reading, issues of suffering and theodicy are inevitably wrestled with however they are a result of historical circumstances. The way in which Job is formulated in the book, paints a different picture with different answers than represented in the previous books of the Torah.

As mentioned above, in my research I stumbled upon David Wolfers' provocative translation and commentary, *Deep Things out of Darkness*. He argues Job ought to be understood as an allegorical story of the events that took place during the eighth century BCE, culminating in the siege of Jerusalem in 701. Wolfers dates Job to the early seventh Century wherein the character of Job can be read as an allegorical figure representing the people of Judah and their King Hezekiah during the Assyrian conquests. He argues Job is a "supremely conscious employment of a literary device, in a work whose every aspect is sculptured with professional craft."[49] The argument I lay out in the following chapter is very near this in style as I am arguing Job is an allegorical figure for the people of Israel post-exile (Babylonian Exile) who have been given provisions to re-enter their land and rebuild their temple. Our arguments coincide in their employment of Deuteronomy 28 and Job as a commentary on the Deuteronomic Covenant, though they diverge in their readings of how this occurs throughout Job and for what purpose. The two arguments also diverge in method. Where Wolfers claims an expertise in language and uses his translation to make his argument, I use my expertise in psychoanalytic literature to make a different, more symbolic argument.

According to Fokkelman the only way our reading can "succeed" is by entering into a pact with the author.[50] In this double trajectory we first follow along with the narrator's line of judgment and second we keep our ears perked, listening for moments of judgment or personal persuasion alluded to by the narrator. For instance, in the first verse of the prose as the

---

49. Wolfers, *Deep Things out of Darkness*, 15, 52–53.

50. Fokkelman, *Book of Job in Form*, 16.

character of Job is introduced, he is located in a place, the land of Uz. But then immediately, within the same verse, we get a judgment, "That man was complete and righteous. He feared Elohim and turned away from evil." Right away the author wants the reader to know something of this man, the protagonist in the story, namely his upright and blameless (*tam or tammim*) character. Fokkelman states, "Our writer . . . has chosen the name of a legendary hero from prehistoric times. The name was appropriate both for his overall purpose and his manner of exposition. The Book of Job is an exercise in thinking, an example, a case." He goes on to argue that a "thought-experiment" is being played out in Job as the author is constructing an absolutely perfect man, complete, blameless and upright, and then is cutting him down undeservedly with the most atrocious consequences.[51] Throughout the book of Job it is not the historical events nor their accuracy that are paramount but rather the way words are used in the story to persuade and move an audience, the way the words tell a story into which the participants are invited to enter and be surprised by.

Job is the only book in the canon that takes the name of the main protagonist, about whom is the story.[52] Meaning, the book of Job is not rhetorically presented as a history book or a book about Torah, Covenant or instructions, or a prophetic book that would traditionally take the name of the heroic protagonist (or satirical failure; i.e., Jonah) of some historical moment. Nor is Job a book comparable to traditional wisdom books wherein there are explicit instructions given for the main character or reader to follow and adhere to, even if subversive as in Proverbs or Song of Songs. Rather the book of Job is about the character of Job, be him fictional or factual, and his struggle to proclaim his innocence, or rather, the injustice of the evil that has come upon him in the face of dire suffering.

The literary composition invites the reader to enter into an ancient debate where each character is introduced and given a turn to speak and chance for rebuttal. Paying attention to its dialogic quality and what arises in between the dialogues, and the larger dialectic it highlights within the Hebrew canon, is where the symbol starts to emerge. The symbol arises precisely by including the improbably other, the affective experience of the Exile or the trauma culture that points to the underside of the dominant historical narrative, even if both "cultures" are embodied in the Judean community. As Job carries the cut-out experience of the Exile, the affective experience

51. Ibid., 20.

52. For example, while Esther is about the life of Queen Esther, the majority of the book is about Israelite and Persian relations in the postexilic era 486–65 BCE a historical novella that includes historical and interpretive information not only about the life of the protagonist.

silenced from the dominant historical narrative, the voice of dissent, anger, rage and disappointment that challenges any notion of the goodness of God, he simultaneously mandates his protest be written in stone (19: 23–24). What remains now is the analysis of what I understand to be key phrases or conversations within the book of Job that point to the new symbol arising, the symbolic history of the Exile and the Divine imaged therein.

7

Living in the Gap

Explorations into the Hinge of Evil

O that my words were written down! O that they were inscribed in a book! O that with an iron pen and with lead
they were engraved on a rock forever!

—JOB 19:23–24[1]

If you have value as an artist it's probably going to be in
your capacity to let things inside you get past things that are
placed there to keep you from telling the truth. The more
you see things as clearly and coldly as you can, the more
value you're going to have.

—TONY KUSHNER[2]

WHEN ONE BEGINS TO confront that which has been cut off from consciousness, yet before integration is possible and the way forward is clear, a gap is
created. The gap is between what is known, what has previously governed
or taken precedence in one's life, and what is unknown, what has been left
in the shadows. This gap is simultaneously life threatening and life giving.
To choose to live in it, consciously, even if only momentarily, one creates
space between one's self and another, actual external others separate from
one's own projections upon those others. This space created allows for oth-

1. NRSV.
2. Quoted in Green, "Intelligent Homosexual's Guide to Himself," 38.

ers to be able to be experienced as others in their own right, independent of the perceiver's internal reality. The gap created here is between what one has always known and a glimpse that such knowledge has been subjectively informed. An awakening to that which one has previously believed has been created by the subject as a means for survival but not based on the reality of the object perceived. Before the gap, one's particular rules were failsafe. One is consciously identified with what is "right" according to the subject's personal and societal standards. Consciously identified with noble notions of the self or the accepted way of living (one's ruling principle).[3] This gap opens up at the point when one's ruling principle begins to falter.

The reasons for this falter are abundant and varied. Growth, death, life-transitions, or trauma—personal or collective—are just a few events that could initiate such an opening. Anything that challenges one's previous *Weltanschauung*, or worldview, creates enough dissonance wherein one is thrust into the abyss, and one's previous roadmap is no longer applicable. This gap, though opened up, may either be traversed or ignored. Denying the gap does not make the reality of what it opens up disappear, but rather, it may continue to press this reality further into the shadows where it is not nurtured, tended to, or brought into the light. Stepping into the gap, while it can feel life threatening, alarming, or terrifyingly empty, if tolerated and maintained, can also bring with it a kind of depth wherein previously disallowed substantive material can provide a new way of living that enables one to find truth in the midst of life's horrors.

Ann and Barry Ulanov describe the gap as the space "between what we want and what we get, between what we ambition and what we realize, between where we should be and where we are, between the ideal and the reality" and in this space, "we see the positive and negative collide" and we "recognize they live next to each other."[4] Ann Ulanov contends that the gap opens up the path toward symbolic death, "the space of darkness in time, the time of searing light in space, the gateway to what our symbols symbolize."[5] The gap does not offer easy solutions nor does it offer neat and tidy ethical, moral, or theological positions. That was the previous *modus operandi* in one's ruling principle. Rather, the gap may serve as a womb, nurturing the previously cut-out aspects of the Self. The gap opens into this womb, which more often negatively feels like a chasm or abyss, where there is nothing to be done or known.

3. Jung, *Red Book*, 264.
4. Ulanov and Ulanov, *Healing Imagination*, 27.
5. Ulanov, *Unshuttered Heart*, 218.

In this space, one can simply be and observe. The Ulanovs remind us that the only thing to do in the gap is to let it happen, see what happens and reflect upon what happens.[6] In the No-thing space[7] one cannot do anything, cannot pull herself up or continue in the same way as before, for the previous way has ceased working. These unconscious aspects of one's personality, which lurk in the shadows and are awaiting in the abyss into which the gap thrusts, include affect, particularly what is felt as negative affect; aggression, desire, passion and rage, previously not linked up with external reality. By resting in the gap, and observing what happens there, these unconscious aspects are slowly *re*membered. They are brought into consciousness and can become members once again with the body, individual and collective. But first, there is living in the gap.

Winnicott describes the gap as space, space between subject and object wherein one transitions from relating to external others as subjective objects, created out of projections of the subject's self and perceptions, to objective objects, others as subjects in their own right with their own experiences. As explained in chapters 4 and 5, it is within this space one can use objects that are subjectively imbued and objectively affirmed by others' recognition of them, allowing the subject to create space between herself and her internalized objects, first her care-givers and her first symbols or transitional objects such as her bear or blanket, later her cultural objects such as myths, traditions, and art. In maintaining their symbolic value these subjective objects accompany the individual in this gap-living space and enable the individual to create meaning that allows for difference and individuality. Eventually these objects are experienced objectively, meaning outside of the subject's projective relation to them. Once objects are objectively perceived they can be consciously used within the gap to help individuals establish a sense of external reality in which to live and live related with others different from one's own person. However, trauma can threaten this space and short-cut its tenure causing these objective objects to lose their symbolic value. Instead, such objects maintain their subjective quality without enabling the individual to transition and live in the shared world of external reality. As I have already argued, at some level, this was the fate of the Deuteronomic Covenant as it was adapted and adopted amongst some, primarily the elites who were themselves exiled, in the exilic and postexilic communities of Israel.

It is my view that the book of Job traverses the gap. The cumulative events of exile and the final atrocious Babylonian Exile left Israel bereft

---

6. Ulanov and Ulanov, *Healing Imagination*, 20.

7. Ulanov's term for the space opened up by the gap. *Unshuttered Heart*, 218.

of former symbols. The Covenant, as one of the symbols created out of years of living under Assyrian oppression, was maintained during exile. However, the way in which it was maintained disallowed the affective experience of rage at the injustice of the Babylonian trauma as it imbibed the belief that Israel was to blame due to its own wickedness. The national historical narrative, influenced by the symbol of the Covenant, inscribed this belief. However, there was another narrative that arose in the rubble. It is my argument that the book of Job arose as a new symbol, a symbol of Israel and Israel's relationship to the Divine, precisely because of the narrator's willingness to place Job's story in the chasm opened up by the gap between what Israel thought would happen, salvation or restoration upon its land, and what, in actuality, did happen, Exile and utter decimation of their temple and their city, Jerusalem.

The prosaic *inclusio* of Job (1–2 and 42:7–17) frames the gap into which the book's poetic core (3—42:6) plunges. The prosaic *inclusio*, with its choice descriptions of the protagonist, elicits an image of Israel that *remem*bers the eradicated experience of the Exile and through the poetic core the narrator's (or narrators') imagination, articulated in the dialogue between Job and the diverse characters within the book, provides a bridge upon which Israel, and readers today, may be able to traverse the gap opened up by trauma. This chapter will explore how the book of Job opens the gap into what Ulanov calls, the No-thing space, the abyss, the space where Israel is forced to wrestle with the death of the previously conceived notion of the Covenant. And yet, the book of Job simultaneously imaginatively provides a bridge, through its poetry that allows Israel and readers of the Bible today to imagine new ways into relationship with one's abolished experiences and thus, into relationship with one's whole personality (all the dissociated parts now included), community, and God, reestablishing Covenantal life through different means. In the words of Alice Miller, the character of Job in the book of Job maintains "the courage to see," which "may be nothing else than the courage to feel the plight of (his) own history." After that, "everything else is easier to bear."[8]

Job's Deconstruction of the Deuteronomic Covenant[9]

As it has been shown, the book of Job may be read as a symbolic history of Israel, a history that affectively remembers the traumatic disruption of

8. Miller's personal correspondence with Donald Capps, August 9, 2005. Quoted in Dykstra's article, "Unrepressing the Kingdom," 407.

9. Clines, "Deconstructing the Book of Job"; Burrell, *Deconstructing Theodicy*, 19.

the Exile and, through its integration of this affective experience, which includes anger, aggression and desire, reveals a new image of God, a God beyond the constraints of the Covenant. Perhaps more accurately, the character of Job may be read as the symbol of the community or nation of Israel through the Babylonian Exile and upon return to Judah during the Persian period, representing the affective experience of the trauma of exile, and in a way, constructing another identity and another image of God that serves as a counter-story to the dominant identity and god-image formulated in the DH. The first step to begin exploring the symbolic function of the book of Job is to place Job in dialogue with the Deuteronomic Covenant emphasized in Deuteronomy 28 in order to show the literary parallels that enable us to read Job as an alternative history. An alternative history that while familiar with, and in many ways in service to, the Deuteronomic Covenant, ultimately challenges the rhetoric and assumptions of the Covenant and eventually asserts a different posture of "obedience." Job's "obedience" is not one of compliance but of confrontation. The surprise that emerges from the deconstruction of the concretized symbol of the Covenant is the synthetic and prospective[10] function of evil that ends up resuscitating the symbol allowing it to live once again, not in the previous way but by integrating good and evil, obedience and purity with aggression and desire as a response to God's *hinnäm*.

The book of Job pulls the Covenant onto center stage and undresses it through the narrated traumatic losses of the character of Job showing that underneath the prestige of the Covenant was nothing but Fool's Clothes.[11] Israel in Exile, on the "borderlands of discourse" due to the horrific and jarring events of the Exile wrote their history, narrated their identity, in an effort to understand. One of the narratives constructed found a way to place the evil into a tangible category of other, even if the other or others were part of Israel's own community (the evil Kings or those that followed after other gods). This narrative has been described above as the narrative of Covenant Religion. Another narrative construction resisted the relatively neat and orderly story of the Covenant and chose instead to sit within the gap that the evil of the Exile opened up. This narrative did not replace the previous one, but instead offered another view that taps into the affective experience of life, always experienced but often silenced or cut out through trauma. This

10. A key distinguishing aspect of Jung's analytic method is his bifocal technique that utilizes both the analytic reductive, tracing everything back to primitive instincts, and the synthetic constructive, developing the surfaced material and images into a process for differentiating the personality. In Jung's view both techniques are necessary for any analysis and the two are complementary. Jung, *Psychological Types*, ¶427.

11. Davoine and Guadillere's explanation of this, described in chapter 5.

experience is articulated in the book of Job through allegory—a fictional story employing vocabulary and images reminiscent of the story of Exile purported within the dominant historical narrative of a servant of Adonai who had undue harm heaped upon. Further, in addition to the affective experience that gets included in the story of Job, another view of God emerges. When God speaks toward the end of the poetic core, it is not the God of the Covenant who speaks, an exacting God adamant about right obedience and loyalty. This God that speaks is not the God of the Covenant who is willing to smite entire nations on behalf of Israel's obedience to the Covenant or smite Israel as a result of Israel's disobedience. Rather, this God is the God of the skies, the weather, the helpless and ravenous animals, even of the monsters that roam the earth and seas. The God that responds to Job's demands for a judge and witness on behalf of the evil Job experienced either at the hands of God or due to God's neglect to protect him as the Covenant promised, is not immediately concerned about Job's circumstances. Rather, this God acts outside of the Covenantal mandates and shows God's freedom to act on behalf of the whole universe, *hinnäm*. This God does not deny a relationship with Job, for God does in fact show up, speaks to Job face-to-face, and sees Job's situation. However, the God in Job does not seem concerned with Job's actions, as does the God of the Covenant. In this way, the narratives must be held in tandem even if one is deconstructing the other. For it is in the presence of the other narrative that each one can exist.

Literary Parallels between Deuteronomy 28 and the Book of Job

I am not the first to place these two texts side by side nor am I the first to pick up on literary parallels between the two.[12] As mentioned above David Wolfers takes this approach understanding the afflictions *hassatan* produces in Job's life read in the prologue as a direct parallel to the Deuteronomic curses in Deuteronomy Chapter 28. Given the Deuteronomic curse was a harbinger of national disaster he asserts Job, as portrayed in the prologue, can be interpreted as a national disaster.[13] This then becomes the premise for his entire interpretive methodology. Given the obvious parallels he re-examines the entire book of Job through this lens. Before coming across Wolfers' monograph I had made a similar chart noting the parallels between Job and Deuteronomy 28.[14] These parallels beg our attention. The following

12. Wolfers, Clines, Ticciati, Weinfeld.

13. Wolfers, *Deep Things out of Darkness*, 116.

14. Along with this chart I made another chart noting the parallels between Job

section will articulate the significance and use of the word *tam* providing a picture of one way in which Israel imagined the state of Israel after the Exile whether it was one of compliance or of self-advocacy. However, first I will elucidate the parallels between Job and Deuteronomy 28 in order to strengthen the hypothesis that one of the functions of the book of Job is to investigate the national archive concretized therein.

Job	Deuteronomy 28
1:1 That man was *tam* and *yashar*, fearing Elohim and turning from evil . . .	1b Adonai your Elohim will set you *most high above all the nations of the land.*
8 And Adonai said to Hassatan, "Have you set your heart toward my servant Job? For there is *none like him in all the land*, a man *tam* and *yahsar*, fearing Elohim and turning from evil.	
1:2 There were born to him, *seven sons and three daughters.* And he had *seven thousand sheep, three thousand camels, five hundred yoke of oxen, five hundred donkeys* and very many servants; that man *was greater than all the children* of the east.	2 All these blessings will come upon you and will overtake you when you obey according to the voice of Adonai.
	3–5 Blessed will you be in the city and in the open field, and blessed will be the *fruit of your womb* and the *fruit of your beasts.* The *increase of your cattle and the young of your flock.* Blessed will be your basket and your kneading trough.

and Lamentations, which led me to lean toward the exilic/postexilic date for Job's final construction as well as toward an interpretive decision to understand Job in light of the national catastrophe of the Babylonian Exile that the poems of Lamentations lament. Though this kind of intertexual work Seow cautions against, as it is often difficult to determine direction of influence. Seow, *Job 1–21*, 41. However, Seow himself makes similar observations drawing links between Job and Jeremiah (Job 3:3, 10–11//Jer 20:14–8; Job 10:18–9// Jer 20:14–9; Job 19:7//Jer 20:8; Job 19:24//Jer 17:1; Job 21:7–20// Jer 12:1–3) and between Job and Lamentations (Job 6:4//Lam 3:12; Job7:20//Lam 3:12; Job 19:7–8//Lam 3:7–9; Job 30:9//Lam 3:14). Seow, *Job 1–21*, 41–42.

Job

Deuteronomy 28

1:9 Hassatan answered Adonai, "Is it without cause that Job fears Elohim? Is it not *because you put a hedge about him and about his house and about all that is to him, surrounding them. You bless the works of his hands and his cattle overflow in the land.*"

v. 11 *And Adonai will make you abound in prosperity in the fruit of your womb and in the fruit of your cattle and in the fruit of your ground in the land* that the Lord swore to your ancestors to give you.

12:23 He exalts nations, then destroys them; He expands nations, then leads them away.

9 Adonai will establish you for himself to be a holy people just as he swore to your fathers, "When you keep the commandments of Adonai your God and you walk in his ways,

10 Then all the peoples on earth shall see that the name of Adonai is proclaimed over you and they shall be afraid of you.

25 Adonai will cause you to be defeated before your enemies. By one road you will go forth against him indeed by seven roads you will flee before him and you will become and object of trembling to all the kingdoms of the land."

63 And it will be, just as Adonai took delight in you by doing good for you, and by multiplying you so Adonai will take delight in you by causing you to perish and by destroying you and you will be plucked from off the ground that you are entering to posses.

12:24 Removing the mind from the heads of the people of the land and causing them to wander in confusion, not on the path. *They grope in darkness, without light he makes them wander like a drunkard.*

29 *You shall grope about at noon as blind people grope in darkness, but you shall be unable to find your way*; and you shall be continually abused and robbed, without anyone to help.

Job	Deuteronomy 28
19:7–20 He has walled up my way so that I cannot pass, and he has set darkness upon my paths. He has stripped my glory from me, and taken the crown from my head . . . He has kindled his wrath against me . . . He has put my family far from me, and my acquaintances are wholly estranged from me . . . My bones cling to my skin and to my flesh . . .	
1:14–19 The oxen, donkeys and sheep, camels were all carried off and the servants were killed by the edge of a sword and Job's children were all killed by a great wind that came across the desert and crushed the house in which they were feasting. One by one all of Job's possession and children were stripped from him, in front of his face.	31 Your ox shall be butchered before your eyes, but you shall not eat of it. Your donkey shall be stolen in front of you, and shall not be restored to you. Your sheep shall be given to your enemies, without anyone to help you. Your sons and daughters shall be given to another people, while you look on; you will strain your eyes looking for them all day but be powerless to do anything.
1:7–8 So Hassatan went out from the presence of Adonai, and inflicted loathsome sores on Job from the sole of his foot to the crown of his head. Job took a potsherd with which to scrape himself, and sat among the ashes.	27 And YHWH will strike you with boils of Egypt and with piles and with scurvy and with itch of which you are not able to be healed.
	35 evil boils cover the body "from the sole of your foot to the crown of your head"
6:4 For the arrows of the Almighty are in me; my spirit drinks of their poison; the terrors of Shaddai are arrayed against me.	67 in the morning you will say, If only evening will be given and in the evening you will say if only morning will be given because of the trembling in your heart which you dread and the sight of your eyes which you see.
7:4 If I lie down I will say, "When shall I arise? But the evening is measured out and I am sated of tossing."	

Obviously, some of the above parallels are more precise than others. Still more appear as allusions rather than direct parallels. However, it is undeniable, when viewing the parallels side-by-side that Job is familiar with and I would argue, explicitly conjuring up the *paraenesis* of Deuteronomy 28 as well as other parts of the Deuteronomic Covenant and its unique History. The very first verse parallels the character of Job with the nation of Israel and then moves quickly to describe the ways in which Job has been blessed. Job is a man of great wealth and progeny, the kind of blessing promised explicitly within Deut 28: 3–5 and 11. In Job 1:9 *hassatan*[15] raises a pertinent question directly related to the *paraenesis* in Deuteronomy 28: "Is it *hinnäm*, without cause, that Job fears Elohim?" According to the Deuteronomic Covenant, God is the cause of such blessings, making Israel abound in prosperity should Israel obey God's commandments. Thus, Adonai is the one who gives blessings and heaps out curses based on Israel's obedience. Therefore, the question asked by *hassatan* indicates the narrator's familiarity with and strategic use of the Covenant in posing *hassatan*'s question. For, of course Job would obey God since God promised abundant blessings upon those who follow all of *seper-hatorah*, an establishment of Covenant Religion. This is the very tenet being questioned within the book of Job. What is the meaning of Covenant when devastation, rather than abundance, befalls the vassal community?

Two times, in vv. 27 and 35, Deuteronomy 28 indicates Israel will be made an object of horror for all the kingdoms/peoples. By setting Job up in a dramatic way, as Adonai's *tam* and *yashar* servant, unlike any other in all the land, the prologue essentially makes Job an object lesson. Literarily, Job's friends, still operating under Covenant Religion, view Job as an object lesson of disobedience. The friends, who go to visit the wise and blameless elder, do not even recognize him, at first. However, after the dialogue begins, familiarity is gained and the friends venture to make long speeches wherein they remind Job that such evil would not become an innocent person, upholding for Job, the tradition of the Covenant. The friends may differ regarding their perspectives on the possibility of human perfection, the definition of disobedience, and the role of the Torah. However, ultimately together, they uphold the previous wisdom of the Covenant, if you obey God you will be blessed abundantly, if you disobey God, you will suffer great curses. They plead throughout for Job to confess his hubris, as pride is one of the great offenses of the Deuteronomic Covenant. In presenting Job as an

15. The only other place the noun *hassatan* is used with the definite article is in Zech 3:1–2, a text that is dated to the late sixth century BCE This occurrence and the way in which it is used within Zech alongside *mal'ak yhwh* in dualistic fashion connote Persian influence, pointing to a later date for the book of Job. Seow, *Job 1–21*, 42.

object lesson, an object of horror upon which to gaze, rhetorically the reader is asked to contemplate what kind of lesson, if any, is emerging from the events that befell the protagonist as the events mirror the curses (the effects of eventual Exile) in Deuteronomy 28 (compare boxes 4–7 above).

As Craigie interprets Deuteronomy 28, "The curse of God reverses the history of salvation: God had brought his people out of Egypt, where they served an enemy; but because in the course of time they rejected God's love, they would be assigned once again to serve an enemy, forfeiting all the privileges of the covenant."[16] One can read Deuteronomy 28:68 to see how Craigie makes his own assertion, "Adonai will bring you back to Egypt in the ships by the way which I promised you would never do again, nor would your eyes see. And you will sell yourselves there, to your enemies, as servants and maidservants, but there will be no buyer." Job too undergoes a kind of reversal of blessing. Adonai's *tam* and *yashar* servant, surrounded and protected by Adonai becomes an object of horror as, according to the narrated prologue, he has his blessings stripped away from him.

However, in Job's case, based on the prologue, it is not due to any disobedience on Job's part, nor as a result of Job rejecting God's love, which would be an offense against Covenantal Religion. Rather, it can be deduced from the prologue, the circumstances that befell Job came as a result of God's *hinnām* or because God was incited by *hassatan*.[17] This story provides another way of interpreting the events of the Exile. By using similar Deuteronomic language, explicitly or thematically, the narrator situates Job in an "exilic-like" crisis and provides another interpretation. Job's circumstances elicit images of the Exile all throughout the book, as can be read in some of the examples in the above chart. Additionally, the very fact that the book of Job is set up in a far away place and in a past time situates Job outside of the "land," mirroring the Israelite experience of forced removal and relocation outside of Judea. This enhances its symbolic quality allowing it to reflect upon the events that actually took place within and outside of the land, from outside of the actual experience.

Newsom reads the prosaic prologue/epilogue *inclusio* as one of the "voices" within the book of Job and states that this voice, "ambitiously undertakes to expose and resolve a hidden contradiction within the religious ideology of ancient Israel."[18] She argues that the prose tale ought to be read together as one of the voices within the book of Job whose purpose is to "articulate a form of piety that persuasively resolves the threat of incoherency,

---

16. Craigie, *Book of Deuteronomy*, 348.

17. Cooper, "Reading and Misreading the Prologue to Job," 67–79.

18. Newsom, *Book of Job*, 51.

to manifest a world in which piety and blessing exits in complementarily, not mutual subversion."[19] In other words, Job will eventually be blessed for his *tam* and *yashar* lifestyle at the end of the book, for this paradigm fits within the moral world of the prose tale.

I argue however, that the prosaic epilogue, similar to the prosaic prologue, educes Deuteronomic language and ideology that is ultimately deconstructed, yet not destroyed or done away with entirely, but re-enlivened, re-engaged in a more whole and conscious way. In the epilogue, God's wrath is kindled, though not because of Job's disobedience to the Covenant, not due to Job's persistence, divine inquiry or anger at God for what had come upon him, but rather it is kindled against Job's friends Eliphaz, Bildad and Zophar for not speaking what was right about Adonai. Adonai's wrath is not kindled against the friends based on their covenantal disobedience but against their false speech. Thus, Job is ultimately "rewarded" in the end, seemingly presenting a moral picture that comports with the Deuteronomic Covenant, however what he is "rewarded" for is quite different than the exilic and postexilic adaptations to the Covenant. Job is not ultimately rewarded for his obedience to the Covenant but, rather, for *establishing a new way of speaking to God*. This new way addresses God directly as Job refuses to take the blame for atrocities that befell him. This new way gives voice to anger and rage, which allows for the capacity to mourn his loses.

Job 42:7 reads: "After Adonai spoke these words to Job, Adonai said to Eliphaz the Temanite: My wrath has been kindled against you and against your two friends; for you have not spoken to me that which has been established by my servant Job." This verse is complicated for two reasons. First, though it often translated as " . . . for you have not spoken of me what is right, as my servant Job has," it does not say, in the Hebrew, you have not spoken *of* me but rather *to* or *toward* me. Secondly, the verb נכונה is the niphal form of the verb *cwn*, which means to establish or stand firm. It seems the point being made here, is not so much an action but a posture. Job made his claims directly *toward* God, perhaps realizing there was no intercessor or even companion to be found in his friends. In doing so, Job *established* a way of posturing oneself in front of God, seeking God face-to-face rather than through someone or some other ceremonial rite. This relates back to one of the shifted nuances of the Deuteronomic Covenant in contrast to the Sinaitic one as discussed above in chapter 3.

The Deuteronomic Covenant sought to establish sacrificial offerings as personal practices for the purpose of social welfare rather than institutional practices in service to the temple or the priestly class. In this way,

---

19. Ibid., 56.

the epilogue portrays Job as a follower of the Covenant. Through his anger, aggression, rage and confrontation with the Divine, he becomes the new prototype of Covenantal obedience and thus is able to offer sacrifices on behalf of his friends. His friends, upholding the national narrative, believed repentance was Job's only road to salvation. Job does not model the kind of repentance his friends expect. Job proclaims, "Therefore I will revoke and I will mourn upon dust and ashes" (42:6). The word revoke, *m's*, comes close to indicating an action of repenting as it indicates a change from a former attitude or an act of compassion or pity. This is the closest the narrator will come to having his protagonist repent. However, the meaning of this word has been the subject of much scholarly debate. Most translate this verse as Job's repentance and complete surrender.[20] *M's* is an intransitive verb that lacks a direct object and thus, it is unclear what Job revokes.[21] Does Job in fact repent? Does he revoke the words he spoke before questioning God and calling God to account? Or does he revoke his actions of having religiously abided by the Deuteronomic Covenant, to which he testified on his account in chapters 29–31, which did not, after all, prove failsafe?

Newsom suggests that the ambiguity of Job's words in 42:6 provide something like a Bakhtinian understanding of a "loophole," that is, "the retention for oneself of the possibility of altering the ultimate, final meaning of one's words . . . this potential other meaning, that is, the loophole left open, accompanies the world like a shadow."[22] She reviews the various potential translations summarizing that one could read the verse as humiliation (the traditional translation and interpretation, "I despise myself and repent in dust and ashes"),[23] as a symbol of mourning ("Therefore I retract my words and repent of dust and ashes"), as the human condition (I retract my words and have changed my mind concerning dust and ashes),[24] as symbols of religion being thrown off, ("I despise and repent of dust and ashes"), or as a cessation to the ongoing dialogue between a man and his God, ("I quit, and

20. Cf. Curtis, "On Job's Response to Yahweh"; Wolfers, *Deep Things out of Darkness*, 461–63; Meunchow, "Dust and Dirt in Job 42:6."

21. One major problem with translating *m's* is determining its object. Buttenwieser, *The Book of Job*, 292; Patrick, "The Translation of Job XLII 6," 370; Terrien, *Job*, 269–270; Morrow, "Consolation, Rejection, and Repentance"; Wilde, *Das Buch Hiob*, 402; Patrick, "Job's Address to God."

22. Newsom, *Book of Job*, 29; quoting Bakhtin, *Problems of Dostoevsky's Poetics*, 233.

23. Ancient translations are perhaps even more severe and rich with imagery. The LXX at Job 42:6a reads, "wherefore I consider myself vile (despise myself) and I melt," and IIQtgJob reads "wherefore I am poured out and dissolved," which both take *'em'as* as derived from *m's*. Muenchow, 597–98.

24. Similar to Wolfers translation, *Deep Things out of Darkness*, 373. Also, see Habel, *Book of Job*, 575; and Scheindlin, *Book of Job*, 155.

I am consoled over dust and dirt").[25] Newsom suggests this loophole allows the conversation between a man and his God not only to be unfinalized in this chapter but unfinalizable for the book as a whole.

I contend that this loophole contributes to the book's symbolic nature and can be interpreted to mean that Job, here, is rejecting his former way of living, having been taken over by the cultural complex constellated in the Deuteronomic Covenant previously maintained in his life, as a symbol of the community of Israel. Though the prose tale elucidates images of a servant whose perfect and complete obedience to Adonai elevated him above all others on the earth, as Israel was called throughout Deuteronomy and the DH, the poetic center struggles to bring to consciousness the experience of loss, trauma, and devastation experienced in the life of Israel during the years of Exile. Therefore, 42:6 may be understood as a climax of understanding. The complex made conscious, integrated through the active struggle in the poetry, allows Job to mourn.

Jolande Jacobi, analytical psychologist who worked with Jung and expounded upon his theories, explains that once complexes become conscious, and not merely conscious as in known but conscious as in taken in and processed or metabolized consciously, emotionally assimilated, then the complex can be corrected. The complex no longer holds numinous qualities wielding its magical power over the life of the individual but it can become a conversation partner informing and teaching the individual resulting in a redistribution of psychic energy.[26] The ability to assimilate affect, transform it into emotion, link it up with the reality of a situation opens one up into the gap, the space where one's life, experiences, ideas, values, religious constructs, and symbols can be seen and experienced outside of one's self, outside of the unconscious hold within which they were previously enmeshed. Through Job's persistence and rage, calling God to court and going so far as to making an oath with God to proclaim his purity (chapter 31), the book of Job is situated in relation to the Covenant and the complex constellated through Exile and offers another melody.

While it is necessary to continue drawing out the symbolic allusions between the book of Job and the DH in order to give further evidence of this argument, the conversation will now shift. We will turn now from looking at direct parallels and ways in which the book of Job deconstructs the *paraenesis* in Deuteronomy 28 specifically, to highlighting allusions between

---

25. This final view is proffered in Fokkelman, 193 and is not referenced in Newsom, *Book of Job*. However, all the others are summarized in Newsom, 29. Habel provides another summary of possible interpretations in his commentary, *Book of Job*, 577.

26. Jacobi, *Complex, Archetype, Symbol*, 21.

the book of Job, particularly the *character of Job*, and the national narrative constellated in the DH in general.

The Meaning and Use of *Tam* in the Book of Job

Manisha Roy, a Jungian analyst, suggests that highly creative people are "nourished by a wealth of unconscious material, which they use as ingredients for their creative expression" and that "cultural complexes offer ideas for the artist to recreate, replenish and embellish by using new symbols from the culture in some form or other."[27] She continues,

> the author uses her imagination to work on a cultural complex with cultural material and transforms it to another level, even leading to the possibility of transcending (or at least lessening the effects) of the complex. Both the author and the readers reconnect with the complex in a new and creative way. At the same time the archetypal energy blocked in the complex, finds expression in human life and need not burst forth negatively.[28]

The author (or authoring community) of Job can be thought of through Roy's description. In a highly creative fashion the author(s) of Job nuanced a story that "recreates, replenishes and embellishes" the ingredients of the unconscious, the affective experience of the Exile, by using Job as the symbol of Israel in Exile and the story of Job as a symbolic history. In this way, the author(s) are able to work with the cultural complex that rigidified the tenets of Covenantal Religion and petrified a particular god image. This is not to say Job replaces or does away with the Covenant but rather, it re-enlivens the Covenant by creating space between the Covenant (and the Covenantal history being formulated throughout the historical books), and the God of the Covenant. In the words of Roy, the authors (or author) of Job use their imagination to work on the cultural complex rigidified in the dominant historical narrative and transform it allowing the Covenant to transcend the complex.

Job's character in the book of Job confronts Israel's cultural complex, the covenantal perfectionist complex constellated during the Babylonian Exile as explained in chapter 4, by decidedly not explaining away the reasons for his calamity. The author's portrayal of Job can be understood in light of what was discussed in chapter 4 as a representation of Job in the grip of a cultural complex. This is not to say that this was the author's

27. Roy, "When a Religious Archetype becomes a Cultural Complex," 76.
28. Ibid.

intention, rather, this is one possible present-day interpretation of the author's portrayal of Job, primarily when read beside the historical books. As the narrator describes, Job religiously arose every morning to offer sacrifices in order to maintain his *tamim*. However, by depicting the calamity thrust upon him by the adversary, *hassatan,* with the approval of Adonai God, the narrator could be understood as forcing the Job in the story, to confront the tenets of Covenant Religion. One way to articulate the narrator's literary move today, in light of Jungian analytical psychology, is to say the narrator sets the stage for Job to confront the complex of Covenant Religion in whose hands he was gripped.

We must investigate further the meaning, significance, and prominence of the word *tam*.[29] This word, used to describe Job's character and actions has diametrically opposed meanings within the Hebrew. It can convey the meaning of complete, as in having all one needs, or blameless, in a sense, perfect. *Tam* can also mean complete as in being over, the end, referring to being finished which can carry both positive and negative connotations. "Thus the root *tmm*, which is inherently ambiguous, simply denoting an absolute conclusion, gives rise to a well-developed semantic dichotomy. Around one pole are grouped the positive senses of perfection and completion, while around the other are gathered the antonymic senses of cessation, decline, and total destruction."[30]

The ambiguous meaning of the root *tmm* is significant for out of its ambiguity a symbol arises. I conjecture that the use of *tam* to describe the character of Job gives us a clue as to the allegorical use of Job in the book. As a man complete and upright, there is no other like him in all the earth. It is not too difficult to imagine the people of Israel describing themselves as such a community. As the Covenant assured, Israel was chosen by God to be God's elect people. The claim to be like no other on the earth resonates with the claims laid out in Deuteronomy.[31] This notion of being God's elect is a complicated subject. It has been proposed that this particular theology arose amongst postexilic Israel most concretely.

---

29. Fokkelman, *Book of Job in Form*, 199.

30. Kedar-Kopfstein, Benjamin. "תמם, *tamam*," 703.

31. Deut 4:7–8 "For what other great nation has a god so near to it as Adonai our God is whenever we call to him? And what other great nation has statues and ordinances as just as this entire law that I am setting before you today." Perhaps most poignantly in 7:7 "It is not because you were more numerous than any other people that the Lord set his heart on you and chose you—for you were the fewest of all peoples. It was because the Lord loved you and kept the oath that he swore to your ancestors, that the Lord has brought you out with a mighty hand, and redeemed you from the house of slavery, from the hand of Pharaoh king of Egypt."

Thomas Römer says, "the Deuteronomistic ideology during the Assyrian and Neo-Babylonian domination (could be described as) 'intolerant Monolatry.'[32] He continues, "At the beginning of the Persian period there was apparently a switch among the elite to a more radical monotheism as is especially shown in the polemic against cultic statues and the deities of the nations in the so-called Second Isaiah (Isa. 40–55) . . . The idea of Yahweh as a creator god does not appear in the Assyrian and exilic layers of the Deuteronomistic History. Rather, this is clearly related to the switch to monotheistic ideology."[33] He goes on to say, "If Yahweh is not only Israel's tutelary deity but also the only 'real god' of the universe (Deut 4:35 & 39) how does one explain his special relationship to Israel? The answer is given by the idea of election: Yahweh has chosen Israel as his special people. In the late monotheistic texts of Deuteronomy, creation is often linked to election (4:37); this is the case in Deut. 10:14–22, which has also been written during the Persian era."[34]

The argument here however, focuses on the description of this elect group as being *tam*, perhaps another postexilic nuance. The dominant narrative, as analyzed above, condemns Israel for not being *tam* and *yashar*. As it is frequently repeated throughout Deuteronomy and the historical books, Israel is condemned for neglecting to "obey/hear the words of Adonai and keep/observe all that was written in *seper-hatorah*," and therefore incurring God's wrath at the hands of foreign oppressors under whom Israel met its demise.

While the narrative of election becomes vital for the rebuilding of Israel under the rule of Persia, equally important is the reiteration of the Exile as punishment for disobedience of the Covenant to assure future obedience and thus future protection. Thus, the DH condemns Israel for not being *tam* and *yashar*. The words *tam* and *yashar* are not used specifically within Deuteronomy and the historical books to describe Israel's disobedience. Instead the words *shema* (hearing/obeying) and *shemar* (guarding/keeping) are used. I contend that this adds to the symbolic nature of the analogy. By using *tam* Job is not quickly equated with the events described or foretold within the Covenantal historical narrative. As it is written in 2 Kgs 23:26–27 (NRSV),

> Still the Lord did not turn from the fierceness of his great wrath,
> by which his anger was kindled against Judah, because of all

32. Römer was referencing Pakkala's, *Intolerant Monolatry in the Deuteronomistic History*.

33. Römer, *So-Called Deuteronomistic History*, 173–74.

34. Ibid., 174.

the provocations with which Manasseh had provoked him. The Lord said, "I will remove Judah also out of my sight, as I have removed Israel; and I will reject this city that I have chosen, Jerusalem, and the house of which I said, My name shall be there."[35]

What is significant about the use of *tam* in the book of Job however, is contemplating its subversive connotation. If Job is allegorically representing Israel as I suggest, it is not the Israel as described in the Covenantal narrative, the Israel who sinned greatly, followed other gods, did not uphold the Covenant and was thus punished. Rather, Job represents *tam* and *yashar*, Israel as the followers of the Covenant who *nonetheless* became recipients of God's great wrath and were utterly finished.

Tam is not only used to describe the character of a person or a sacrifice offered as complete and blameless but it is also used to describe the end or destruction of a people or nation. I suggest the use of *tam* in the book of Job could be used in order to evoke the sense of destruction the chosen people of Israel, as described in the Covenant, felt after the Exile and decimation of their temple and land (2 Kgs 23:26–27; 24:20). Not only was Israel potentially blameless and upright, and according to their Covenant, loved by God like no other in the land, but they also met their demise, were finished at the hands of the Babylonians. An interesting note to make is the use of the *tmm* in the qal infinitive construct form in the book of Deuteronomy. In 2:15 *tmm* is used to describe the hand of God against the original exodus generation who grumbled in the desert unwilling and afraid to go into the land of Canaan. "Indeed, the Lord's own hand was against them, to root them out from the camp, until all were finished (*tumam*)." The two other times it is used in Deuteronomy are in 31:24 and 30 referring to the words of the Torah written down by Moses (to the very end—*tuma*) and sung by Moses to the whole assembly, to the very end (*tuma).* The use of *tmm* in Deuteronomy thus indicates the word is readily understood to mean completion, end or finality, even the very end of something, and at times, the end of a community of Hebrew people as a result of God's anger. Thus, paradoxically, Israel is both blameless and destroyed or finished. Using *tam* to describe Job allows Israel to use the Covenant once again, to work through what I described above as the cultural complex of perfectionism or perfect obedience to *seper-hatorah*, which rigidified the Covenant in the exilic and postexilic redaction of the dominant historical narrative. In the character of

35. As asserted in Deut 28:15, "If you will not obey Adonai your Elohim by diligently observing all his commandments and decrees, which I am commanding you today, then all these curse shall come upon you and overtake you." The curses that follow include loss of land, produce, progeny, animals, health at the hands of the earth, foreign enemies and God.

Job Israel asserts its blamelessness, denies its grave disobedience inscribed in the history, and acknowledges the feeling of completion, as in being utterly destroyed. The prolific use of the word *tam* and the way in which it is used within the book of Job is the next area of inquiry.

As suggested before by Fokkelman, the narrator gives us a judgment about the character of Job immediately after introducing him. The judgment at first glance renders an almost untouchable character. Clines even suggests that Job in fact has nothing to say about the meaning of suffering for people in general because the first sentence of the book makes it explicit that Job is not like every other person but instead is rather exceptional, perfect in every way.[36] If the reader was uncertain about Job's special character she need only wait until 1:8 when Adonai admits that in fact there is no one like Adonai's servant Job in all the earth. The same sentiment remains throughout much of the book. Adonai repeats this admission about the complete and upright servant in Job 2:3 in response to *hassatan's* hunt, this time twice. "Adonai said to *hassatan*, 'Have you set your heart toward my servant Job? There is no one like him in all the earth, a *tam*[37] and *yashar* man who fears God and turns from evil. He still persists in his *tummâ*[38] though you incited me against him, to swallow him without cause (*hinnäm*).'"

Throughout the book, it is *Adonai* who considers and describes Job to be *tam* (complete/blameless) and to have *tummâ* (integrity). Job's *tam* is mentioned four times in the prologue, three out of the four times by *Adonai* directly, clearly indicating one function of the prologue is to exonerate Job's character, for from the very mouth of *Adonai* comes the judgment of Job's *tam* character. Another point of conjecture is the narrator's choice to use the tetragammaton. Although the prologue's setting takes place in the midst of a gathering of the sons/children of Elohim,[39] it is not Elohim who speaks to *hassatan* regarding the *tam* of his servant, but *Adonai*.[40]

36. Clines, "Deconstructing the Book of Job," 72.

37. Here *tam* is used as an adjective.

38. Here *tummâ*, is the root *tmm* used in verbal form meaning integrity or uprightness.

39. This phrase is often translated as heavenly beings.

40. In the book of Job, the tetragammaton Adonai is mostly used in the prologue, epilogue and the divine speeches in 38—42. Only once is Adonai used within the poetic core, a reference made by Job himself in 12:9. It is significant to note that none of Job's friends, nor Elihu, nor the wisdom poem in chapter 28 make reference to Adonai although an array of other names, ones more archaic or universally used to designate a deity, are utilized throughout including Eloah, Shem, Shaddai, El and Elohim. In Job there is great diversity in the names of God used. Shaddai: 5:17, 6:4, 14; 8:3, 5; 11:7; 13:3; 15:25; 21:15, 20; 22:17, 23, 25, 26; 27:10, 11; 29:5; 31:2, 35; 32:8; 33:4; 37:23; 40:2. Eloah used about 60x in the Hebrew Bible appears 40 of those times in Job; Shem

The other occurrences of *tam* within the book of Job deserve further attention. The next time *tam* is mentioned outside of the prologue, in adjectival form, is by Bildad the Shuhite who declares, "God will not reject a *tam* person, nor take the hand of evil doers" (8:20). And in 9:20, 21 & 22, this time in Job's reply to Bildad once again asserting his innocence, he determines it is all one in the same, whether you are *tam* or wicked you are subject to El's destruction. As Bildad maintains the voice of the Covenant, telling Job, "if you seek God and make supplication to Shaddai, if you are pure[41] and upright surely then he will rouse himself for you and restore you your rightful place." Bildad's speech/response takes on the form of a public speech with language of disputation likened to Deuteronomy 4:32 and 32:7[42] further indicating the prevalence and perspective of the Covenant tradition alive and well within the mind of the author(s), and presumably the original hearers, of this text. Job's response to Bildad, directly critiques the upheld notion within the Covenant, for his life testifies that obedience and disobedience alike will be punished. As an example of Covenantal obedience, *tam*, Job's life stands as a counter-example. *Tam* is counted the same as *rasha* (wickedness) and both are subject to destruction (9:20).

The significance then, for the narrator's judgment about the *tam* character of Job, unlike any other in all the earth, is poignant. Rabbinic interpretations of the book of Job have circled around the notion of whether Job was an Israelite or Gentile based in part on the description of his character.[43] I contend that rather than determining Job's ethnicity, it is constructive to contemplate the symbolic function of Job, as the picture of Israel after the destruction of Jerusalem and the temple, especially given how the narrator sets up the story juxtaposing the Job of the prosaic *inclusio* with the Job in the poetic core of the book. The narrative description of Job as *tam*, unlike any other in all the earth, elucidated in the prologue, is exactly what is challenged in the poetic center and precisely what Job seeks to defend.

Thus, Job as symbol begins to emerge. The way in which Job is described as *tam*, unlike any other on the earth, evokes images of Israel's

---

which is most prevalent in Dtr and DH appears 11x in Job 1:21, 3:17, 19; 18:17; 23:7; 30:8; 34:22; 35:12; 39:30; 40:20; 42:14; and Elohim, perhaps the most common name used for God in the Hebrew Bible, appears only 11x in Job and predominately in the prologue either referring to Job's "fear of Elohim" or to the "sons of Elohim" (more commonly translated as heavenly beings). Outside of these references Elohim is only used by Eliphaz, Wisdom (28:18) and Elihu, who interestingly do not use the divine designation. We will come back to chapter 12 and Job's use of the tetragammaton in the section following.

41. Significantly *tam* is not used here.

42. Clines, *Job 1–20*, 201.

43. Baskin, "Rabbinic Interpretations of Job," 101–10.

uniqueness and particularity that formulate in the theology of Israel's election that begins to emerge during the later editorial stages of the Deuteronomistic History. The book of Job seems to utilize images already circulating within the community to tell a different story, a different history from the dominant history reported in the DH. It seeks to inscribe the affective experience cut off from the dominant historical narrative thus told, arguing that whether elect or not, obedient or not, *tam* or *rasha* all are equally subject to destruction. While, on the one hand, Israel conceives itself as an elect community, particular to the one and only Adonai-Elohim, and re-formulates the Covenantal tradition to ensure Adonai's control over the atrocities of the Exile (by blaming themselves for such atrocities indicating God's ordination of the Exile rather than the alternative—God's impotence in the face of the Babylonians) another symbol starts to materialize that serves as a witness to the utter inconceivability of the exilic experience.

Israel is finished (*tam*), utterly destroyed, despite their (*tam*) uprightness, justice and blamelessness, just as the wicked are destroyed. The protagonist portrayed by the author through the voice of Adonai, as like none other on the land, is about to incur the devastating wrath of God, utter destruction, regardless of his *tam*, regardless of his election. Thus, Israel stands on the ash heap, reflecting upon the nation that once was great. Israel stands decimated and dispersed. In an ironic tone the chosen one, unlike any other upon the land, is now finished. It is now that the stage is set for us to enter the poetic dialogue, as the symbolic is aroused. Through the language and metaphors employed we traverse further into the symbol to see what new images, new history may be discovered or born in the process.[44]

Self-Advocacy:
The Symbolism of Words and Speech in the Book of Job

Another key theme in the book of Job repeated throughout is Job's self-advocacy. Though too, the way in which Job advocates for himself differs between the prosaic *inclusio* and the poetic core. It is this juxtaposition that will now be analyzed.

---

44. The other two times *tam* occurs in the Book of Job are during Elihu's speech, 36:4, 37:16—each reference is to *tamim daʾot* perfect knowledge being with or in Job's presence—a reference, most likely to God (though it is possible Elihu considers himself to be *tamim daʾot*, but I am not convinced by this argument).

Job of the Prosaic Inclusio

In the prologue narrative, the narrator assures the readers that Job "did not sin and did not give unsavoriness (*tapel*) to Elohim" (1:22).[45] The only words uttered out of Job's mouth throughout the narrative buildup within the heavenly realm and its earthly aftermath indicate Job's acceptance of the ill that has come upon him, blessing the name of Adonai and testifying that good and the evil are to be accepted from *haelohim*. The prologue recounts how Job became victim to a great atrocity, though did not sin with his *lips* (*spt*). Interestingly, Job is voiceless/speechless in the prosaic epilogue. Though the narrator of the epilogue indicates that Job spoke correctly about Adonai (2 times this is mentioned within 42:7–8), in contrast to the friends and will thus serve as their intercessor according to their folly, he is given no voice of his own in the epilogue. Once again, a passive protagonist, Job receives double what he had before, is blessed by Adonai and by his family and friends, once again enjoying elevated status and a long life before dying a blessed man in his old age. The prologue and epilogue frame Job as a silent, helpless victim in the battle of some archetypal drama that Job seems to have no control over. Job's self-advocacy takes the form of acceptance and blessing humbly receiving whatever should come his way, for good or ill.

As the symbol of Israel, post exile, what can we glean from the character of Job in this prosaic frame? On the one hand, Job, the blameless/complete and upright man, who religiously observes the Covenant, ritually rising and offering burnt offerings according to all the possible sins of himself and his children, seems humbly to accept the good and evil from *Ha-Elohim*. However, Job, the finished and destroyed man, perhaps has no other option but to take that which has come to him. Religious obedience, ritualistic observance, and sacrifice did not keep Job from experiencing utter decimation of all that was precious to him. The symbol being evoked leads us to wonder if the narrator is using the prologue and epilogue to

45. The word *tapel* or *tapla* (unsavoriness) requires a note of analysis. This word, the root *tpl*, occurs only seven times in the Hebrew Bible, in Job 6:6, Lam 2:14; Ezek 13:10, 11, 14, 15; 22:8. A separate root *tpl* II is posited to occur in Ezekiel and the concrete noun *tipla* occurs 3 times: Jer 23:13; Job 1:22; 24:12. The interesting thing about this word is its similarity to the word *tipilah*, meaning prayer. The very few occurrences of *tpl* occurring in the rare form as it is used in Job are clearly all from the exilic period, which connects the writing of Job to the time period of exile or after. These occurrences reference the false prophets that portrayed deceiving visions ensuring safety for Israel rather than urging Israel to repent, seeing Israel's destruction near at hand (Lam 2:14), the prophets of Samaria prophesying by Baal unsavoriness (Jer 23:13); and in Ezekiel the prophets of Israel concerning Jerusalem who prophesied peace when there was no peace and thus spread "whitewash" or "unsavoriness" upon the walls of the temple. The word can be translated as unsavoriness, foolishness, or emptiness. Marböck, "תפל, *tapel*."

image an Israel faithful to the Covenant. As the history of exile is being explained throughout exilic and postexilic redactions to the Covenant narrative in Deuteronomy and within the historical narratives in Joshua—Kings, Job of the prologue becomes an image of the obedient Israel, Israel that lives according to the Covenant, advocating for themselves through their righteous obedience of the Covenant. The Job of the epilogue, in contrast to the Job of the prologue, becomes the intercessor for his friends as a response to establishing something true of Adonai through Job's willingness to confront God face-to-face regarding Job's experience of inexplicable evil. But what of the Job pictured within the poetic core?

Job of the Poetic Core

The first verse within the poetic core informs the reader of the narrative shift. The Job of the prosaic *inclusio* has left the story, or so it seems, and the Job of the poetic core enters. It is this dramatic shift in Job's character portrayal that has led scholars to postulate the book of Job as a composit of two different sources.[46] In the poetic core Job's self-advocacy takes a dramatically different tone. His lips speak of the violence he has incurred and his words are used to testify to the injustice, to name the trauma and to plea, at times to demand an answer from the God of the Covenant by calling him to court. This Job is not willing to accept the good and the bad that come from God without revealing his complaint.

Beginning in 3:1, "Job opened his mouth and cursed his day (the day he was born)." Arousing images of creation and the Leviathan, Job 3 and Job 41 serve as their own *inclusio* within the poetic core. Echoing the proclamation, "Let there be light" (Gen 1:3) Job offers an anti-proclamation, "Let that day be darkness!" In a reversal of "and there was morning and there was evening the first day," (Gen 1:5) Job pleads about the day of his birth, "Let it not rejoice among the days of the year; let it not come into the number of the months" (Job 3:6). Beckoning images of the primordial deep, the watery chaos of Gen 1 wherein Leviathan dwells, Job calls for the one who can rouse up Leviathan, presumably God, to come and curse the day of his own birth. The imagery being evoked in chapter 3 of Job, the first of Job's speeches in the poetic core, leads to death, pleading for death to come, or for life never to have been tasted, "Why is light given to one in misery, and life to the bitter in soul, who long for death, but it does not come," (3:20–21a). Instead, Job pronounces he feels fenced in and surrounded, a pronouncement that normally indicates a sense of protection (Ps 139). However here,

46. Pope, *Job*, xxiii–xxx.

it indicates a feeling of being trapped and unable to escape the pain that has been brought upon him. Uttering a pain so deep, Job wishes he had been a stillborn, to never have been born would be better than to have seen the light of his first day.[47]

What do the poet's words portray through the character of Job? Desperation or depression, a wish never to have been born or looked upon by God, never to have received God's light which now blinds and does not show the way toward comfort. For the arrows of Shaddai are in him; the poet describes how Job's spirit drinks of their poison and how the terrors of Eloah are arrayed against him (6:4). The poet describes Job as resource-less, desperate, without strength, or patience or any hope of his ending well (6). The words and speech uttered from his lips become Job's only tools, the last of what he has, by which he advocates for himself. He pleads with God to grant his desire and crush him, cut him off (6:8). He advocates for his death as he maintains that he is innocent (6:30). It is his very advocacy, the words uttered from his lips that his friends hold against him and count as his sin (6:26; 8:2). Yet, he does not restrain his mouth, he speaks in the anguish of his *ruach* (breath/spirit) and complains in the bitterness of his *nephesh* (life/ life force) (7:11).

Job is not claiming to be *without* sin; that was Adonai's claim in the prologue. Instead, Job admits that he is not without sin, but questions why it is that his sin should deserve such severe punishment from God, why he has become God's target, why God will not pardon his transgression and take away his iniquity (6:21). He admits that no mortal can be just before God (9:1) and yet still maintains his innocence and his *tam* almost as if there are two different measuring sticks, a mortal one and an immortal one. In terms of human goodness and righteousness, Job is innocent but will be destroyed nonetheless, void of any external advocate.

Beginning in chapter 9 the remainder of Job's speeches contain legal language and metaphors that leave the poetry reading like a legal dispute.[48] Job continues to assert that God must be the one who brings disaster, gives the earth into the hands of the wicked and covers the eyes of the judges who might be able to be advocates for the innocent. Job maintains his innocence, not perfection. Though he confesses his fear in speaking *directly to God*, the one he holds responsible for calamity that has come upon him (9:27–35), he begins to formulate his case.[49] In chapter 10 Job conjures up a proposal for what he might say to God as he begins to give free utterance to his complaint

---

47. Mathewson, *Death and Survival in the Book of Job*.

48. Seow, *Job 1–21*; Newsom, *Book of Job*; Ticcciati, *Job and the Disruption of Identity*.

49. Ticciati, *Job and the Disruption of Identity*; Seow, *Job 1–20*, 543.

(10:1). As Davoine and Guadilliére state, "Madness marks the moment and the dynamics of the passage in which one subject tries to exist by inscribing a real that is not transmissible."[50] What they mean here is the moment when the unknown that lives in the body, an experience one has had that has not yet been made conscious, begins to emerge into consciousness, an effort to graft the experience into one's lived reality, is marked by madness or utter confusion and impossibility. One can feel this as one reads the narrated character of Job in the poetic core—the feeling of madness or impossibility at the indescribable pain he is experiencing not only due to his physical circumstances but do also to the decimation of his worldview. He is trying to exist, to utter his experience, by inscribing a real that is not transmissible because it was not allowed into the dominant narrative. He is calling out for his pain to be recognized and answered. However, he is amidst a community so shaped by the history told in Covenant Religion that regardless of Job's seeming blamelessness before he was "cursed," the only interpretation possible for such circumstances continues to silence the pain and perceived injustice of the situation. As the symbol of Israel, Job's own madness[51] marks the dynamics of the passage of Israel trying to allow a new story to exist by inscribing a *real* at the root of the experience of the Exile. What I mean by madness is that which the author is able to portray in the poetic core of the raw, gut, affective experiences of the trauma that befell him as narrated in the prosaic prologue. When psychoanalysts use the term "mad" or "madness" we mean a psychological state that is often categorized by the medical community as psychological illness. However, psychoanalysts, particularly those I am using in this work, have a different perception of madness, seeing the prospective function of madness. Rather than seeing madness/illness as something to cure I stand in line with the tradition of analysts that seeks to see what the illness is communicating.

I want to come back to a point mentioned above regarding the use of Adonai. To reiterate, the tetragrammaton in the prosaic narrative deserves attention particularly because the only other time the divine name is used outside of the narrator indicating the speech of Adonai, it is used by Job, himself, to testify to Adonai's wrath. He proclaims it is by Adonai's hand the horrors have befallen him, "Who among all these does not know that the hand of Adonai has done this?" (12:9). The narrator inscribes Job showing an effort to hold his ground and assert his own understanding in the face of his friends' taunts and claims to wisdom. In his response, Job (12) echoes

---

50. Davoine and Guadilliére, *History through Trauma*, 51.

51. Ulanov, *Unshuttered Heart*, 187–211.

the creation narrative of Genesis 1,[52] yet again, as he explains that while he is just (*ṣaddîq*) and *tamim*, God has made him a laughingstock (*sochaq*) to his companions.[53] Even the animals (sixth day of creation), the birds of the air and fish of the sea (sixth day of creation) and the plants of the earth (third day of creation) can testify that what has come upon Job has come from the very *yad*, hand, of Adonai (12:7–10).

Chapter 12 is significant for other reasons as well. Starting in verse 13 a picture is painted through the poetry that begins to reveal clues to the destruction of the Babylonian Exile experienced by those living in Jerusalem. Verses 13–25 portray a version of reality that declares a God (Eloah) who is wisdom and strength (12:13) but in God's counsel and understanding, tears down that which no one can rebuild; withholds waters and causes the waters to overwhelm; humbles counselors, judges, kings, priests, princes, and elders alike; reveals a great darkness from the depths and is responsible for making nations become great and then destroying them all the same (Job 12:23//Deut 28:10, 25, 63). Picturing the affective experience of the events of the Exile, Job stands as the symbol of Israel, once great and revered, now decimated and a laughingstock among the nations at the *yad* of Adonai.

For a moment, one might think she were reading straight out of Lam 3:1–15 (NRSV):

> I am the one who has seen affliction
> under the rod of God's wrath;
> he has driven and brought me
> into darkness without any light;
> against me alone he turns his hand,
> again and again, all day long.
>
> He has made my flesh and my skin waste away,
> and broken my bones;
> he has besieged and enveloped me
> with bitterness and tribulation;
> he has made me sit in darkness
> like the dead of long ago.

---

52. Priestly Source

53. Another interesting parallel is this image and the word used, *sochaq*. While *sochaq* is derived from the playful word, *tsachaq*, which was derived from the word "to laugh" (also the name Isaac), here it juxtaposes laughing as Job becomes a character to mock or laugh at, a laughingstock in the midst of his sorrow. The word is used in the same way in Lam 3:14; Jer 20:7; 48:26, 27 and 39, again, indicating ties to the exilic experience.

He has walled me about so that I cannot escape;
    he has put heavy chains on me;
though I call and cry for help,
    he shuts out my prayer;
he has blocked my ways with hewn stones,
    he has made my paths crooked.
He is a bear lying in wait for me,
    a lion in hiding;
he led me off my way and tore me to pieces;
    he has made me desolate;
he bent his bow and set me
    as a mark for his arrows.
He shot into my vitals
    the arrows of his quiver;
I have become the laughingstock of all my people,
    the object of their taunt-songs all day long.
He has filled me with bitterness,
    he has sated me with wormwood.

I note Lamentations 3 here to draw a parallel to the poetic language used to describe what is agreed upon in the scholarly world, as response to the experience of the Babylonian Exile. While Judea or Israel are not mentioned explicitly in chapter 3 of Lamentations, the poem stands in the middle of the book of laments over the city of Jerusalem. In Lamentations 3 the *geber*, the everyman or the strong man, is used allegorically to represent the strength and leadership of Israel who was once potent, upon the destruction in 586 BCE becomes impotent.[54] He, like the character of Job, feels the sting of the arrows of God's quiver (Job 6:4; Lam 3:13) and becomes a laughing-stock among the nations/friends (Job 12:4; Lam 3:14; Jer 20:7). The allusion to becoming a laughingstock and feeling the sting of the arrows of God's quiver direct the reader's attention to the exilic experience being lamented in the book of Lamentations evoking similar images for Job sitting on the

54. R. B. Salters illuminates that critical scholarship is divided over the identification of the *geber*. One camp believes that the *geber* is an individual sufferer, either an actual sufferer or an illustrative sufferer, speaking/suffering on behalf of the nation. The second camp views the *geber* as a collective, the people of Israel. Salters *Critical and Exegetical Commentary on Lamentations*, 185. Also see O'Connor, *Lamentations and the Tears of the World*; and Hillers, *Lamentations*, for further discussion of the *geber* in Lamentations 3.

ash heap. While the evidence of precisely when and where the book of Job originated is sparse, there are certain literary allusions within the text, such as the above example in Lamentations, within both the prose and the poetry sections, that lend toward reading this book as a symbolic expression of exile, perhaps written or redacted later, but reflecting upon the events of the Exile nonetheless.

Working with chapter 31, the final chapter of Job's speech directed to Adonai, will elucidate a final analogy within the poetic core. Habel titled this chapter, "Job's Oath of Purity."[55] His title for the chapter is based on the first line and the argument following. Job 31:1 reads, "I cut a covenant according to my eyes."[56] Evoking linguistic imagery of Covenant making, the narrator of Job places the book firmly within the Covenant tradition. The poetry following is Job's plea of innocence, as if in a court room, measuring himself up to the ordinances of his culture articulated in the Deuteronomic Covenant, and proving himself innocent.

Job claims to be free of disobedience on account of adultery (vv. 1–12) (// with commandments 7 & 10 in Deuteronomy). He exonerates himself based on the responsibility he took over care of his servants, the poor and the widowed (vv. 13–23) as acts of social welfare, key aspects of the Deuteronomic Covenant (see chapter 3 of this work). Job confesses his innocence regarding the commandment of idolatry (vv. 26–28)[57] (commandments 1 & 2 in Deuteronomy) and the Deuteronomic emphasis against hubris (vv. 24–25) (see chapter 3 of this book). He makes a case for his continual love and concern for his neighbor, the foreign traveler and kin (vv. 29–34), another major tenet of the Deuteronomic Covenant (again, see chapter 3 of this book). Finally, the very act of Job's self-advocacy, taking his *rîb*, his dispute, directly to God (for lack of any other advocate) and demanding an *anâ*, an answer, fits in line with one of the prominent Deuteronomic nuances of the Covenant. As discussed in chapter 3, the Deuteronomic Covenant accentuates that sanctity is due to the *intentions* of the *person* who consecrates an offering rather than being contingent upon the intervention of a priest or priestly ceremony. Job had no advocate though he looked for one and asked, pleaded even, with his companions to be one on his behalf. Without an advocate, Job becomes his own advocate and takes his *rîb* to Adonai directly.

> 'O, that I had one to hear me! Here is my signature! Let Shaddai answer me! Let the man of my dispute write a document! If not, upon my shoulder I shall lift it, I shall bind it around as

55. Habel, *Book of Job*, 423.

56. In Ancient Israel a *berith* (covenant) was cut not made.

57. Habel, *Book of Job*, 41–42, 437.

a crown belonging to me! I will declare to him the number of my steps and like a prince I will confront him! If, against me, my ground cried out and its furrows wept together, If I have eaten its strength without payment and if I have enraged the life of its owners, May thorns grow instead of wheat and foul weeds instead of barley.' The words of Job are finished (*tamu*). Job 31:35–40

Chapter 31, the final of Job's "speeches," seals the Covenantal image through which to view the character of Job in the poetic dialogue.[58] Habel writes that the "outer frame (38:1–3, 38–40) recalls traditional covenant motifs which underscore that Job's oath of purity is grounded in a past commitment to pursue the principles of his way (38:1). Maintaining the image of *tam* yet again, the narrator indicates that Job's words are *tamu*, Job is finished. Having pleaded his case, confronted God on his own behalf, is he now complete? Finished? Has Job proven himself to be blameless? In poetic beauty, the narrator maintains Job's *tumma* as the closing image of his speeches.

Grappling with the God Speeches: Symbolism Emerging from the Space between God and Job

The speeches of God, from out of the whirlwind (38:1) have perplexed many readers and been the subject of multiple books ranging from the field of biblical scholarship, philosophy, psychology, cultural studies, theology, and art.[59] What is analyzed through various different methods, is the question of what God is actually saying, if anything? Or, what does the author want us to know about this God? In a surprising twist, God shows up. Much to the chagrin of Job's friends and the young Elihu, who argued against Job's hubris for his desire to confront God face-to-face, God, in fact, answers Job's request.

God answers Job in a similar disputation style evoking, yet again, images of creation reminiscent of Job's speech in chapter 12. I argue that the author's construction of the God speeches at the end of the poetic core function to reconstruct the meaning of the Covenant by showing a God that is truly beyond it. God's speeches in no way shame Job or function

---

58. Habel, *Book of Job*, 428.

59. Perdue, *Wisdom in Revolt*, 197–98; Brown, *Character in Crises*, 89–90. Timmer, "God's Speeches, Job's Responses"; Blake, *Blake's Job*; Jung, "Answer to Job," in *Psychology and Religion*, ¶¶553–70. Frost, *Masque of Reason*.

to "put Job in his place" nor silence him.[60] Instead, by the author's choice to image God in this particular way, through God's response to Job, Job's *tumma* is maintained. In maintaining Job's *tumma* throughout the book, the author creates the necessary space between the God image proffered in the book of Job and the God imaged in the Covenant. In Job's boldness (at the hand of the author) to contemplate this new image arising, due to the space provided, Job "revokes" (42:6) his former image, the image maintained by the national narrative in the Deuteronomic Covenant, and is able to mourn his loss and pain. Before Job knew God only by what he had heard of God. After the confrontation and the space created in the gap between what was formerly known and what was yet to be known, Job saw God with his own eyes. His knowing shifts senses and becomes his own knowing in contradistinction to his friends' and community's way of knowing. Herein lies the path of Individuated Religion.

Job 38–41 elicits images of God as a mother who bore the world into being and took tender care of it and all its creatures and continues to watch over all that happens upon her surface and in the skies from the weather to the constellations in the universe.[61] Chapter 39 moves from the heavens and the earth the creatures that roam upon the earth and fly about in the sky, not the wise and distinguished animals but animals often thought of as vulnerable or not smart, (goats, deer, donkeys, oxen, ostriches, horses), or conversely, predators (hawks and eagles).[62] The short interlude in chapter 40, where Job speaks to God, has traditionally been interpreted as God putting Job "in his place," as he covers his mouth and refuses to answer any further.[63] I argue this is where Job recognizes the true distance between who he thought God was and who God is in reality, outside of Job's subjective (Covenantal) experience of God. Job was not "put in his place" but rather, was allowed an experience with the real, the known but not yet thought about or integrated experience, his own reality of his suffering and the reality of the Divine outside of his own construction of the Divine. The narrator does not stop there however, but allows the dialogue to continue, indicating the ability to remain in the gap opened up through Job's suffering and in the No-thing space.

The final two chapters of God's speech move from the weak, vulnerable and scavenging animals that roam the earth to the monsters that roam the earth and sea. In an ironic tone the language of the covenant is again

60. Lacocque, "Deconstruction of Job's Fundamentalism."

61. O'Connor, "Wild, Raging Creativity."

62. Newsom, *Book of Job*, 244–48.

63. Pellauer, "Reading Ricoeur Reading Job"; and, Olson's response, "Silence of Job."

elicited as God asks Job, "Will it (Leviathan!) make a covenant with you to be taken as your servant forever?" The narrator utilizes covenantal imagery in order to deconstruct Job's (Israel's) understanding of Covenant. The question being asked here is, who is the covenant maker? God or Israel? In Covenant Religion Israel ultimately became the creators and sustainers of the Covenant, finding a way to make sense of the atrocities of the Exile and trying to secure such events from ever happening again by rigidifying the tenets of the Covenant that became concretized and then canonized within Deuteronomy and the national History told in the books of Joshua–Kings. The God speeches serve to remind Israel, God is perhaps the maker of Covenants, but not the Covenant itself.

The length and the flow of the God speeches, where they come in the book and how they are juxtaposed with the various previous arguments between Job and his friends, sharing familiar images and languages, serve to create a kind of denouement that has led readers to assume Job's silence at the end is the hermeneutically appropriate stance. However, reading this book as a fictional tale, an artistic expression that rewrites Israel's history, the God speeches serve as an opening. This opening is into the space where previous symbols failed due to their neglect of affect and thus, the inhibition of mourning. In this way, the final stanzas of the book of Job allowed its author, its ancient community and communities across the ages to gain consciousness of the cultural complex of perfection, constellated in the Deuteronomic Covenant, in a new and creative way. The archetypal energy previously blocked was able to find expression within the story and now amongst reading communities today. This new way was through confrontation, disputation, anger, rage, and finally, mourning.

8

Psychoanalytic Explorations into the Significance of *Tam*, Individuated Religion, and the Role of Job in Relation to the National History

We divert our attention from disease and death as much as we can; and the slaughter-houses and indecencies without end on which our life is founded are huddled out of sight and never mentioned, so that the world we recognize officially in literature and in society is a poetic fiction far handsomer and cleaner and better than the world that really is.

—WILLIAM JAMES,
VARIETIES OF RELIGIOUS EXPERIENCE[1]

IT IS NOW TIME to explore a psychoanalytic analysis of the symbolic significance of *tam*, which, I argue, frees up the cultural complex constellated within the historical narrative of Covenant Religion. Once again, the work of Carl Jung, Ann Ulanov, and Donald Winnicott will aid in an analysis of the word *tam* used to describe Job and its implications for reading Job as a symbol of Israel throughout the Babylonian Exile. Furthermore, the new god-image that emerges at the end of Job through the Divine speeches is analyzed for its symbolic value as it opens the way for an Individuated Religion, juxtaposed with the Covenant Religion of the dominant historical narrative. The symbols that emerge in the book of Job do not replace Covenant Religion or the dominant historical narrative articulated in the DH but, rather, they re-imagine the original symbol of the Covenant and

---

1. James, *Varieties of Religious Experience*, 90.

the God to which the Covenant points. For within the symbol of Job and the new god-image that emerges in relation to him lies the mutative agent, the symptom or image that enables change and new growth within Covenant Religion as it was adopted by the dominant historical narrative reported in the Deuteronomistic History.

Psychoanalytic Explorations into the Significance of Tam

Jung's concept of the archetypes, mentioned in chapter 4, provides a framework for understanding universal and historical ideas or images that traverse the span of time and distance. Perhaps the greatest of these images or concepts for Jung is the archetype of the Self. Jung describes the Self,

> . . .as an empirical concept [that] designates the whole range of psychic phenomena in [a person]. It expresses the unity of the personality as a whole . . . In so far as psychic totality, consisting of both conscious and unconscious contents, is a postulate, it is a transcendental concept, for it presupposes the existence of unconscious factors on empirical grounds and thus characterizes an entity that can be described only in part but, for the other part, remains at present unknowable and illimitable.[2]

As has been discussed throughout this work, Jung held fast to the idea that conscious living is only a small part of one's whole existence. That which is not conscious, has been repressed or comes to an individual from the collective, is the other part of life that begs attention. The components left out of consciousness, those unseemly aspects of self, those opposite our conscious personality, or belonging to the other half of life will continue to pound at the door of consciousness until they are admitted, related to, reckoned with and integrated.

Jung maintains that,

> the elevation of the human figure to a king or a divinity, and on the other hand its representation in subhuman, theriomorphic form, are indications of the transconscious character of the pairs of opposites. They do not belong to the ego-personality but are supraordinate to it. The ego-personality occupies an intermediate position, like the *"anima inter bona et mala sita"* (soul placed between good and evil). The pairs of opposites constitute the phenomenology of the paradoxical self, man's totality.[3]

2. Jung, *Psychological Types*, ¶¶789–90.
3. Jung, *Mysterium Coniunctionis*, ¶4.

So long as one pretends these other aspects do not exist, and do not exist within one's own Self, the individual will continue to be taken over by them all the more. Or worse, the collective will become the container for these divorced parts of Self and whole communities will be forced to hold unconscious parts of others ending in schisms, religious and political othering, even war. The Self is larger than the ego and contains one's inferior function, that which is opposite one's ruling principle.

The Self is the center of the psyche. Jung explains,

> The energy of the central point is manifested in the almost irresistible compulsion and urge to become what one is, just as every organism is driven to assume the form that is characteristic of its nature no matter what the circumstances. This center is not felt or thought of as the ego, but if one may so express it, as the self. Although the center is represented by an innermost point, it is surrounded by a periphery containing everything that belongs to the self—the paired opposites that make up the total personality . . . The self, though simple . . . is also a conglomerate soul.[4]

The course by which the ego is able to recognize consciously and contain elements coming from the unconscious that belong to the individual, allowing the individual to create space between him and others, him and his society or community, and him and his national and religious creeds is described by Jung as individuation. The "process by which a person becomes a psychological "in-dividual . . . a separate, indivisible unity or 'whole.'"[5] This process entails integrating contents from one's unconscious into one's consciousness, by way of the ego. The ego, in Jung's summation, is only a small part of the individual's total being, wherein consciousness rests. The way toward individuation begins through the gap described above, creating a moment when an individual begins to pull back her outer projections and her own personas and takes time in the space between.

I suggest that Israel, in its personification in the narrative character of Job, is confronted with all that has been left out of consciousness, of that which made up Covenant Religion inscribed in the book of the Covenant and in its national History. The book of Job stands in contrast to the dominant, national History as a different history, one that is able to integrate the affective experience of the Exile rather than dissociate it by controlling it through wise words or strict dogmas of righteousness. By choosing a non-Hebrew name, and setting the story in a distant time and place, and then poignantly employing the word *tam* to describe this character the creators

4. Jung, *Archetypes and the Collective Unconscious*, ¶634.
5. Ibid., ¶490.

of this story create enough space to acknowledge the experiences of exile and the Babylonian Exile's ramifications in order to imagine different possibilities for moving forward. I term one of the varied possibilities Individuated Religion. By this, I do not suggest some form of individual religion, but rather, a collective expression that began to take seriously the pain and disruption of the Exile instead of introjecting shame and guilt *per* Covenant Religion. This new narrative makes use of the previously silenced affective responses of aggression, rage, and desire in relation to the disillusioning experience of Exile and enables Israel to imagine a new relationship with Adonai through the Covenant.

In choosing to describe the protagonist as *tam*, the narrators of this story (consciously or not) bring in that which was left out of Covenant Religion, the utterly destroyed, decimated, and finished Israel, who understood itself to be blameless and simultaneously destroyed in the face of such catastrophe. This is a move toward wholeness or toward the Self, in Jung's terms, but understood here in the sense of the collective or the community of Israel. Jung would not describe the Self as a collective artifact and may in fact warn against such an assumption postulating that being absorbed into the collective is what one individuates from. However, Jung's notion of the Self as an archetype, a universal content of the collective unconscious outside of the personal, allows us to understand this originating principle as not only a symbol for the individual but for the community as well. Given the ANE socio-cultural context I argue there is a collective experience being re-imagined in the book of Job, not an individual experience. I use Jung's understanding of the Self and the process of individuation as a way of explaining how a community might, like an individual, differentiate from the collective dogmatistic narratives, or gain awareness of the prominent cultural complexes that keep a community from becoming integrated and whole and thus able to create more room for that which is other and different. By including that which was left out, namely aggression, rage, anger, and desire, Job confronts God and begs, even demands, God to confront him face-to-face. The god previously imaged in Covenant Religion spoke through a burning bush, a cloud, an imageless voice, or through the voice of God's prophets or leaders but not face-to-face with Israel. Ann Ulanov makes a similar comment about the book of Job in her book *The Unshuttered Heart*, saying, "So great the shift, (referencing Job 42:6), that the religion of the ear changes to the religion of the eye. The ego, that eye in which consciousness is located, through which consciousness beholds reality, now becomes a means to look at consciousness, an organ through which consciousness—its place and its limits—is perceived."[6] Job, as the symbol of Israel, re-imagines his relationship with Adonai. Rather than ignoring or denying his felt experience of the trauma Job is able to use this energy to deconstruct the dominantly held notion of the Covenant, asserting his "blamelessness" (*tam*) in the face of being "finished" (*tam*).

Given my argument that the character of Job can be understood as the symbol of the community of Israel in Exile, there is one final image evoked left to be explored. Another way in which the root word *tmm* is used within the Bible is to mean a complete or whole sacrifice being offered up to Adonai. I suggest that this story plays a vital role in its relationship to the DH within the Hebrew canon. Rather than assuming some kind of conscious intent from the creators of the book of Job to imagine another way to tell the story of exile symbolically through the character of Job, I propose that the inclusion of the book of Job within the Hebrew canon has even further implications, which go beyond consciousness. In Job, the devastation of the Exile, symbolically elucidated in the prologue wherein Job has all of his possessions, family (aside from his wife), and health taken from him, in the poetic core is met with rage and aggression, and that which enables mourning. Jung describes that "every psychic process has a value quality attached to it, namely its feeling-tone. This indicates the degree to which the subject is affected by the process of how much it means to him (in so far as the process reaches consciousness at all). It is through "affect" that the subject becomes involved and so comes to feel the whole weight of reality."[7] Affect, though undeniably present in the national narrative told through the DH, is repressed and inaccessible and thus the energy turns inward and finds the blame within the victimized culture, Israel in Exile.

In the symbolic history of Job, affect is the way through which Job begins to come to terms with and express the whole weight of reality. The way toward wholeness, for postexilic Israel, was to recognize the reality that the national narrative silenced intolerable and unjustified devastation. This recognition inevitably led to a kind of symbolic death, a sacrifice of the symbol of Covenant, as the previous symbol made sense of the Exile through internalizing blame. This death, or sacrifice, was necessary in order to be able to approach the reality behind the Covenant. Ann Ulanov, expounding upon Jung, reminds us that if we are to approach the reality behind our images and picture of god or our "theories of the ultimate" then we must experience a symbolic death, it is a death to what we thought was reality from our

---

6. Ulanov, 216. See also, Deut 4: 11–12; 5:2–5.

7. Jung, *Aion*, ¶61.

one-sided conscious perspective.[8] The role the book of Job plays within the Hebrew canon is not only summed up in the character of Job as the symbol of Israel in exile and the book of Job as a symbolic history of its foreclosed events, but it brings in what Jung explains as the shadow, what I have referenced thus far as the left-out parts of the exilic experience. It is the inclusion of the book of Job within the canon, and in relation to the DH, which can be understood as the shadow of the Covenant, that allows for the new to appear. Such inclusion in turn re-enlivens the very symbol of Covenant Religion that was destroyed due to Israel's encounter with the reality of exile. The symbolic function of the book of Job can be understood in terms of its relation to the dominant history finally redacted sometime after the Exile that upheld, what I call, Covenant Religion and also in relation to Adonai, as a God not bound by the Covenant but a God that transcends all.

The shadow, according to Jung, is that which we hate in others and think does not belong to us. In Jungian theory, symbolic death occurs when we confront what we do not consciously think belongs to us. We work hard creating personal and societal systems or norms that insure we never have to confront what we reject in ourselves as bad. To accept all of this is like a symbolic death. The unseemly parts we believe ourselves free of, are thrust into the gap where all our notions and perceptions of what is true must be reevaluated.

The Job of the prosaic *inclusio*, particularly the prologue, holds the former position, Israel's identification as the blameless and perfect servant of Adonai. Job's silence indicates his acceptance of the evil experienced, reminiscent of the way of Covenant Religion. In the poetry however, Job is anything but silent. Job's refusal to accept the blame for the evil that befell him and his persistence in calling Adonai to court to account for what has happened paves the way for Israel to destroy its national symbol—the Covenant as articulated within the dominant history. The history told through the lens of Covenantal disobedience pressured Job to repent of his sin(s) that led to such devastating effects. His transgression of the collective and dominant story can be understood as his own evil. It was his own confrontation with the shadow of the dominant history—finding a reason for the atrocity of exile within Israel's community rather than mourning the inexplicable pain and devastation that came without cause (*hinnäm*)—that eventually allows him to be brought back into relationship with the symbol of the Covenant as something real, outside of Israel's projection of it, and into relationship with the God the symbol sought to symbolize.

---

8. Ulanov, 216; Jung *Nietzsche's Zarathustra*, Vol. 1, ¶39.

Madness and Creativity:[9]
The Book of Job in Relation to the National History

Jung himself incurred a great interruption in the height of his career. This interruption, felt by Jung as madness or even psychosis, though it was not finally a psychosis that he had feared, ended up proving to be essential for his personal growth, life, and career and in fact laid the groundwork for all of his later theories that developed into what is now known as Analytical Psychology.[10] The breakdown that occurred between November 1913 and April 1914, narrated and imaged through his paintings until 1927, was Jung's own personal experience with the unconscious, what Jung referred to as his own experience in Hell.[11] Jung describes the breakdown as a dismantling of the ruling principle. The ruling principle is that which is considered by an individual and society to be the right, guiding, productive, acceptable, benevolent, or just principle by which we live. The ruling principle is all that one consciously holds onto as the "good" and that one strives to achieve. Our good ethics, strong morals, and our personified selves make up the ruling principle. The ruling principle is then guarded by certain rituals, observances, norms and/or laws. Our personality types are determined by this, we function socially in particular ways in order to strengthen the ruling principle.

In our struggle toward "goodness," personal and social, all that threatens the good or all that is perceived as other and hence bad is cut off from consciousness, relegated to the shadows where it lies contaminating all else, personal and collective, that lies in the dark. Erich Neumann, an analytical psychologist and philosopher who practiced in Tel Aviv until his death in 1960, wrote many books on Jungian Analytical theory and philosophy including *Depth Psychology and a New Ethic*. He articulates in this book his understanding of the role of the *new ethic* saying, "When evil works unconsciously and emits its radio-activity underground, it possesses the deadly efficiency of an epidemic (the old ethic); on the other hand, evil done consciously by the ego and accepted as its own personal responsibility does not infect the environment, but is encountered by the ego as its own problem and as a content to be incorporated into life and the integration of

---

9. This is the title of Ann Ulanov's most recent book that I have referenced throughout, *Madness and Creativity,* a compilation of her lectures given at the Carolyn and Ernest Fay Series in Analytical Psychology at Texas A & M University, which were based on her years of clinical experience in relation to main themes in Jung's *The Red Book.*

10. Jung, *Red Book*, vii.

11. Ulanov, *Madness and Creativity*, 35; Jung, *Red Book*, 264.

the personality like any other psychic content."[12] Jung urges that the work of the individual is tied to the collective. That our personal work, descending into all that has been cut off and relegated to the shadows in our life, that which we hate in our neighbor that inevitably belongs to our own person, is as important and beneficial to society and culture as a whole, as it is to the individual doing the work. Neumann calls the former way of living, the 'old ethic' and the way of integration, suffering evil rather than cutting it off and throwing it out upon others, as the 'new ethic.' He suggests, "the problem and the level at which the solution emerges are manifested in the individual; both, however, have their roots in the collective."[13] By "restoring our personal life in that space, space is made in the culture itself for self and symbol to be refound or found for the first time."[14]

However, the breakdown of the ruling principle, the confrontation with the inferior function, that which has not been tended, is nearly impossible. What must be severed is the identification with what we have upheld as the only way, the ruling principle, which has in a sense become a god in and of itself. But sacrificing this identification with the good can feel like death when it has been tended to as if it is life itself. What is sacrificed is our identification with our ideals and Jung posits that this is sometimes precisely the work of evil. Consciously, one may not ever be able to sacrifice living according to one's ruling principle. Therefore, evil intrudes, comes upon us, surprises us and does the work seemingly outside of ourselves. The evil one could not ever do, is found in her very midst. Ulanov elucidates, "Evil cuts the cord of identification with what we have formed as the meaning of life. Evil does it . . . We need evil to help us do the unthinkable, the unbearable that we are helpless to do by ourselves. Something else forces us to find the way for us, a way we easily choose to avoid because it is unknown or, if known dimly, it is too much, frightening, so different from our plot for our lives."[15]

The Deuteronomic Covenant can be seen as the ruling principle within the canon. It upholds what is thought to be good, structuring, organizing and nurturing but becomes identified with as a god in and of itself or the only way toward right life with God. This perception created a certain ideology in postexilic Israel that split the good and the bad, rather than allowing the two to be held together. The split happened, I

---

12. Neumann, *Depth Psychology and a New Ethic*, 104; Jung, *Civilization in Transition*, ¶¶400–433; and Ulanov and Ulanov, *Religion and the Unconscious*, 164–67.

13. Newmann, *Depth Psychology*, 30.

14. Ulanov, *Madness and Creativity*, 24.

15. Ibid., 35–36.

conjecture, as a result of the collective traumas of the many exiles experienced throughout Israel's history but most dramatically upon the Babylonian Exile wherein the Temple was destroyed. This is not to suggest that the established Covenant was bad or wrong. As Ulanov reminds us, our ethics are not bad and wrong, "They are good, our versions of the good, our 'heroic' constructions that confer meaning on us. But they are not conclusive. When we lose them, when they prove ineffective, we lose our sense of meaning we have relied upon."[16]

The Deuteronomic Covenant initially formulated in late pre-exile or early exile became the structuring element amongst the Exiles, the way in which the community maintained its unity and integrity (*tummâ*) while living in foreign land under foreign rule. Newsom describes this as the role of didactic literature, which is the lens through which she interprets the prosaic *inclusio* of Job. "Didactic stories are instruments of persuasion that directly attempt to form their readers by recruiting them to certain beliefs and shaping their attitudes and behaviors,"[17] I maintian that this is precisely the role of the national History given in the Covenant narrative throughout the historical books. But this conclusive ideology found someone or some community to blame in order to make sense of the trauma. It elevated the tenets of the Covenant to the place of the divine. At the hands of the trauma a complex was constellated. Israel found the blame within Israel's own community and leadership and as a result silenced the pain and trauma experienced under foreign oppression and hostile takeover. Therefore, in order for Israel to re-enter the land and have any hope for renewal, Israel was required to confess the wrongdoings of the past and present and live unswervingly according to the instructions of the Covenant. Once confession and obedience were practiced, Israel's Covenantal relationship with Adonai would be restored and they would be blessed.

Obedience, confession, and ritual became the ruling principle. Within the complex the Covenant, once used as a way into a relationship with Adonai or a way to image God, became a god. In Jung's terms, what the Covenant symbolized—a relationship between Israel and Adonai—regressed to identification of the Covenant with God. Hence, what prevailed was a literal interpretation of the Covenant and an exhortation to perfect obedience should Israel have any hope of renewal and restoration as a nation upon their former land, a kind of symbolic equation (see Chapter 4). Therefore, challenging the regulations and instructions in the Covenant, seeking to transgress them, would be an implausible possibility. In seeking

16. Ibid., 17.
17. Newsom, *Book of Job*, 42.

to transgress the rules and regulations of the Covenant one would transgress God. The consequences for such actions would be utterly devastating. The challenge to the Covenant narrative, and thus to Covenant Religion, arrives in a story about a man from the land of Uz, a far away place in a seemingly far away time—a tale that ushers in metaphorical evil, Job's transgression of the Covenant, in order to assist in dismantling the national History's construction of the good.[18]

Jung reminds us in *The Red Book* that once one engages with his inferior function and transgressing his ruling principle, one can "no longer separate good and evil conclusively, neither through feeling nor through knowledge."[19] When growth ceases, good and evil become separate entities again and are projected onto particular codes, individuals, or whole groups of people. Thus we can label some people good and others bad. As Jung reminds us, "As soon as growth stops, what was united in growth falls apart and once more you recognize good and evil."[20] Ulanov continues, "Living our own particular paths individually and together sponsors our growth, and our growth offers some protection against evil split off from good."[21]

In the Persian sponsored version of the Deuteronomic Covenant evil and good are split. The book of Job works with the images of the Covenant that split good and evil, but ultimately offers a different approach and therefore arrives at a different place due to the space made between his personal experience and his loyalty to Covenant Religion. The Job of the prologue obediently observes his and his culture's ruling principle, the Covenant, rising early to offer up burnt offerings just in case one in his family had sinned. Job is the *tam* and *yashar* servant of Adonai, unlike anyone on earth. As a picture of perfection, Job of the prologue holds all that is good, a faithful and obedient servant of Adonai who is blessed with all the things important to ancient Israelite culture and dictated within the Deuteronomic Covenant; progeny, land, animals, and status. Job maintains his *tam* even though all of this is suddenly ripped away from him.

18. A note about the location of Uz. While the exact location of Uz still baffles scholars Wolfers provides a nice summary of the arguments regarding the geographical reliability and other textual references to Uz within the Hebrew canon. He argues the location discredits the argument that Job was not an Israelite. While I do not think such an argument is paramount, what is more intriguing about Wolfers' argument is his attention to the two other references to Uz in the canon, namely Lamentations and Jeremiah further indicating a connection to the same time period in which Jeremiah and Lamentations were written, during and just following the Babylonian Exile.

19. Jung, *Red Book*, 231 quoted in Ulanov, *Madness and Creativity*, 30.

20. Jung, *Red Book*, 246, 247, 249, 301, quoted in Ulanov, *Madness and Creativity*, 30.

21. Ulanov, *Madness and Creativity*, 30.

The New Image that Emerges

But one question that surfaces in the prologue for readers is, "Why did Adonai allow such evil to fall upon this blameless and upright servant?" Ulanov suggests, "Our complex confronts us with the bad we do not know where to put. And its hinge makes us fall into evil itself."[22] Meaning, whenever we confront that which we consider evil for us personally we are dropped into the collective experience of evil *qua* human. Having held fast to the Covenantal notion that obedience would be rewarded with a good and prosperous life, Job's demise and his refusal to accept blame for the events that befell him becomes his own personal evil (in his transgression of Covenantal compliance) that acts as a hinge, the way into the evil experienced in exile.

Whereas in Covenant Religion, evil is found within the disobedient kings of Israel due to their disobedience of the Covenant for following after other Gods and forsaking Adonai, in the book of Job evil shows up in spite of Job's obedience to the Covenant. The bad that comes upon Job as introduced in the first two chapters of the book is first met with Israel's ruling principle, obedience and submission, functioning autonomously within Job. The blameless and upright man takes what comes to him without protest. I maintain that the evil that befalls Job in the prologue is the hinge that thrusts Job into his own inferior function—that which challenges the goodness of the Covenant—showing up in the character of Job portrayed in the poetry. Within the poetry, Job's aggression, passion, and desire to have the injustice of his circumstances seen and validated by Adonai help to deconstruct the upheld good of the Covenant. In the poetic core Job holds the bad, namely anger, aggression, and refusal to repent. This allows him to question the God of the Covenant and take this God to trial. His friends continue to hold the good as the logic of the Covenant that finds a way to explain his circumstances without questioning God or the Covenant. Job's friends repeatedly turn to Job's actions and character to place the blame for the evil that has come, allowing them to rest in the logic of the Covenant without having to wrestle with the bad that has inexplicably intruded.

As a symbolic history, the character of Job in the prosaic prologue is set up to represent compliant Israel, a representation of Israel's special relationship with Adonai based on Israel's obedience to the Covenant made between the two as portrayed in the initial layer of the Deuteronomic Covenant fashioned after Assyrian Vassal Treaties and Hittite Loyalty Oaths. However, quickly the story moves from Job the compliant or patient to Job the angry or aggressive, the Job of protest. Once the story is set up and the

---

22. Ibid., 32.

symbol is evoked, the symbol evoked through Job the *tam* and *yashar*, unlike any other in all the earth, the story takes a surprising twist as the hinge opens the characters and its readers into a new symbol. This new symbol evoked through the imagery of the Covenant, ultimately explores the notion of God's actions *hinnäm*, without cause, upon the *tam* (blameless) and *rasha* (evil) alike, which maintains ambiguity holding good and evil together and, finally, calls for a reevaluation of Covenant Religion. The new god-image that emerges is not one of a God poised and ready to destroy or bless according to Israel's actions but a God who acts seemingly without cause (*hinnäm*), not based on action or inaction. The image that emerges is of a God who watches over all of creation—the great and the small, and witnesses all events—the good and the bad. This new image is not of a God who is easily offended or perhaps even perfect, but rather a God willing to sit in the muck and count it as "right" when one of God's servants confronts God directly with his own disappointment, fear, and rage.

"Seeing that our ruling principles are not ultimate truth but at best our constructions of truth, not to be equated with truth, that our images of God are images, not God, throws us into a gap that opens between order and what is beyond order."[23] This is the gap opened up in Job. What was held onto as ultimate truth, the dominant Covenantal motif that became particularly rigidified amongst some in postexilic Israel as can be read in the books of the Deuteronomistic History and in later redactions to some of the prophets and in Ezra–Nehemiah, crumbles in Job. What is challenged is the notion that obedience connotes reward. What is ultimately proffered is that God acts *hinnäm*, without cause, not in response to obedience or disobedience, and thus is able to withstand the entire range of human experiences, good and bad, without destroying the bad or rewarding the good.[24] In this way the story of Job becomes a counter-story by its willingness to engage the deep pain of disillusion, the disillusionment that accompanied a collapse of what was once held onto for survival, and to sit in the gap in which the hinge door of evil opened.

The gap, the place of madness wherein one feels she is falling into pieces, dissolving or disintegrating, facing her own complex and seeing it for a complex as opposed to truth can be utterly terrifying as one can feel all she ever knew and cherished is false.[25] Yet, sitting in the gap can open up new space, space for living and living creatively. Forced to reckon with the disillusion of the felt good (through the atrocity of the Exile) as known

23. Ibid., 20.

24. A view proffered originally by Cooper as discussed in chapter 6 above.

25. Ulanov, 50–53.

in the Deuteronomic Covenant, the story of Job hovers over the place of madness, and the character of Job brings with him a new perspective, and hence a new path gets ignited in relation to the Deuteronomistic History or the dominant history held within the historical books of the canon.

Robert C. Dysktra, a professor of Pastoral Theology at Princeton Theological Seminary recently published a beautiful article in which he describes his notion of *linguistic body-blocking*.[26] Dykstra writes specifically for a modern community regarding the repression of affect in development and the impact of shame upon one's natural and instinctual thoughts and questions. He urges the Church toward *Unrepressing the Kingdom* (the title of his article). His argument is helpful here as well and helps further the current point. He describes *linguist body-blocking* as distracting the child (or grown up) from the developing individual's natural inquiry and curiosity due to another's maintenance of certain social cues and fear of them being trespassed. He maintains, based on his use of psychoanalytic theorists Michael Billig[27] and Adam Philips,[28] that this distraction shames the individual and linguistically blocks the individual from her natural feelings, desires, and interests just as in body-blocking when a parent physically blocks the child from seeing something the child is naturally curious about.

He gives a profound example of a social experiment conducted by *Washington Post* journalist Gene Weingarten by way of introduction. In this experiment Weingarten stationed world-renowned violinist Joshua Bell, who had, three days earlier, filled the house at Boston's Symphony Hall where seats were top dollar, in jeans and a ball cap playing selections such as Schubert's most captivating "Ave Maria" on his $3.5 million Stradivarius, in L'Enfant Plaza subway station in downtown D.C. Weingarten's experiment was, in his words, one "in context, perceptions and priorities—as well as an unblinking assessment of public taste: In a banal setting at an inconvenient time, would beauty transcend?"[29] Dykstra cites a revealing observation made by Weingarten. When Ave Maria was being played, a preschool aged child who could not help but be captivated by the beauty of the sound, pulled his mother closer and closer to the music. In the mother's rush to go about her busy day, she obscured the child's view from the music in order to distract him, hop the train, and get to work. Dykstra uses this example as a way of introducing the notion of *body-blocking* and its subsequent,

26. Dykstra, "Repressing the Kingdom," 391–409.

27. Billig, *Freudian Repression*.

28. Phillips, *On Balance*.

29. Weingarten, "Pearls before Breakfast"; quoted in Dykstra, "Repressing the Kingdom," 392.

linguistic-blocking, and their relation to shame. In blocking the child from his natural inquiry and desire to hear the music, the mother literally blocked the child from pursuing his interest and continuing his gaze. Dykstra goes on to explain how this kind of blocking occurs not only in bodily movements but linguistically as well. Using Billig and Phillips Dykstra describes how blocking one from her natural curiosity results in shaming the individual or leaving the individual to feel ashamed for her gut reactions, inclinations, and natural inquiries. He ultimately is addressing the Church or religious institutions to be conscious of ways they silence individual's natural questions and curiosities (the kingdom of God within) whether these questions and curiosities have to do with early traumatic experiences, personal or collective, or religious inquiry in general.

Dykstra uses an example of Fredrick Buechner, novelist and Presbyterian minister, in his description of his personal work through his early tragedy of losing his father to suicide and the trauma of his mother never allowing him to speak of it. In therapy, later in life, Buechner was encouraged to write about his early childhood memories with his non-dominant, left hand as a way to gain access to his early experiences of this loss and the questions he was disallowed. Buechner explained that this activity allowed him to remember forgotten parts of his childhood and to "recapture feelings connected with them."[30] In this method, Buechner was not so much accessing actual events, but rather affect and perceptions associated with the events that were never cathected. Through this process a new narrative of the trauma arose. In a sense, he was rewriting the trauma.

Dykstra's ideas and admonitions further Jung's notion of the inferior function, as that part of the personality repressed and lying in the shadows, and Davoine and Guadilliére's discussion of the cut-out unconscious that which was never allowed integration. His modern-day examples are helpful for explaining further the role of the book of Job in light of the Deuteronomic canon. Using Dykstra's analogy, the Deuteronomic Covenant, adapted and adopted in postexilic Israel, linguistically blocks the natural affective experience of the trauma of exile from being integrated into Israel's written history. Continuing with Dykstra's line of thought, Job is written as if from the non-dominant, "left hand,"[31] what Jungian analysts would attribute to the unconscious, which enables the *unthought known* to surface within the canon. When the unthought known is included in consciousness the loss is able to be mourned.[32] The poetic core, as described

---

30. Buechner, *Telling Secrets*, 98; quoted in Dykstra, 397.

31. Ibid.

32. Freud, "Morning and Melancholia."

above, truly accentuates this "non-dominant, left hand" perspective that enables previously cut-out and disallowed perspectives and feelings to be integrated into the story of Israel's history. As was shown in the brief history of interpretation provided in chapter six, scholars continue to circle around prominent themes such as the nature of suffering, the goodness of God, the question of evil—what is it and where does it come from—and retribution theology. All of these point to the fact that one cannot read the book of Job without experiencing dissonance and being forced to, at least momentarily, ponder evil and its ramification.

What is the symbol that is emerging? Furthermore, what is the symbol saying? Through the conglomeration of the various images, words, phrases and dialectical exchanges outlined in chapter 7, there are a multitude of possibilities. One possibility is symbolic death, which is enabled through Individuated Religion as proffered in the symbolic role of the character of Job. The book of Job opens up into the No-thing space where the author does not rush to fill the gap. The hinge of the affect of rage and confusion, the feeling of being threatened that the poetry makes space for allows, perhaps forces, readers to plunge into this experience. However, while the author does not rush to fill the gap, something emerges nonetheless. Perhaps the symbol that emerges simply serves as the inferior function, the desire and rage disallowed by the dominant narrative. The hope in the national History is always for return, never for dissolution. Through the book, Job pleads with God, not only for God to show up and contend with Job, but also for Job to be allowed to die, forever. He complains that he is surrounded, hemmed in, by God, in a reversal of Psalm 139, there is no where he can go from God's presence, nowhere he can hide. Rather than being comforted by this reality, Job feels it as agonizingly painful. Job cannot escape God's watchful eye that seems to scrutinize even the most diligently obedient life. Job speaks for the regressive function, the dark side of the Covenant, the side that grapples with the unjustifiable intrusion of evil. What we read in Job is not the dark side of God as has been proffered by some, but rather, the shadow side of the symbol of the Covenant.[33]

Jung in his "Answer to Job," contends how Job's confrontation of God awakens the unconscious God who, by the nature of being an unconscious entity, was amoral and did not yet have an understanding of life afforded by the work of consciousness. By imaging God as unconscious Jung places the bad that happens to Job and evil in general in God, the one who created from the place of the amoral unconsciousness rather than from differentiated consciousness. He argues it is God's encounter with Job that finally urges

---

33. Jung, *Psychology and Religion*, ¶¶553–758.

God to become incarnate, human, and thus conscious through the figure of Christ. I find Jung's analysis of Job to be deeply personal and subjective as Jung admits up front that he is not a theologian nor a biblical scholar. He seems to have found a way to process his own experience with his father and his break with Freud.[34] Jung argues that the Book of Job witnesses Adonai's obsession with faithfulness (*tam*) though ironically it is Adonai's faithlessness that is the mutative agent within the book. I contend that it was not Adonai's obsession with faithfulness but a worldview born out of the Covenant and deeply entrenched within postexilic Israel that imaged God as the angry vassal lord who hid his face from Israel due to Israel's disobedience. Therefore, what emerges is not a change within God but a change in the image of God portrayed by the Israelites.

Where Covenant Religion within the national History upholds the notion of blamelessness—one can be blameless if he follows *seper-hatorah*, ensuring God's goodness and blessings upon him—the book of Job dismantles this vision of good by ushering in evil, which forces its deconstruction. The evil of the trauma that blew in from out of nowhere and destroyed Job's life and led him to reevaluate his understanding of what was right and good, that in which the Covenant Religion had instructed him. To turn once again to Winnicott on transitional objects, the fictional quality of the book of Job frees the Covenant to be used, once again, as an object that could help Israel come to terms with the objective reality of the Exile as an atrocious evil that happened to them *hinnäm*, without cause—not due to their own evil or disobedience. Freeing the Covenant from its rigid constraints as a consequence of exilic and postexilic redactions allowed Israel to place the Covenant outside of their subjective experience. As Winnicott says, when one is able to place an object outside of one's projections one, in a sense, destroys the object and *vice versa*. When one destroys an object (in fantasy) one places the object outside of herself, establishing its externality, making the object real. Winnicott describes the sequence as follows:

1. Subject relates to object.

2. Object is in process of being found instead of placed by the subject in the world.

3. Subject destroys object.

4. Object survives destruction.

5. Subject can use object.[35]

34. Stein, *Jung's Treatment of* Christianity, 165.

35. Winnicott, *Playing and Reality*, 120–21.

He goes on to say, "The object is always being destroyed. This destruction becomes the unconscious backcloth for love of a real object; that is, an object outside the area of the subject's omnipotent control."[36]

The story of Job takes up the symbol of the Covenant, and in fantasy (through its poetic imagery), destroys it. Yet, the Covenant survives Job's destruction of it, as is portrayed in the God speeches and the final prosaic conclusion wherein Job is affirmed for his willingness to confront God directly, which allows the object to be placed outside of Job's (Israel's) subjective experience of it making it useful once again, useful for relating to that which was beyond them and greater than their experiences. Once the stage of object usage is reached, "projective mechanisms assist in the act of noticing what is there, but they are not the reason why the object is there."[37] The Covenant, surviving Job's destruction of it, is now able to be regarded as an object in its own right and used as a means toward greater recognition—of Israel in relation to others and in relation to the Divine. Now the Covenant can be used as a resource, a symbol pointing to the Divine outside of and not bound by the Covenant and thus not bound to Israel's actions of obedience or disobedience. The Covenant's survival provides Israel the ability to use the Covenant as an objective object that helps Israel relate to one another and to the Divine as an objective other outside of Israel's subjective experience of God.

By picturing Job as *tam*, blameless/finished, Job embodies the cutout, affective experience of Israel in Exile. In maintaining his *tumma* Job is portrayed as the one character in the book whose anger, aggression, and relentlessness evokes a response from God face-to-face. Not only is it the evil that befell Job, it was Job's own evil. By this I mean his trespass of the Covenant by arguing for his *tammim* and denying his responsibility for the evil that befell him. This defiance allowed for the *new* to enter. The new is in part a renewal of the old that is the Covenant. In the end of the book Job still made sacrifices on behalf of others, though not because the others were disobedient to the Covenant but instead because they did not speak what was right about God. However, the new is also a new god-image, an image of *hinnäm*, a God that acts without cause, not in response to obedience or disobedience, but on behalf of and in spite of the *tam* and *rasha* alike. This God imaged is one beyond the confines of the Covenant and yet, the Covenant still serves Israel as a means through which they can be in relationship with this God.

---

36. Ibid., 126.
37. Ibid., 121.

I contend, Job is able to make the sacrifices at the end of the story, because of his confrontation with his own evil at transgressing the Covenant. What was felt to be evil, namely Job's refusal to take the blame for the confounding events of trauma, is integrated in the character of Job. In amalgamating his pain, anger, desire, and resistance, upholding the eradicated experiences of the trauma of the Exile in the life of Israel the story of Job allows Israel to mourn the confounding experience of exile that the dominant History previously silenced.

9

Reimagining in Order to Reimage God

An Application for Today

We need stories in order to live.

—Joan Didion

Anyone who has had a family member or friend die at a young age from cancer or a tragic accident, lost a baby before she was born or at birth, lived in a war-torn ghetto or in the country responsible for unnecessary bombings, or worked as a Chaplain in a hospital and seen the complete randomness of death, loss, and tragedy that befalls those that work hard to live perfectly healthy and safe does not question how a story like Job is constructed and canonized as sacred text. The randomness of tragedy is not a modern epidemic and the quandary of the order of the universe, the nature of suffering, the questions of whether or not there is a God attentive and attuned to such tragedies are not new questions. As you can read, from early Jewish and Christian writers to those today, these questions continue to surface when one picks up the book of Job. There are as many answers to these questions as there are people who ask them. It is my hope that in articulating this new perspective, specifically related to the life of ancient Israel and the concept of history making and history telling within the Hebrew canon, one might find a new lens into these questions that affect all of humanity.

The book of Job opens into the gap, the No-thing space, wherein the dominant history of Israel, based on Covenant ideology formulated in Deuteronomy, itself experiences a symbolic death, the death of the symbol of the Covenant as it was imaged in the national narrative and purported to make sense of the trauma of exile by blaming it on Israel's disobedience. The character of Job, as the symbol of Israel, is thrust into the gap after the atrocities befell him and he remains in the gap for the majority of the book. Through the book's poetic core Job's affect enables him to voice the pain of such devastating loss, reject responsibility for such circumstances, and ultimately to confront Adonai for the wrath Job incurred that his friends contend is a result of his disobedience. Yet, it is Job's ability to integrate such affect, voice it, and give it space that allows him to experience a reality beyond the symbol of the Covenant. At the end of the book's poetic core Adonai shows up and speaks to Job, in the same poetic way in which the narrator chose to portray Job. God's speech conjures images of creation that remind the listener and the reader today of a larger reality that surpasses the symbols we construct to make meaning of suffering, meaning that enables growth and identification. Rather than interpreting God's appearance and the Divine speeches as a further shaming of Job, wherein one conjectures their meaning was to silence Job, I contend God's words assure Israel that Adonai can and does survive the deconstruction of the reigning interpretation of the Covenant and sees Israel in the midst of the devastating experience of exile and the arduous process of reconstructing meaning.

This very process of deconstruction, which calls for a re-imagining of Israel, Adonai, and history as it is constructed in the national narrative formulated in the biblical books of Joshua—Kings, rather than rendering the covenant inadequate, presented Israel with another way to engage with the reality beyond the Covenant. This other way that freed the Covenant from its dogmatistic renderings, recognized God's actions *hinnäm*, without cause, and allowed Israel to grapple with a reality beyond the Covenant, a reality where God acts and creates in the world, without cause, meaning, not in response to obedience or disobedience. This new image of God, though admittedly sounding somewhat grim, allows Israel, and those who are in relationship with these sacred texts today, to recognize the Divine, and the symbol of the Covenant, as objective others, not as subjective objects that one creates remaining bound to the subject by way of his actions and experiences.

The book of Job emerges in the space between Israel and the experience of exile, between Israel and Israel's Covenantal image of God, as an object that allows Israel to destroy the codified beliefs of retribution inscribed within the Covenant Religion and thus the Covenantal history. Winnicott describes the work of destruction within the intermediate space between subject and object, early on the space between baby and mothering-one, as the transformative process that establishes external reality for the subject. As Winnicott says, the transition from object-relating to object-usage is the ability for the subject to say, in a sense, "'I destroyed you . . . and the object is there to receive the communication. From now on the subject says to the object: 'I destroyed you.' 'I love you.' 'You have value for me because of your survival of my destruction of you.' 'While I am loving you, I am all the time destroying you in (unconscious) fantasy. Here fantasy begins for the individual. The subject can now use the object that has survived . . . and is now placed outside of the area of omnipotent control."[1] In this sense, the book of Job functions to enable Israel to loosen the Covenant from its subjective tangle of projection and identification and places it in the world of external reality. What this does in relation to the national History and for the Hebrew canon as a whole is it places God outside of Israel's obedience or disobedience and thus frees Israel from the grips of an oppressive and shaming God-image.

This move is vitally relevant and important for those who seek meaning within the sacred texts of the canon regardless of one's religious or belief system. The work of the book of Job is found in how it dismantles our quest for explanations of evil or for innocent suffering, or our desire to find these answers and explanations within ourselves, others, or God. The narrated character of Job does this work for Israel as he confronts God regarding the injustice of his experience and is met by God in a face-to-face encounter through the whirlwind. The encounter does not answer Job's interrogation directly and thus it leaves scholars and readers of the text today in a quandary for how to interpret its message.

I suggest this ambiguous move, the narrator's unwillingness to give a specific or direct answer, provides the new god-image. This new God being imaged is not partial to right action or obedience, is not moved by sacrifice or perfection as in the image proffered in the Covenant, but rather, is a God that sees and holds all beings, all processes, all experiences in view and acts on account of all of creation, without cause, rather than in relation to one aspect of creation alone. This God is not concerned with rigid obedience nor is this God swayed by perfection. The view remains somewhat inconclusive in that there is no person, system, or place wherein one can put the bad. This means that one cannot blame herself, or her neighbor, her children, her partner, her nation, or her God for the evil experienced. The evil in the book of Job simply is. The prologue imagines the evil coming from *hassatan* at the approval of Adonai. However, Adonai of the poetry does not mention *hassatan* and changes the focus entirely. In Adonai's non-answer to the "problem of evil" in the world one is left in the tension of knowing evil exists and yet also knowing the world is much bigger than one's personal picture of it. This view actually changes one's understanding of and relationship to

---

1. Winnicott, *Playing and Reality*, 121. See also Winnicott, *Psychoanalytic Explorations*, 238–40.

evil while simultaneously changing one's understanding of God. The book of Job, read symbolically, allows readers today a way to wrestle with the impossibility of evil, internal and external, knowing God also sees it and knows it and has not caused it to happen as a result of any action nor can God cause it to happen upon others at the bequest of the righteous. Job, read in this way, does not provide a way to escape evil or to rectify it in our present situation. Rather it allows us to acknowledge its reality and to grapple with its impossibility.

Job's relation to postexilic Israel and the story's presence and relation within the Hebrew canon are not the only ideological relationships altered. Just as scholars of the book of Job have inevitably, whether intentionally or not, used Job as a way to argue for or against the goodness of God or the presence of suffering and evil in our world in light of God's goodness and what the faithful person's response ought to be, I also venture to make a statement about the role of Job for faith communities today. I argue the new image being proffered asks for its readers to grapple with God's *hinnām* and thus reckon with the reality of evil within and without. The narrated character of Job personified a communal struggle and thus provided an image for community renewal. So too, any individual today who situates herself in the gap opened up through the book of Job and herself and wrestles with the deconstruction of the symbols, personal and collective, contributes to society. Jung's concept of individuation is precisely this—our personal work toward wholenss contributes to society. It is not merely individualistic or a move toward individualism but rather a move into greater connectedness and community through differentiation and through our personal processes. As Ulanov says, "By restoring our personal life in that space, space is made in the culture itself for self and symbol to be refound or found for the first time."[2]

Reading the Counter-Narrative Today: Implications for Pastoral Theology

What has been argued in this work is an alternative interpretation of the book of Job serving as a symbolic history within the Hebrew canon and its importance for an understanding of the symbol of the Covenant as it is constructed in Deuteronomy and throughout the Deuteronomistic History. However, this is only one possible interpretation. I do not argue that there is only one way to interpret the book of Job, nor is there one meaning. I believe, choosing to read the book of Job as a symbolic history of Israel

2. Ulanov, *Madness and Creativity*, 24.

has, at least, two functions. First, it opens up the foreclosed parts of Israel's history allowing readers of the Hebrew Bible another picture of Israel's history of exile, culminating in the Babylonian Exile of the sixth century BCE. Read as a symbolic history the book of Job does not offer chronological details or any "authorized" version of Israel's history of monarchy, division, economic position in the ancient Near East, or national collapse. Instead, it stands as an archive of the trauma of the Babylonian Exile. As an archive it stands peripherally, but nonetheless beside, the national narrative wherein the symbol of the Covenant collapses into concretized notions of obedience and perfection due to unrecognized and immaterialized affect. By standing beside the national narrative portrayed through the books of Deuteronomy—Kings, Job stands as the inferior function to the Covenant's ruling principle, ultimately serving the Covenant by dismantling its concretized notion of the good. Understood in this way, Job remains in the canon, not as part of the Torah or the history but rather, in the writings, most dominantly understood as wisdom literature. This grants Job, in a sense, a prophetic quality within the Hebrew canon as it contains that which the Covenant left out.[3]

However, this is not the only function of reading Job as a symbolic history. The second function is for reading communities today and that holds implications for pastoral theology. This second function works in at least three specific ways. It allows reading communities to acknowledge and access the presence and reality of evil that comes from outside ourselves that intrudes upon the everyday and interrupts our community's understanding of the good, without the need to explain it away, rationalize its reality, or look for causes. It provides a model for mourning as it is through Job's affect that he is able to access the Divine.[4] It is his affective response of anger and despair (his *own evil* in relation to Covenantal Religion), that causes him to confront Adonai. Further Job's confronting Adonai is counted as truth in the end of the book. Twice in chapter 42 it is God who proclaims Job is the one who spoke what was *right/established* concerning God. Through the character of Job, one is able to see the prospective function of one's own "evil," in trespassing societal norms and inhabiting that which is disallowed by one's community. Grasping such a prospective function enables readers today to place their own stories and methods of (hi)story-making beside the sacred text. Analyzing the ways in which ancient Israel constructed its own history indicates potential ways in which one may construct her own

---

3. Birch, et al., *Theology of the Old Testament*, 381–424.
4. Houck-Loomis, "Good God?!?," 701–8.

history today in order to make sense and meaning out of or simply acknowledge the inexplicable reality of past trauma.

As Fokkelman says, "Biblical poetry is always fiercely emotional, but at the same time it is emotional in such a way that it reaches out for the universal, mostly successfully. Job's fate and his emotions are not strange to us, and the Book of Job explores the extremes for us. And 'we'—we are of all times."[5] The first way in which the book of Job functions for the reading community today is that it acknowledges and accesses the presence and reality of evil that intrudes upon the everyday and interrupts our understanding of the good. Without getting lost in the details of the Job of the prose versus the Job in the poetic core, the fictional narrative is intentionally set up in a way that draws the reader to contemplate why such "bad things happen to good people." Westermann asserts this existential question undergirds the book of Job and that focusing on the "problem" of evil (though it cannot be disputed that the dialogue throughout Job indeed wrestles with this problem) rather than the existential question shifts the focus of the book from lament to disuptation. He argues we must start with the question and the presence of lament that undergirds the book.[6] This is not an unfamiliar question in religious communities nor is Job an unfamiliar book in which one would turn to as a way to contemplate or mourn hardships that befall a person or community.

Reading Job as a symbolic history maintains its symbolic and allegorical nature. This frees the story from being concretized as an actual story about a factual character. As was argued in chapter 2, symbols arise within human consciousness by way of the unconscious, providing a bridge between self and other, or ego and one's larger Self, or one's consciousness and one's lost parts of history eliminated and repressed due to the affective weight of their trauma, between one's self and what is beyond. Understood as a symbol, the story of Job provides readers today a bridge in which to engage an evil that has come upon them or their community, something that has disrupted one's own *going on being*.[7] To acknowledge such evil, without explaining it away by taking on the blame for the events or shunting the blame upon someone else, enables one to access the outrage, despair, and anger associated with evil events falling on one. But by accessing the affect perhaps previously unintegrated one's community is offered the chance to become integrated. This integration is possible due to the gap created between what was previously constructed as the *truth* of one's life or experi-

5. Fokkelman, *Book of Job in Form*, 21.

6. Westermann, *Structure of the Book of Job*, 1–13.

7. Winnicott, *Maturational Processes*, 47–54.

ence and the disruption of that truth. By contemplating the gap opened in the book of Job, a reader or community today reflecting upon her or their own story in conjunction with Job's, is able to trepidatiously traverse the gap because of a felt companionship with the character and story in the text.

Not only does the book of Job allow one to contemplate the consequences of evil that intrude from the outside, without justifying it, but it also allows one to access her own "evil," her shadow, that which remains unintegrated. Integrating these left-out parts of one's personality and being, as is read in the story of Job, allows one to see and thus know God face-to-face. The character of Job acted uncharacteristically for faithful followers of Covenant Religion. Job's friends questioned him time and again about his own wordiness (8:1; 11:2–6; 15:2–3; 18:2). They questioned his assumption of blamelessness (4:7, 17; 11:4; 15:14), his anger and outrage at the injustice felt (15:3–6; 18:3) and his despair, chiding that God would not pervert justice nor would any human being be without wickedness (22:1–3; 25:4). It can be said that Job holds the evil for his community. Traditional wisdom asserted that no mortal was truly just before God and therefore Job's claim of innocence was his folly. Due to the narrator's creativity and willingness, Job transgresses Covenant Religion and maintains his integrity, asserting his innocence and speaking out against God's felt neglect. The ramifications of this for ancient Israel, specifically in terms of how this allowed the pain of exile to be inscribed has already been discussed. However, Job's willingness to transgress the Covenant has yet another function for the reading community today. Job's ability to claim his anger and aggression and use it in relation to his community and his God is an encounter with the national History's and therefore Covenant Religion's inferior function, and relates to that which is felt to be "bad" or perhaps even "evil" in faith communities today. The book of Job thus, not only witnesses to external evil and its ramifications upon the story of Israel's history told in its national Covenantal narrative, but it witnesses to individual and communally constructed evil in our world today and the need for it to be integrated, linked back into the unity of being.

Evil in this way does not have one definition but rather depends upon the human individual and each individual's societal context. For Job, it was his affect experienced through his anger and aggression toward God due to God's initial silence and the Covenant's justification (upheld by Job's friends) for Job's suffering. His resistance to concede to the blame attributed to him and his willingness to testify to God's silence and felt betrayal of their Covenant, in essence—his transgression of Covenant Religion, was Job's personal evil. His protest was considered sin under Covenant Religion as it is articulated and upheld within the Deuteronomistic History. This is not to somehow morally categorize certain actions or circumstances as evil *per se*, but to analyze how our own constructions of good create, in a sense, certain other constructions of evil that we then inhibit ourselves and others from inhabiting. Job's friends considered Job's actions morally outrageous, and were thus able to project their own feelings of anger and aggression upon their friend Job ridding themselves of their own anger at the injustice experienced in their midst (symbolizing Israel's own anger at the injustice of the Exile).

This concept draws us back to what was described as the fourth methodological assumption in chapter 2, that is, the third that comes in the shadow of the fourth. The third is the new that is experienced through the transcendent function, the image or experience that emerges in between inner and outer, subject and object, the symbol that draws the bridge to one's larger more whole Self that includes conscious and unconscious contents. The new that emerges is the new image of God, and thus a new relationship that comes by way of the shadow. As Ulanov expounds, "The transcendent function is a natural psychic process of going back and forth between opposites to create a third out of the two."[8] In the work being described here, the transcendent function can be understood on two different levels. First, one can understand the dialectical relationship between the book of Job and the Deuteronomistic History or Individuated Religion and Covenant Religion. Understood in this way, neither history (the national History of the Deuteronomic Covenant or the symbolic history of Job) trumps the other. Instead, the two remain side by side together in the canon. It is the going back and forth between the two. On the one hand, the story is that of the Deuteronomistic History or Covenant Religion that structures a firm way of living, relying, in part, on internalized shame in order to maintain hope of renewal based on that structure. On the other hand, the story is the story of Job that dismantles this former structure showing its holes and disrupting its foundation. While the book of Job proffers an Individuated Religion in contrast to Covenant Religion, it is not Individuated Religion *per se* that is the new symbol that arises, but the God experienced through Job's own shadow, and thus Israel's shadow.

The new that arises in the dialectical interchange between Covenant Religion and Individuated Religion is a new image of God experienced through the servant Job who is *tam*. God's blameless servant unlike any in all the land is finished or decimated (*tam*) and yet still maintains his integrity (*tammim*), not through ritualistic abidance of the law (Covenant Religion) but through his anger and aggression, which allowed him to access

8. Ulanov, *Unshuttered Heart*, 163.

the Divine, to see God with his eyes, establishing (הַנּוֹכֵנ) something true. That which was established was not a codified belief system that provided assurance for safety, prosperity, or well being based on a particular set of actions or rituals but rather, an experience of God that was beyond that which was imaged in the Covenant. This alternative image of God showed a God that could contain the good and the bad, the disappointment, anger, and aggression, the experience of utter loss and devastation, and not flee from it or provide excuses for such horrible experiences.

In the narrator's choice to include a response from God, a face-to-face exchange, a significant shift is made from Covenant Religion. An individual servant of Adonai dares to address Adonai face-to-face and pleads his innocence. The response given is not decimation as is imagined within the Covenant[9] but a divine encounter. In the encounter Adonai paints a picture of creation that includes the weakest and most vulnerable creatures and the largest, strongest, and most wild creatures side-by-side with the celestial and environmental processes. God speaks to the needs of all of these animals and the awareness of all that goes on within the earthly and heavenly realm. Giving voice to such processes expands the image of God. While Adonai is Israel's God, Adonai is imaged in Job as the creator and sustainer of all the animate and inanimate processes in the universe. This enlarged view of God does not shame Job or put Job "in his place," as others have suggested but rather serves to situate Job, as Israel, as the everyman (*geber*) between the reality and the ideal, between the tension of living in what can feel like the painful reality of now, giving voice to inexplicable evil while assuring that such evil is not deserved and does not go unnoticed but does not necessarily have a resolution either.

Jung finds the third in the spontaneous and creative solution that comes through consciously bearing the tension of the opposites, in the gap-living space. As he says, "The solution, seemingly of its own accord, appears out of nature. Then and then only is it convincing. It is felt as 'grace.' Since the solution proceeds out of the confrontation and clash of opposites, it is usually an unfathomable mixture of conscious and unconscious factors, and therefore a symbol, a coin split into two halves which fit together precisely."[10] Winnicott finds the third in the space between subject and object, between internal and external realities, in the space where objects are found and, in health, eventually used to adapt to external reality. In a

9. One of the consequences for Israel's disobedience in the Deuteronomic Covenant is that God will hide God's face from them (Deut 31:17–18, 32:20). Deut 34:10 suggests that there has not been another prophet since Moses who has known God face-to-face.

10. Jung, *Memories, Dreams and Reflections*, 335.

creative solution, the author(s) of Job picture a man who is blameless and upright yet holds the symbolic value of being utterly destroyed regardless of this blamelessness and the way in which he maintains his integrity is through a suspension of his Covenantal rituals. Though he still maintains a relationship with the Covenant, as is imaged in the language utilized throughout the book, it is Job's surrender to his own felt evil, his anger and aggression toward his unjust circumstances, an attitude his community believed to be dangerously wrong in opposition to the usual interpretation per Covenant Religion as the circumstances being a result of sin or disobedience, that allows for a confrontation with God. This confrontation births a new god-image, an image of the expansiveness of the divine, the divine who holds in mind all of creation and is not bound by the subjective confines of the Covenant. Through the book of Job the Covenant becomes an object able to be *used* rather than simply related to, used in the Winnicottian sense as it survived Job's destruction.

The second way in which the transcendent function is at work is through the dialectical interchange between the two and three within the text and the two and the three within the reader or reading community today. By two and three within the text I mean the *two* histories being told through the Deuteronomistic History and the symbolic history in Job and the *third* that arises, the *tam* servant who has a face-to-face encounter with the Divine creator. The ambivalent symbol of representing wholeness and blamelessness on the one hand and decimation or completion on the other hand, portrayed in the character of Job gives rise to this new god-image—an image of expansiveness and *hinnäm*. Similarly, by the two for the reader or the reading community I am referring to the different histories that get constructed as a way of trying to make meaning out of life's difficult circumstances. Often it is the case that we have our own version of a "national narrative." This is the history we tell ourselves, and others, about how we have come to be where we are now. Sometimes these (hi)stories are delicately constructed to mask, or silence, painful parts of one's past or as a way to justify or explain how or why things happened the way in which they did. Other times these (hi)stories are adopted from cultural or communal narratives that are traditionally used as ways to explain the unexplainable or to keep a society or community functioning predictably. These histories are likened to the national narrative read within the Deuteronomistic History explained in the first half of this work.

One of the exercises I do, in my work with graduate students training for ministry, is life-writing/history telling. This is a three-step exercise. First, I have students give a reasonably complete account of their life thus far. Without drawing attention to anything specific I ask them to write a brief account of their life history (in five pages or less); where they have come from, what their growing up was like and how they got to where they are now, their family structure, etc. I think of this assignment as gathering their "national narrative" or formalized history, likened to the DH repeated throughout the historical books of the canon. After they turn in this assignment, I have them recall the most transformative, or *one* of the most transformative, moments in their life. I have them journal briefly about this during class time and then ask them to write a more formal account of this event to turn in. I ask that this account include as much detail as possible, the sensory and affective surround and a timeline of events. The paper is turned in, in narrative form. The purpose of this second exercise is to ask the previous question in a different way to see what response it evokes. For many, the transformative moment did not make it into their "history," or it was glossed over by the more dominant aspects of their "history." The work of articulating this moment serves to reconnect the affect of the experience. The third and final assignment is another "history" of their life, this time including the details of the transformative moment, as best as can be remembered and the before and after of said event. There is flexibility with the final assignment in terms of its form. Students are allowed to be as creative as they wish and can choose to perform a musical piece, creative writing, poetry, visual art or any other medium through which they wish to tell their history. This practical exercise is meant to parallel the two histories I posit can be read within the canon in order to show the nuances of the two more clearly and personally. The final assignment is essentially a rearticulation of the first assignment but the two "histories" can be looked at and analyzed for what was missing in the first, and how the second gives a new picture of one's own image of Self, one's view of others within her life, and her image of God. The final assignment is meant to parallel the way I imagine Job was written, as a symbolic history that included the felt experience of the Exile, which made way for a god-image that re-enlivened the Covenantal image of God.

Spreading this writing exercise out over the course of the semester, while pairing it with readings from Deuteronomy and Job, trauma literature, and discussions on the symbolic value of history-making, my hope is slowly to bring consciousness to ways in which we *make* history as a means of coping with or covering over painful moments of our past. Here is the *two* within the modern-day reader or reading community, the official "history" and the unofficial subjective history, the stories or the affective experiences to these stories, that often get left in the shadows. The third that comes in arises between the reader's two histories (the "national History" as the first history told in the beginning of class and the second history or "symbolic history" told after time was spent contemplating and articulating a radically transformative experience) which is possible by placing the biblical stories next to the reader's stories, forming yet another *two*. The third that comes is unique to each reader and it comes through the shadow of that which has been left out.

As Jung writes and Ulanov expounds, the third is only experienced through the shadow of the fourth. Ulanov believes that, "Our work personally and collectively . . . is sorting out the fourth that engineers the third wherein healing locates. For all the stuff, the *materia prima* that does not get included in conscious living, bundles into the fourth. Just as we cannot find the healing third except in the shadow of the fourth, we cannot get to the fourth without going through the shadow of undifferentiated life stuff lying in the unconscious."[11] As stated before, we find in the fourth, all that we consider bad or evil, that which seeks to dismantle our ideas of the good.[12] We find the inferior function, or the regressive personality, and it is precisely this part of the personality that ushers in the process of individuation and an experience with that which is beyond our religious and moral structures.[13] The book of Job holds the fourth for the Hebrew canon as it contains that which was left out of the Deuteronomic Covenant, namely, anger, aggression, passion, and a refusal to accept blame for the atrocities that had come upon him and thus makes way for an experience with the third, the image that transcends.

When placing one's own story in relationship to the story(*ies*) within the biblical canon we are brought into relationship with our own shadow. Jung states, "The clash, which is at first of a purely personal nature, is soon followed by the insight that the subjective conflict is only a single instance of the universal clash of opposites."[14] That is, the gift of the sacred texts of the Hebrew canon and in particular the inclusion of both the Deuteronomic and Joban portrayal of God is that they are revealed to contain the opposites without eradicating either one, i.e. Covenant Religion and Individuated Religion, the god of the national (Deuteronomistic) history and the god of the book of Job, and ultimately, good and evil. In maintaining the tension of these opposites, the canon itself elicits the third. Ulanov reminds that, "the third reveals the larger fourth, emerges from the fourth, is sponsored by the fourth."[15] By the

11. Ulanov, *Unshuttered Heart*, 169.

12. Jung, *Psychology and Alchemy*, ¶¶123, 297; Ulanov, *Unshuttered Heart*, 170.

13. Jung, *Psychology and Alchemy*, ¶192; Ulanov, *Feminine in Jungian Psychology*, 144; Ulanov, *Unshuttered Heart*, 170.

14. Jung, *Memories, Dreams, and Reflections*, 335.

15. Ulanov, *Unshuttered Heart*, 167.

canon containing such stories as Job, and other stories, which include affect and actions traditionally (which varies of course based on the particularities of different traditions) seen as bad or wrong or are placed in any familiar human experience and struggle, it (the text) holds the fourth for the reader and reading community until it is able to be integrated.

Ulanov believes this is our work now, collectively and personally. We find the fourth in what we consider destructive, evil, any fundamentalist or dogmatistic approach that falls into a kind of split way of thinking and being. In splitting, one maintains the idea of the good for one's self, thinking she can get rid of the bad which is then thrown onto another individual or entire community where it can be killed off in order to secure one's identification with the good. This kind of splitting happens throughout the Hebrew canon as various communities (Hittites, Girgashites, Amorites, Amalekites, Canaanites, Perizzites, Hivites and Jebusites), Israel's own community (particularly the Kings of the North and the Southern King, Manasseh), and, at times, God (parts of Lamentations and Job) are scapegoated with the bad. The national narrative in the historical books of the canon maintains a story that encourages Israel to rid the community of the bad and thus inherit the land and all the blessings promised in the Covenant, Israel's symbol of the good.

The fourth is the grist of our complexes. It is the undifferentiated material that lies in the unconscious and thrusts itself into daily living unexpectedly.[16] The fourth is that which does not align with our individual and communal ideals of the good and thus is repressed and thrust onto others leading us to relate to others through projective identification, projecting aspects of our self upon others and then identifying with these projections of ours in others as if they really belong to them, when it actually belongs to us. Unconsciously, we then see and relate to others for the bit of evil that they hold for us, and thus we hate and demonize them and try to control them or to rid them of this bad that we have not held within our own self. Lying in the shadows, it is not allowed light to grow and become integrated, thus it remains regressed and stunted.

However, there is another function of the fourth—the constructive and protective function. Ulanov reminds us of the "necessity of growth beginning in the dark."[17] She speaks of the role of the analyst at moments when the analyst holds something of the patient in the shadows, rather than impinging upon the analysand's process by offering interpretations too soon. In this way, the grist of the analysand is protected and held until she is ready and able

---

16. Jung, "Autonomy of the Unconscious," in *Psychology and Religion*, ¶155.
17. Ulanov, *Unshuttered Heart*, 175.

for integration.[18] Developing a relationship with this grist brings freedom from the grip of complexes that enslave us into certain ideas of the good and perpetuate scapegoating of the bad.[19] This is the gift of our sacred texts. They contain the opposites, do not provide easy answers or simplified solutions, muck up our tightly held notions of right and wrong or good and bad and they show us alternative ways to engage. Through the grist, one learns to engage through his inferior function, his non-dominant hand. In this way, he is brought back into relationship with parts of his self, his experience of his past and his experience of the present, which while remaining un-integrated gathered energy bound to the unconscious complex.

Reading Job as a symbolic history enables readers to contemplate their own ways of constructing histories out of which they construct identity and ways of being in relationship with others. This is a dialectical process where by engaging with the book of Job in this symbolic way one may be able to get linked back to one's own experience of trauma or experiences of loss and pain that were thrown out of consciousness due to the severity of pain they caused or the disruption to one's conscious way of living. The link is provided symbolically, opening up more space to engage allowing for the ability to cathect once again due to the availability of affective energy with which to utilize. By contemplating the evil Job experienced and Job's own ability to hold the evil, what was felt to be evil by the dominant narrative, namely denying responsibility and crying out in anger and disappointment, the book of Job is the hinge into evil that allows readers today a portal into evil's reality and its ineffability. It keeps evil present disallowing reading communities from denying its presence and impact upon the everyday. It also reminds us we are not void of the evil ourselves and in fact shows the prospective and useful function of evil for depth, growth, and wholeness. Not only does reading Job in this way allow us to contemplate our own evil and the reality of evil in the world, but also it is through one's engagement with the contents of the fourth that the new arises, and the new that arises in Job is an image of a face-to-face encounter with one's Divine creator. This kind of encounter, excluded from Covenant Religion due to Israel's disobedience (Deut 31:17–18, 32:20), established a new way of imaging God and a new way of imaging the Self (and community) in relation to the Divine. As stated above, this new god-image is one that can hold the reality of evil without placing the blame upon anyone else or taking the blame personally, it is an image that maintains ambivalence and the vastness of human experience, acting on account of all of creation *hinnäm*, without cause.

---

18. Ibid., 175.

19. Ulanov, *Spirit in Jung*, 57–60.

Finally, reading the book of Job as a symbolic history, as a counter-narrative to Covenant Religion that arises through Job's Individuated Religion, makes space for destruction and thus an experience with reality, outside of one's subjectivity. It is precisely the Covenant's ability to withstand Job's destruction of it that places it outside of Job's; i.e., Israel's, subjectivity, and thus allows it to become a resource for living.[20] Through Individuated Religion, proffered in the book of Job, Job deconstructs the Deuteronomic Covenant and the tenets of Covenant Religion founded upon the *paraenesis* of the blessings and curses that were originally adopted from ANE vassal treaties and loyalty oaths used as a way of constructing identity and making meaning through the turmoil of national development and its later collapse. It was precisely that which was viewed as evil, namely aggression and destruction, that allowed the Covenant, and as a result, God, to survive, to be placed outside of Israel's subjective experience and be used once again as a resource for living. This new that arises through Job's story is a vision of God that is beyond Israel's, and therefore beyond our own, subjective experience of this God—a God that acts *hinnäm*, without cause, irrespective of creation.

In the epilogue, Job continues to make sacrifices out of piety. However, his sacrifices at the end are on behalf of his friends' piety rather than on his own. It is because of the new god-image that emerges in the end of the book of Job that enables Job to become the intercessor for his friends. Because of his willingness to wrestle with the Covenant, Job was brought into relationship with his own unconscious material, the complex of *tam* or perfectionism/blamelessness before it included aggression and anger. By going through the shadow of the fourth, the book of Job makes room for the third, the new thing that is the transcendent not bound by the Covenant, the Divine creator who acts without cause. In the book of Job, Adonai is not *the* Covenant but is placed, once again, outside of and beyond the Covenant. Through Job's aggression, desire, and refusal to accept blame, Job established a new way of relating to Adonai without abandoning the former symbol of the Covenant but by creating space between Adonai and the Covenant thus reminding postexilic Israel of the vastness and ineffability of Adonai. Therefore, Adonai makes Job the intercessor for others.

In this way, the book of Job, read as a symbolic history, serves as a resource for faith communities today in both content and process. The book itself contains our own foreclosed parts of history. In the author's willingness to situate Job hovering in the abyss opened up by the traumatic events in the prologue, the author opens the hinge door of evil through which postexilic Israel, and readers and reading communities since then, are brought back

---

20. Winnicott, *Playing and Reality*, 120–27.

into relationship with that which is cut off and thrust onto others and put outside of consciousness. The book of Job, and its relation to the Hebrew canon, read as a counter-text, challenges faith communities today to evaluate ways in which their ruling principle (dogma, liturgies, dominant scriptural interpretations, etc.) dominates congregational life, linguistically blocking peoples' expressions that do not align. The questions that arise, for faith communities, out of this study are: How do we make room for alternative (hi)stories? What are ways in which faith communities can be containers for the good *and* the bad, maintaining a relationship with what is felt to be evil, both external and internal, so as not to thrust it upon other individuals, groups or entire nations? How do our liturgies and dominant theologies disallow other voices or experiences of God? Finally, how can faith communities utilize sacred texts, and the histories behind them, in order to creatively re-imagine the Reality that is beyond their symbols?

The new image of God that emerges in the book of Job is not bound by creed, nationality, or personal experience but rather images God as one who acts without cause, meaning, one whose actions are not dependent upon one's beliefs, rituals, obedience or disobedience. This image of God is not a God who turns God's face away due to aggression, or felt rebelliousness or disobedience, but remains present amidst horrific evils, sees them and the suffering, and still maintains a perspective that is larger than the evil experienced. From direct encounter, God meets us in our experience, in all of our reactions to calamity. This new image stands beside the God imaged in the Covenant, not as a replacement God but as another image of God, another source through which ancient Israel made sense out of their experiences in exile. This alternative god-image in the book of Job frees the Covenant from the confines of its conditionality. Rather than God being swayed by our obedience or disobedience, personal or collective, God's actions are not correlated with our actions and therefore cannot be measured according to human understanding. However, and more importantly, the Joban god-image reveals a God willing to show up in the midst of human experience to witness the pain, the horror, and the joys—the vicissitudes of human experience.

As I have mentioned throughout, it is not that Individuated Religion, offered in the book of Job, replaces Covenant Religion or stands above it, but rather it is the existence of both narratives that enables the Hebrew canon, with its polyphonic voices, to remain a living symbol. In its ability to hold the, often, jarring tensions and ambiguities it remains alive and available for the plethora of human experiences. At any given time, an individual or a community or one part of an individual or community may need the kind of ordering god-image that promises restoration and salvation should one live obediently. At times, we may need to blame others, or ourselves, in order to make meaning and find resolution for harm done. At other times, one may need to question this conditionality that has provided meaning and order. What the god-image of Individuated Religion offers is a way to step outside of collective expectations; ways of living that have become rigidified due to a cultural complex. By offering multiple god-images and histories that include different experiences and varying affects the Hebrew canon holds the tensions that sometimes we cannot. Ultimately it does not offer a linear or even teleological perspective but rather remains alive due to the canon's ability to contain the opposites, as shown in Covenant and Individuated Religions addressed in this work, and thus it can stand with and for us throughout the range of human experience.

Bibliography

Albertz, Rainer. *A History of Israelite Religion in the Old Testament Period.* Vol. 1. Translated by John Bowden. OTL. Louisville: Westminster John Knox, 1992.

————. *Israel In Exile: The History and Literature of the Sixth Century B.C.E.* Studies in Biblical Literature 3. Atlanta: SBL, 2003.

————. "Foreword." In *Interpreting Exile: Displacement and Deportation in Biblical and Modern Contexts,* edited by Brad E. Kelle et al., 2–5. SBL Ancient Israel and Its Literature 10. Leiden: Brill, 2012.

Albrekston, Bertil. *History and the Gods: An Essay on the Idea of Historical Events as Divine Manifestations in the Ancient Near East and in Israel.* Coniectanea biblica: Old Testament Series 1. Lund: Gleerup, 1967.

Albright, William F. *The Archaeology of Palestine.* Harmondsworth, UK: Pelican, 1960.

Alter, Robert, and Frank Kermode, eds. *The Literary Guide to the Bible.* Cambridge, MA: Belknap, 1987.

Arav, R. "Bethsaida Excavations: Preliminary Report, 1994-96." *Bethsaida: A City by the Shore of the Sea of Galilee.* Vol. 2, *Bethsaida Excavations Project: Reports & Contextual Studies,* edited by Rami Arav and Richard Freund, 1–110. Kirksville, MO: Truman State University Press, 1999.

Bakan, David. *Disease, Pain and Sacrifice: Toward a Psychology of Suffering.* Boston: Beacon, 1971.

Bakhtin, Mikhail. *Problems of Dostoevsky's Poetics.* Edited and translated by C. Emerson. Theory and History of Literature 8. Minneapolis: University of Minnesota Press, 1984.

Barry, Peter. *Beginning Theory: An Introduction to Literary and Cultural Theory.* 3rd ed. Beginnings. Manchester: Manchester University Press, 2009.

Baskin, Judith R. *Pharaoh's Counsellors: Job, Jethro, and Balaam in Rabbinic and Patristic Tradition.* Brown Judaic Studies 47. Chico, CA: Scholars, 1983.

————. "Rabbinic Interpretations of Job." In *The Voice from the Whirlwind: Interpreting the Book of Job,* edited by Leo G. Perdue and W. Clark Gilpin, 101–10. Nashville: Abingdon, 1992.

Bender, Thomas, ed. *Rethinking American History in a Global Age.* Berkeley: University of California Press, 2002.

Benjamin, Jessica. *The Bonds of Love: Psychoanalysis, Feminism, and the Problem of Domination.* New York: Pantheon, 1988.

————. *Shadow of the Other: Intersubjectivity and Gender in Psychoanalysis.* New York: Routledge, 1998.

Berne-DeGear, Lizzie. "Revisiting Texts of Tension: A Method of Interpretation for Scripture Scholars." Personal copy.

Berquist, Jon L. *Judaism in Persia's Shadow: A Social and Historical Approach.* 1995. Reprint, Eugene, OR: Wipf & Stock, 2003.

Billig, Michael. *Freudian Repression: Conversation Creating the Unconscious.* Cambridge: Cambridge University Press, 1999.

Birch, Bruce C., et al. *A Theology of the Old Testament.* Nashville: Abingdon, 1999.

Blake, William. *Blake's Job: William Blake's Illustrations of the Book of Job with an Introduction and Commentary by S. Foster Damon.* Hanover, NH: University Press of New England, 1982.

Blenkinsopp, Joseph. "The Bible, Archaeology and Politics; or The Empty Land Myth Revisited." *JSOT* 27 (2002) 169–87.

———. "The Narrative in Genesis–Numbers." In *Those Elusive Deuteronomists: The Phenomenon of Pan-Deuteronomism,* edited by Linda S. Schearing and Steven L. McKenzie, 84–115. JSOTSup 268. Sheffield: Sheffield Academic, 1999.

Bollas, Christopher. *The Shadow of the Object: Psychoanalysis of the Unthought Known.* New York: Columbia University Press, 1987.

Brown, William P. *Character in Crisis: A Fresh Approach to the Wisdom Literature of the Old Testament.* Grand Rapids: Eerdmans, 1996.

Budde, Karl. *Das Buch Hiob übersetzt und erklärt.* 2nd ed. Göttinger Handkommentar zum Alten Testament. Göttingen: Vandenhoeck & Ruprecht, 1913.

Buechner, Frederick. *Telling Secrets.* 1991. Reprint, New York: HarperOne, 2000.

Burrell, David B. *Deconstructing Theodicy: Why Job Has Nothing to Say to the Puzzle of Suffering.* Grand Rapids: Brazos, 2008.

Buttenwieser, Moses. *The Book of Job.* London: Hodder & Stoughton, 1922.

Carr, David M. *An Introduction to the Old Testament.* Oxford: Wiley-Blackwell, 2010.

———. *The Formation of the Hebrew Bible: A New Reconstruction.* New York: Oxford University Press, 2011.

Carroll, Robert P. "Exile! What Exile? Deportation and the Discourses of Diaspora." In *Leading Captivity Captive: 'The Exile' as History and Ideology,* edited by Lester L. Grabbe, 62–79. JSOTSup 278. Sheffield: Sheffield Academic, 2001.

———. "The Myth of the Empty Land." *Semeia* 59 (1992) 79–93.

Cassirer, Ernst. *Language and Myth.* Translated by Susanne K. Langer. New York: Dover, 1946.

Christensen, Duane L. *Deuteronomy 21:10—34:12.* WBC 6B. Nashville: Nelson, 2002.

Clements, R. E. *God's Chosen People: A Theological Interpretation of the Book of Deuteronomy.* Valley Forge, PA: Judson, 1969.

Clines, David J. A. "Deconstructing the Book of Job." In *The Bible as Rhetoric: Studies in Biblical Persuasion and Credibility,* edited by Martin Warner, 65–80. Warwick Studies in Philosophy and Literature. New York: Routledge, 1990.

———. *Job 1–20.* WBC 17. Dallas: Word, 1989.

———. *The Theme of the Pentateuch.* JSOTSup 10. Sheffield: JSOT Press, 1978.

Cogan, Mordechai, and Hayim Tadmor. *II Kings: A New Translation with Introduction and Commentary.* AB 11. New York: Doubleday, 1988.

Coggins, Richard. "What Does 'Deuteronomistic' Mean?" In *Those Elusive Deuteronomists: The Phenomenon of Pan-Deuteronomism,* edited by Linda S. Schearing and Steven L. McKenzie, 22–35. JSOTSup 268. Sheffield: Sheffield Academic, 1999.

Coles, Prophecy. *The Uninvited Guest from the Unremembered Past: Exploration of the Unconscious Transmission of Trauma across the Generations.* London: Karnac, 2011.

Cooper, Alan. "Reading and Misreading the Prologue to Job." *JSOT* 46 (1990) 67–79.

———. "Narrative Theory and the Book of Job." *Studies in Religion/Sciences Religieuses* 11 1 (1982) 35–44.

Cooper, Alan, and Bernard R. Goldstein. "Cult of the Dead and Reentry into the Land." *Biblical Interpretation* 1 (1993) 285–303.

Craigie, Peter C. *The Book of Deuteronomy.* New International Commentary on the Old Testament. Grand Rapids: Eerdmans, 1976.

Cross, Frank Moore. "The Themes of the Book of Kings and the Structure of the Deuteronomistic History." In *Canaanite Myth and Hebrew Epic: Essays in the History of the Religion of Israel,* 174–89. Cambridge: Harvard University Press, 1973.

Curtis, J. B. "On Job's Response to Yahweh." *JBL* 98 (1979) 497–511.

Cvetkovich, Ann. *An Archive of Feelings: Trauma, Sexuality, and Lesbian Public Cultures.* Durham: Duke University Press, 2003.

Davoine, Fançoise, and Jean-Max Guadilliére. *History beyond Trauma.* Translated by Susan Fairfield. New York: Other Press, 2004.

Davies, Phillip. R. "Exile? What Exile? Whose Exile?" In *Leading Captivity Captive: 'The Exile' as History and Ideology,* edited by Lester L. Grabbe, 128–. JSOTSup 278. Sheffield: Sheffield Academic, 1998.

———. *In Search of 'Ancient Israel.'* JSOTSup 148. Sheffield: JSOT Press, 1992.

Dell, Katharine. *The Book of Job as Skeptical Literature.* BZAW 197. Berlin: Gruyter, 1991.

Dhorme, Edouard. *A Commentary on the Book of Job.* Translated by H. Knight. London: Nelson, 1967.

Duhm, Bernhard. *Das Buch Hiob.* Die Poetischen und Prophetischen Bücher des Alten Testaments 1. Tübingen: Mohr/Siebeck, 1897.

Dykstra, Robert C. "Unrepressing the Kingdom: Pastoral Theology as Aesthetic Imagination." *Pastoral Psychology* 61 (2012) 391–409.

Edinger, Edward. *Archetype of the Apocalypse: Divine Vengeance, Terrorism, and the End of the World.* Edited by George R. Elder. Chicago: Open Court, 1999.

———. *The Bible and Psyche: Individuation and Symbolism in the Old Testament.* Toronto: Inner City, 1986.

———. *Transformation of the God-Image: An Elucidation of Jung's Answer to Job.* Toronto: Inner City, 1992.

Evans, R. J. *In Defense of History.* London: Granta, 1997.

Fairbairn, W. R. D. *Psychoanalytic Studies of the Personality.* London: Routledge, 1953.

Fewell, Dana Nolan. "Imagination, Method, and Murder: Un/Framing the Face of Post-Exilic Israel." In *Reading Bibles, Writing Bodies: Identity and the Book,* edited by Timothy Beal and David Gunn, 132–52. London: Routledge, 1997.

Finkelstein, Israel. *The Forgotten Kingdom: The Archaeology and History of Northern Israel.* Ancient Near East Monographs 5. Atlanta: Society of Biblical Literature, 2013.

Fokkelman, Jan P. *The Book of Job in Form: A Literary Translation with Commentary.* Studia Semitica Neerlandica 58. Leiden: Brill, 2012.

Frankena, Rintje. "The Vassal Treaties of Esarhaddon and the Dating of Deuteronomy." *Oudtestamentische Studiën* 14 (1965) 122–54.

Franz, Marie-Louise von. *Interpretation of Fairy Tales*. Rev ed. Boston: Shambhala, 1996.

————. *Projection and Re-collection: Reflections of the Soul*. Translated by William H. Kennedy. Reality of the Psyche Series. La Salle, IL: Open Court, 1995.

Freud, Sigmund. *Beyond the Pleasure Principle*. Translated and Edited by James Strachey. New York: Liveright, 1970.

————. *Future of An Illusion*. Translated by James Strachey. New York: Norton, 1961.

————. "Morning and Melancholia." In *General Psychological Theory*, 161–78. New York: Collier, 1963.

————. *An Outline of Psycho-Analysis*. Translated by James Strachey. Mansfield Centre, CT: Martino, 2011.

————. *Totem and Taboo*. Translated by James Strachey. New York: Norton, 1950.

Frost, Robert. *A Masque of Reason*. New York: Hold, 1945.

Geoghegan, Jeffrey. *The Time, Place, and Purpose of the Deuteronomistic History: The Evidence of 'Until this Day'*. BJS 347. Providence: Brown Judaic Studies, 2006.

Gordis, *The Book of Job: Commentary, New Translation, Special Study*. New York: Jewish Theological Seminary of America, 1978.

Gordon, Avery. *Ghostly Matters: Haunting and the Sociological Imagination*. Minneapolis: University of Minnesota Press, 2008.

Green, Jesse. "The Intelligent Homosexual's Guide to Himself." *New York Magazine*, Oct. 25, 2010.

Habel, Norman C. *The Book of Job: A Commentary*. OTL. Philadelphia: Westminster, 1985.

Halpern, Baruch. *The First Historians: The Hebrew Bible and History*. San Francisco: Harper & Row, 1988.

Henderson, Joseph. "The Cultural Unconscious." *Shadow and Self*. Silmette, IL: Chiron, 1990.

Herman, Judith Lewis. *Trauma and Recovery*. Rev. ed. New York: Basic Books, 1997.

Hillers, Dilbert R. *Lamentations*. AB 7A. New York: Doubleday, 1992.

Hogenson, George B. "Archetypes: Emergence and the Psyche's Deep Structure." In *Analytical Psychology: Contemporary Perspectives in Jungian Analysis*, edited by Joseph Cambray and Linda Carter, 32–55. Advancing Theory in Therapy. New York: Routledge, 2004.

Horsley, Richard A. *Scribes, Visionaries and the Politics of Second Temple Judea*. Louisville: Westminster John Knox, 2007.

Houck-Loomis, Tiffany. "Good God?!? Lamentations as a Model for Mourning the Loss of a Good God." *Journal of Health and Religion* 5 (2012) 701–8.

————. "When Fast-Held God Images Fail to Meet Our Needs: A Psychoanalytic Reading of Job Chapters 6 and 7." *Pastoral Psychology* 64 (2015) 195–203.

Hurvitz, Avi. "The Dating of the Prose-Tale of Job Linguistically Reconsidered." *Harvard Theological Review* 67 (1974) 17–34.

Jacobi, Jolande. *Complex, Archetype, Symbol in the Psychology of C. G. Jung*. London: Routledge, 1959.

Jacobsen, Thorkild. *Treasures of Darkness: A History of Mesopotamian Religion*. New Haven: Yale University Press, 1976.

James, William. *The Varieties of Religious Experience: A Study in Human Nature*. 1902. Reprint, New Hyde Park, NY: University Books, 1963.

Janet, Pierre. *Psychological Healing: A Historical and Clinical Study.* Vol. 1. Translated by Eden Paul and Cedar Paul. London: Allen & Unwin, 1925.

Janzen, David. *The Violent Gift: Trauma's Subversion of the Deuteronomistic History's Narrative.* Library of Hebrew Bible/Old Testament Studies 561. New York: T. & T. Clark, 2012.

Johnson, Timothy Jay. *Now My Eye Sees You: Unveiling An Apocalyptic Job.* Hebrew Bible Monographs 24. Sheffield: Sheffield Phoenix, 2009.

Jung, Carl Gustav. *Aion.* Translated by R. F. C. Hull. Collected Works of C. G. Jung 9 pt. 2. Princeton: Princeton University Press, 1951.

———. *Alchemical Studies.* Translated by R. F. C. Hull. Collected Works of C. G. Jung 13. 2nd ed. Princeton: Princeton University Press, 1968.

———. *Analytical Psychology: Its Theory and Practice. The Tavistock Lectures.* New York: Pantheon, 1968.

———. *The Archetypes and the Collective Unconscious.* Translated by R. F. C. Hull. Collected Works of C. G. Jung 9 pt. 1. 2nd ed. Princeton: Princeton University Press, 1959.

———. *Civilization in Transition.* Translated by R. F. C. Hull. Collected Works of C. G. Jung 10. 2nd ed. Princeton: Princeton University Press, 1970.

———. *Memories, Dreams and Reflections.* Edited by Aniela Jaffé. Translated by Richard and Clara Winston. New York: Pantheon, 1963.

———. *Mysterium Coniunctionis.* Translated by R. F. C. Hull. Collected Works of C. G. Jung 14. 2nd ed. Princeton: Princeton University Press, 1970.

———. *Nietzsche's Zarathustra: Notes of the Seminar Given in 1934–1939.* Vols. 1 and 2. Edited by James Jarrett. Princeton: Princeton University Press, 1988.

———. *The Practice of Psychotherapy.* Translated by R. F. C. Hull. Collected Works of C. G. Jung 16. 2nd ed. Princeton: Princeton University Press, 1966.

———. *Psychiatric Studies.* Translated by R. F. C. Hull. Collected Works of C. G. Jung 1. 2nd ed. Princeton University Press, 1970.

———. *Psychological Types.* Translated by R. F. C. Hull. Collected Works of C. G. Jung 6. 2nd ed. Princeton: Princeton University Press, 1971.

———. *Psychology and Alchemy.* Translated by R. F. C. Hull. Collected Works of C. G. Jung 12. 2nd ed. Princeton: Princeton University Press, 1968.

———. *Psychology and Religion: West and East.* Translated by R. F. C. Hull. Collected Works of C. G. Jung 11. 2nd ed. Princeton: Princeton University Press, 1969.

———. *The Red Book, Liber Novus.* Edited by Sonu Shamdasani. Translated by Mark Kyburz, John Peck, and Sonu Shamdasani. New York: Norton, 2009.

———. *The Structure and Dynamics of the Psyche.* Translated by R. F. C. Hull. Collected Works of C. G. Jung 8. 2nd ed. Princeton: Princeton University Press, 1960.

———. *Symbols of Transformation.* Translated by R. F. C. Hull. Collected Works of Carl G. Jung 5. 2nd ed. Princeton: Princeton University Press, 1956.

Jung, C. G. et al. *Man and His Symbols.* Garden City, NY: Doubleday, 1969.

Kalsched, Donald. *The Inner World of Trauma: Archetypal Defenses of the Personal Spirit.* New York: Routledge, 1996.

Kautzsch, Karl. *Das sogenannte Volksbuch von Hiob und der Ursprung von Hiob cap. I. II. XLII, 7-17: Ein Beitrag zur Frage nach der Integrität des Buches Hiob.* Tübingen: Mohr/Siebeck, 1900.

Kedar-Kopfstein, Benjamin. "תמם, *tamam.*" In *Theological Dictionary of the Old Testament,* edited by G. Johannes Botterweck et al., 15:699–711. Translated by David E. Green. Grand Rapids: Eerdmans, 2006.

Kelle, Brad E. "An Interdisciplinary Approach to the Exile." In *Interpreting Exile: Displacement and Deportation in Biblical and Modern Contexts*, edited by Brad E. Kelle et al, 5–38. Ancient Israel and Its Literature 10. Leiden: Brill, 2012.

Kelle, Brad E. et al., eds. *Interpreting Exile: Displacement and Deportation in Biblical and Modern Contexts*. Ancient Israel and Its Literature 10. Leiden: Brill, 2012.

Kille, Andrew. *Psychological Biblical Criticism*. Guides to Biblical Scholarship. Minneapolis: Fortress, 2001.

Kim, Uriah Y. *Decolonizing Josiah: Toward a Postcolonial Reading of the Deuteronomistic History*. Bible in the Modern World 5. Sheffield: Sheffield Phoenix, 2005.

Klein, Melanie. *Love, Guilt, and Reparation, and Other Works 1921–1945*. Writings of Melanie Klein 1. New York: Free Press, 1975.

———. *Envy and Gratitude & Other Works 1946–1963*. Writings of Melanie Klein 3. International Psycho-analytical Library 104. London: Hogarth Press and the Institute of Psycho-Analysis, 1975.

Klein, Ralph W. *Israel in Exile*. Overtures to Biblical Theology. Philadelphia: Fortress, 1979.

Knoppers, Gary N. "In Search of Postexilic Israel: Samaria after the Fall of the Northern Kingdom." In *In Search of Pre-exilic Israel: Proceedings of the Oxford Old Testament Seminar*, JSOTSup 406, edited by John Day, 150–80. London: T. & T. Clark, 2004.

———. "The Vanishing Solomon: The Disappearance of the United Monarchy from Recent Histories of Ancient Israel." *JBL* 116 (1997) 19–44.

Kristeva, Julia. "In Times Like These, Who Needs Psychoanalysts?" In *New Maladies of the Soul*, 27–44. New York: Columbia University Press, 1995.

Kuhrt, Amelie. *The Ancient Near East, c. 3000–300 BC*. Routledge History of the Ancient World. London: Routledge, 1995.

Lacan, Jacques. *The Language of the Self: The Function of Language in Psychoanalysis*. Translated with commentary by Andrew Wilden. Baltimore: John Hopkins Press, 1968.

Lacocque, André. "The Deconstruction of Job's Fundamentalism." *JBL* 126 (2007) 83–97.

Levenson, Jon D. "Who Inserted the Book of the Torah?" *Harvard Theological Review* 68 (1975) 203–33.

Lohfink, Norbert F. "Was There A Deuteronomistic Movement?" In *Those Elusive Deuteronomists: The Phenomenon of Pan-Deuteronomism*, edited by Linda S. Schearing and Steven L. McKenzie, 67–83. JSOTSup 268. Sheffield: Sheffield Academic, 1999.

Longman, Tremper, III. *Job*. Baker Commentary on the Old Testament Wisdom and Psalms. Grand Rapids: Baker Academic, 2012.

Maidenbaum, Aryeh, and Stephen Martin, eds. *Lingering Shadows: Jungians, Freudians, and Anti-Semitism*. Boston: Shambhala, 1991.

Mann, Thomas W. *The Book of the Torah: The Narrative Integrity of the Pentateuch*. 2nd ed. Eugene, OR: Cascade Books, 2013.

Marböck, Johannes. "תפל, *tapel*." In *Theological Dictionary of the Old Testament*, edited by G. Johannes Botterweck et al., 15:740–744. Translated by David E. Green. Grand Rapids: Eerdmans, 2006.

Morrow, William. "Consolation, Rejection, and Repentance in Job 42:6." *JBL* 105 (1986) 211–25.

Matthews, Victor H., and Don C. Benjamin. *Old Testament Parallels: Laws and Stories from the Ancient Near East.* 4th ed. New York: Paulist, 2016.

McKenzie, Steven L. "Deuteronomistic History." In *The Anchor Bible Dictionary,* edited by David Noel Freedman, 2:160–68. New York: Doubleday, 1992.

McKenzie, Steven L., and Patrick Graham. *The History of Israel's Traditions: The Heritage of Martin Noth.* JSOTSup 182. Sheffield: Sheffield Academic, 1994.

McKenzie, Steven L. and John Kaltner, eds. *New Meanings for Ancient Texts: Recent Approaches to Biblical Criticisms and Their Applications.* Louisville: Westminster John Knox, 2013.

Mendenhall, George E. "Covenant Forms." *Biblical Archaeologist* 17/3 (1954) 50–76.

Middlemas, Jill A. "Going Beyond the Myth of the Empty Land: A Reassessment of the Early Persian Period." In *Exile and Restoration Revisited: Essays on the Babylonian and Persian Periods in Memory of Peter R. Ackroyd,* edited by Gary Knoppers and Lester Grabbe, 174–94. Library of Second Temple Studies 73. London: T. & T. Clark, 2009.

———. *The Templeless Age: And Introduction to the History, Literature, and Theology of the "Exile."* Louisville: Westminster John Knox, 2007.

Miller, Alice. *The Drama of the Gifted Child.* New York: Basic, 1981.

———. Personal correspondence with Donald Capps, August 9, 2005.

Morrow, William S. "Consolation, Rejection, and Repentance in Job 42:6." *JBL* 105 (1986) 211–25.

Muenchow, Charles. "Dust and Dirt in Job 42:6." *JBL* 108 4 (1989) 597–611.

Nathanson, Donald. *Shame and Pride: Affect, Sex, and the Birth of the Self.* New York: Norton, 1992.

Nelson, Hilde Lindemann. *Damaged Identities, Narrative Repair.* Ithaca, NY: Cornell University, 2001.

Nelson, Richard. *Double Redaction of the Deuteronomistic History.* JSOTSup 18. Sheffield: JSOT Press, 1981.

Neumann, Erich. *Depth Psychology and a New Ethic.* Translated by Eugene Rolfe. London: Shambhala, 1990.

Newsom, Carol A. *The Book of Job: A Contest of Moral Imaginations.* Oxford: Oxford University Press, 2003.

Ngwa, Kenneth Numfor. *The Hermeneutics of the "Happy" Ending in Job 42:7–17.* Beihefte zur Zeitschrift für die alttestamentliche Wissenschaft 354. Berlin: de Gruyter, 2005.

Noth, Martin. *Deuteronomistic History.* JSOTSup 15. Sheffield: University of Sheffield, Dept. of Biblical Studies, 1981.

———. *Überlieferungsgeschichtliche Studien.* Schriften der Königsberger Gelehrten Gesellschaft. Geisteswissenschaftliche Klasse. 18. Jahr, Heft 2. Halle: Niemeyer, 1943.

O'Brien, Mark A. *The Deuteronomistic History Hypothesis: A Reassessment.* Orbis biblicus et orientalis 92. Göttingen: Vandenhoeck & Ruprecht, 1989.

O'Callaghan, Michael. "A Conversation with John Weir Perry." In *When the Dream Becomes Real: The Inner Apocalypse in Mythology, Madness and the Future.* http://www.global-vision.org/papers/JWP.pdf, 1982, 3.

O'Connor, Kathleen M. *Lamentations and the Tears of the World.* Maryknoll, NY: Orbis, 2002.

————. "Wild, Raging Creativity: The Scene in the Whirlwind (Job 38–41)." In *A God so Near: Essays on Old Testament Theology in Honor of Patrick D. Miller*, edited by Brent A. Strawn and Nancy R. Bowen, 171–82. Winona Lake, IN: Eisenbrauns, 2003.

Oded, Bustenay. *The Early History of the Babylonian Exile (8th–6th Centuries BCE)*. Haifa: Pardes, 2010. (Hebrew)

————. *Mass Deportations and Deportees in the Neo-Assyrian Empire*. Wiesbaden: Reichert, 1979.

Ogden, Thomas. *Subjects of Analysis*. London: Karnac, 1994.

Olson, Alan. "The Silence of Job as the Key to the Text." *Semeia* 19 (1981) 113–19.

Pakkala, Juha. *Intolerant Monolatry in the Deuteronomistic History*. Publications of the Finnish Exegetical Society 76. Göttingen: Vandenhoeck & Ruprecht, 1999.

Patrick, Dale. "Job's Address to God." *Zeitschrift für die alttestamentliche Wissenschaft* 91 (1979) 277–81.

————. "The Translation of Job XLII 6." *Vetus Testamentum* 26 (1976) 369–71.

Pellauer, David. "Reading Ricoeur Reading Job." *Semeia* 19 (1981) 73–83.

Perdue, Leo G. *Wisdom in Revolt: Metaphorical Theology in the Book of Job*. JSOTSup 29. Sheffield: JSOT, 1991.

Perdue, Leo G, and W. Clark Gilpin, eds. *The Voice From The Whirlwind: Interpreting the Book of Job*. Nashville: Abingdon, 1992.

Perry, John. "Emotions and Object Relations." *Journal of Analytical Psychology* 15 (1970) 1–12.

Person, R. F., Jr. *The Deuteronomic School: History, Social Setting, and Literature*. Studies in Biblical Literature 2. Atlanta: Society of Biblical Literature, 2002.

Pope, Marvin. *Job: A New Translation and Commentary*. 3rd ed. AB 15. Garden City, NY: Doubleday, 1973.

Phillips. Adam *On Balance*. New York: Farrar, Straus & Giroux, 2010.

Rad, Gerhard von. *Deuteronomy: A Commentary*. Translated by Dorothea Barton. OTL. Philadelphia: Westminster, 1966.

Revel, J. "Qu'est-ce qu'un cas?" Paper presented at the colloquium "Casus Belli," Ecole des Hautes Estudes en Sciences Socials. Paris, June, 2001.

Ricoeur, Paul. *Freud and Philosophy: An Essay on Interpretation*. Translated by Denis Savage. New Haven: Yale University Press, 1970.

Rizzuto, Ana-Maria. *The Birth of the Living God: A Psychoanalytic Study*. Chicago: University of Chicago Press, 1979.

Rogerson, John. "Jonah." In *Prophets and Poets: A Companion to the Prophetic Books of the Old Testament*, edited by Grace Emmerson, 238–43. Nashville: Abingdon, 1997.

Rollins, Wayne G. *Soul and Psyche: The Bible in Psychological Perspective*. Minneapolis: Fortress, 1999.

Römer, Thomas C. *The So-Called Deuteronomistic History: A Sociological, Historical and Literary Introduction*. New York: T. & T. Clark, 2007.

Rowley, H. H. *Job*. New Century Bible Commentary. 2nd ed. Grand Rapids: Eerdmans, 1980.

Roy, Manisha. "Religious Archetype as Cultural Complex." In *The Cultural Complex: Contemporary Jungian Perspectives on Psyche and Society*, edited by Thomas Singer and Samuel L. Kimbles, 64–78. New York: Brunner-Routledge, 2004.

Salters. Robert B. *A Critical and Exegetical Commentary on Lamentations*. International Critical Commentary. London: T. & T. Clark, 2010.

Samuels, Andrew. "National Psychology, National Socialism, and Analytical Psychology: Reflections on Jung and Anti-Semitism Part 1." *Journal of Analytical Psychology* 37 (1992) 127–47.

Sanders, James. *Canon and Community: A Guide to Canonical Criticism.* Guides to Biblical Scholarship. 1984. Reprint, Eugene, OR: Wipf & Stock, 2000.

Scheindlin, Raymond. *Book of Job.* New York: Norton.

Schneider, Sandra. *The Revelatory Text: Interpreting the New Testament as Sacred Scripture.* San Francisco: HarperSanFrancisco, 1991.

Schreiner, Susan E. "Why Do the Wicked Live? Job and David in Calvin's Sermons on Job." In *Voice from the Whirlwind: Interpreting the Book of Job,* edited by Leo G. Perdue and W. Clark Gilpin, 129–43. Nashville: Abingdon, 1992.

Seow, C. L. *Job 1–21: Interpretation and Commentary.* Grand Rapids: Eerdmans, 2013.

Sherry, Jay. *Carl Gustav Jung: Avant-Garde Conservative.* Palgrave Studies in Cultural and Intellectual History. New York: Palgrave Macmillan, 2010.

Singer, Thomas, and Samuel L. Kimbles. "The Emerging Theory of Cultural Complexes." In *Analytical Psychology,* edited by Joseph Cambray and Linda Carter, 176–203. New York: Routledge, 2004.

Smith-Christopher, Daniel L. *A Biblical Theology of Exile.* Overtures to Biblical Theology. Minneapolis: Fortress, 2002.

———. "Reassessing the Historical and Sociological Impact of the Babylonian Exile (597/587–539 BCE)." In *Exile: Old Testament, Jewish, and Christian Conceptions,* edited by James M. Scott, 8–36. Journal for the Study of Judaism Supplements 56. Leiden: Brill, 1997.

Spivak, Gayatri Chakravorty. "Subaltern Studies: Deconstructing Historiography." In *The Spivak Reader: Selected Works of Gayatri Chakravorty Spivak.* New York: Routledge, 1996.

Stein, Ruth. *For Love of the Father: A Psychoanalytic Study of Religious Terrorism.* Meridian: Crossing Aesthetics. Stanford: Stanford University Press, 2010.

Stern, Ephraim. *Archaeology of the Land of the Bible.* Vol. 2, *Assyrian, Babylonian, and Persian Periods, 732–332 BCE.* Anchor Bible Reference Library. New York: Doubleday, 2001.

———. "The Babylonian Gap: The Archaeological Reality." *JSOT* 28 (2004) 273–77.

Stulman, Louis. "Encroachment in Deuteronomy: An Analysis of the Social World of the D Code." *JBL* 109 (1990) 613–32.

Sugirtharajah, R. S. *Voices from the Margin: Interpreting the Bible in the Third World.* 3rd ed. Maryknoll, NY: Orbis, 2006.

Terrien, S. *Job.* Commentaire de l'Ancien Testament. Neuchâtel: Delchaux & Niestlé, 1963.

Ticciati, Susannah. *Job and the Disruption of Identity: Reading beyond Barth.* New York: T. & T. Clark, 2005.

Timmer, Daniel. "God's Speeches, Job's Responses, and the Problem of Coherence in the Book of Job: Sapiential Pedagogy Revisited." *Catholic Biblical Quarterly* 71 (2009) 286–305.

Tompkins, Silvan. *Affect Imagery Consciousness.* New York: Springer, 1962.

Torrey, C. C. *Ezra Studies.* New York: Ktav, 1970.

Uehlinger, Christoph. "Gibt es seine joschijanische Kultreform? Plädoyer für ein begrüdetes Minimum." In *Jeremia und die "deuteronomistiche Bewegung,"* edited by Walter Gross, 57–90. Bonner Biblische Beiträge 98. Weinheim: Beltz Athenäum, 1995.

Ulanov, Ann Belford. *The Feminine in Jungian Psychology and in Christian Theology.* Evanston, IL: Northwestern University Press, 1971.

————. *Finding Space: Winnicott, God, and Psychic Reality.* Louisville: Westminster John Knox, 2001.

————. *Madness and Creativity.* Carolyn and Ernest Fay Series in Analytical Psychology 18. College Station: Texas A&M University Press, 2013.

————. *Picturing God.* 1986. Reprint, Eugene, OR: Wipf & Stock, 2002.

————. *Spiritual Aspects of Clinical Work.* Einsiedeln: Daimon. 2004.

————. *Spirit in Jung.* Einsiedeln: Daimon, 2005.

————. *The Unshuttered Heart: Opening Aliveness/Deadness in the Self.* Nashville: Abingdon, 2007.

Ulanov, Ann, and Barry Ulanov. *Healing Imagination: The Meeting of Psyche and Soul.* New York: Paulist, 1991.

————. *Religion and the Unconscious.* Philadelphia: Westminster, 1975.

van der Kolk, Bessel A. and Onno van der Hart. "The Intrusive Past: The Flexibility of Memory and the Engraving of Trauma." In *Trauma: Explorations in Memory,* edited by Cathy Caruth, 158–82. Baltimore: Johns Hopkins University Press, 1995.

Van Seters, John. *In Search of History: History in the Ancient World and the Origin of Biblical History.* New Haven: Yale University Press, 1983.

Weinfeld, Moshe. *Deuteronomy and the Deuteronomic School.* Oxford: Claredon, 1972.

————. *Deuteronomy 1–11.* AB 5. New York: Doubleday, 1991.

Weingarten, Gene. "Pearls before Breakfast." *Washington Post* 1A (2007).

Westermann, Claus. *The Structure of the Book of Job: A Form-Critical Analysis.* Translated by Charles A. Muenchow. Philadelphia: Fortress, 1981.

Wehr, Gerhard. *Jung: A Biography.* Translated by David M. Weeks. London: Shambhala, 1987.

Wilde, A. de. *Das Buch Hiob.* Oudtestamentische Studiën 22. Leiden: Brill, 1981.

Wilson, Robert. "Who Was the Deuteronomist?" In *Those Elusive Deuteronomists: The Phenomenon of Pan-Deuteronomism,* edited by Linda S. Schearing and Steven L. McKenzie, 67–82. JSOTSup 268. Sheffield: Sheffield Academic, 1999.

Winnicott, Donald W. *The Maturational Processes and The Facilitating Environment.* London: Karnac, 1965/1990.

————. *Playing and Reality.* London: Routledge Classics, 1991.

————. *Psycho-Analytic Exploration.* Cambridge: Harvard University Press, 1989.

————. *Through Paediatrics to Psycho-Analysis: Collected Papers.* London: Brunner-Routledge, 1992.

Wiseman, D. J. *The Vassal-Treaties of Esarhaddon.* London: British School of Archaeology in Iraq, 1958.

Wolfers, David. *Deep Things Out of Darkness.* Grand Rapids: Eerdmans, 1995.

Yaffe, Martin D. "Providence in Medieval Aristotelianism." In *Voice From the Whirlwind: Interpreting the Book of Job,* edited by Leo G. Perdue and W. Clark Gilpin, 111–28. Nashville: Abingdon, 1992.

Zehnder, Mark. "Building on Stone? Deuteronomy and Esarhaddon's Loyalty Oaths (Part 1): Some Preliminary Observations." *Bulletin for Biblical Research* 19 (2009) 341–74.

Zuckerman, Bruce. *Job the Silent: A Study in Historical Counterpoint.* Oxford: Oxford University Press, 1991.

Made in United States
North Haven, CT
29 July 2022

22004304R00137